GERMAN GENERALS
OF WORLD WAR II

GERMAN GENERALS OF WORLD WAR II
As I Saw Them

By F. W. von MELLENTHIN
German General Staff Officer

UNIVERSITY OF OKLAHOMA PRESS : NORMAN

By F. W. von Mellenthin

Panzer Battles (Norman, 1956)

German Generals of World War II: As I Saw Them (Norman, 1977)

Library of Congress Cataloging in Publication Data

Mellenthin, Friedrich Wilhelm von, 1904–
    German generals of World War II.

    Bibliography: p. 291
    Includes index.
    1. World War, 1939–1945—Germany. 2. Generals—Germany.
3. World War, 1939–1945—Personal narratives, German. 4. Mellenthin, Friedrich Wilhelm von, 1904–
I. Title.
D757.M369   940.54'09'43 [B]   76–62518

FOREWORD

My portrayal of German generals of World War II is based on recollections of the actions, decisions, and behavior of military commanders under whom I served as a general staff officer during the war or with whom I came in contact a number of times. My own experiences were varied, since I took part in the Polish, French, and Balkan campaigns as a young staff officer; I was in the North African Campaign with Field Marshal Erwin Rommel from 1 June 1941 to 15 September 1942 as staff officer (intelligence) and subsequently for my last three months there as acting staff officer (operations), or GSO I, as it would have been termed in the British Army.

At the end of 1942 I became chief of staff in the 48th Panzer Corps, which was in action at Stalingrad, and I then took part in all the big battles in southern Russia, from May 1944 as chief of staff in the Fourth Panzer Army at Baranov, on the Vistula. From September until the end of 1944 I was chief of staff of Army Group G, which was holding a front between Luxembourg and Switzerland. I ended my military career as chief of staff of the Fifth Panzer Army in the Ruhr Pocket at the end of April 1945.

During those long war years I came to know well the commanders under whom I served, with all their points of strength and weakness, and I believe that I can express objective opinions about their personalities without whitewashing their faults. My generation is gradually dying out, and I consider it important that, apart from a study of military history, the younger generation should learn something about the characters and human side of German generals of World War II.

I must ask for some understanding as regards the selection of generals whom I have portrayed. I have dealt with only those personally known to me. The sequence of generals has been purposely chosen without strict adherence to seniority. I have tried to illustrate the great diversity in ability and character to be found among them. Understandably, in completing the book, I have reached some conclusions for the present and the future, which may be drawn from the personalities I have sketched.

A very real help in the writing of the book and a valuable companion in discussions on the subject has been Hans-Jürgen Dingler, with whom I often worked during the war. He was in Russia and, toward the end, in the West as chief of staff of the 58th Panzer Corps. From this comradeship-in-arms a close neighborly friendship developed. I am also grateful to my brother, General Horst von Mellenthin, as well as to Generals Hermann Balck, Hasso von Manteuffel, Walter Wenck, and von Natzmer, who have rendered me valuable assistance through personal interviews and with written records. In addition, thanks are due Colonel Neil D. Orpen for editorial assistance in preparation of the final draft of the book and for the preparation of two maps, the Yugoslavian theater in 1945 and the Murmansk Front in 1943. Finally, thanks are due M. R. Legat, Editorial Director of Cassell & Collier Macmillan Publishers, Ltd., London, for providing prints of six maps from the publication *The War, 1939–1945*.

The maps in this book illustrate the major campaigns or battles in which the generals participated. For the convenience of the reader each map appears in the text at the point at which the operation is discussed in greatest detail. The maps are listed in the front of the book chronologically by theater of war.

Many books have been consulted, and a list of sources is provided at the end of the book.

F. W. von MELLENTHIN

Johannesburg,
South Africa

INTRODUCTION

Many accounts have been published about World War II from the German as well as from the Allied points of view. Insofar as they can lay claim to historical value, they must be based on genuine records, in which case they accurately describe the course of battles and of whole campaigns and record the decisions of military leaders and their consequences. There is seldom an evaluation of the personal attributes and characters of the generals, who were the soldiers in command. In his *History of the Second World War* the British writer Sir Basil Liddell-Hart said, "The best historical presentation would be one of their thoughts and feelings, for which the actual events were only the background, making them physically visible."

A man's actions and omissions spring first and foremost from his character and naturally, but to a lesser degree, from his origins, his upbringing, and his training. How a man appears to his superiors may differ markedly from his image in the eyes of his subordinates, who often see him in quite another light. From the point of view of the Supreme Command, what counted in a general was his success in the field, as was particularly apparent in Adolf Hitler. From the viewpoint of a member of a general's staff, however, what counted was not so much military success as his superior's qualities as a man: his attitude, behavior, upbringing, and education; his concern for his men; and his physical and mental capabilities. If a military commander is well endowed with all these gifts, the men will follow him confidently, even if success is not invariably achieved.

Field Marshal Erich von Manstein summed up the qualities

required of a field commander in these words: "Intelligence, knowledge, and experience are telling prerequisites. Lack of these may, if necessary, be compensated for by good general staff officers. Strength of character and inner fortitude, however, are decisive factors. The confidence of the men in the ranks rests upon a man's strength of character."

This book sets out to discover to what extent certain German generals of World War II measured up to those standards.

NOTE FOR THE ENGLISH-SPEAKING READER

For the English-speaking reader who may not be familiar with the wartime organization and character of the German Wehrmacht, it should be explained that many of the generals with whom I have dealt were products of one or other of the old Kadettenkorps, or Cadet Corps, of which there appears to have been no exact army equivalent in Great Britain. In naval training Dartmouth somewhat resembles the German cadet institution, with its idea of "catching them young" when molding the character of future officers.

It should also be stressed that in prewar Germany—and especially in the days before World War I—General Staff officers were the elite of the army and had all passed through the Kriegsakademie, or War College, which was the equivalent of the British Staff College at Camberley. The General Staff held a position of influence and privilege rather more pronounced than that of the British General Staff, and like the army itself, was by tradition totally nonpolitical.

Translation has presented some peculiar problems in view of differences in German and British military organization and practice. I shall mention only a few of the more obvious instances that appear to have created misunderstanding in a number of earlier books in English about the German forces.

To avoid any doubts about English and German equivalents in rank, throughout this book I have followed the official listing of the War Office for the British forces in 1940:

German Rank	English Equivalent
Leutnant	Second lieutenant
Oberleutnant	Lieutenant
Rittmeister (cavalry)	Captain
Hauptmann	Captain
Major	Major
Oberstleutnant	Lieutenant colonel
Oberst	Colonel
Generalmajor	Major general
Generalleutnant	Lieutenant general
General der	General
Infanterie	
Kavallerie	
Artillerie	
Pioniere	
Panzertruppen	
Nachrichtentruppen	
Generaloberst	(No equivalent)
Generalfeldmarschell	Field marshal

These ranks need no special explanation, except to note that the not uncommon idea that a German Oberst was the equivalent of a British brigadier is not correct. The German Oberst, or colonel, was normally in command of a regiment within a brigade or division. Such a regiment—in the lorried infantry in 1940, for example—consisted of a headquarters and three lorried infantry battalions (all from the *same* regiment) with their own infantry guns and antitank guns. A brigadier in the British and Commonwealth forces, on the other hand, almost invariably commanded a brigade group, which included not only three infantry battalions, all from *different* regiments, but also artillery, engineer, signals, medical, and other units.

A German infantry brigade *included* an infantry regiment, plus a motorcycle battalion and a heavy gun company of six guns in its original form, and was not necessarily commanded by an Oberst. The independent Parachute Brigade that fought at El Alamein was commanded by Major General B. H. Ramcke, and the 15th

Lorried Infantry Brigade in the desert had two light-infantry regiments.

Just as there were no brigadiers in the German forces, so the rank of Generaloberst was unknown in the British forces. Meaning, literally "colonel-general," the rank was held by the most senior of German generals, and has been used in some instances in the text, indicating their seniority.

Difficulty arises in translation regarding artillery terms, in view of the marked differences in organization between the German and British armies during World War II. Though both German and British batteries might have had four guns in the prewar days when British field-artillery units were still organized in brigades, the position from 1939 onward was quite otherwise:

German	Guns	British	Guns
Regiment	48	Regiment	24
Abteilung	12	Battery	8
Batterie	4	Troop	4
Zug	2	Section	2

In fact, a British division had a field regiment for each brigade and could thus count on seventy-two 25-pounders (plus its other guns) in an infantry division, whereas a German division had only one field regiment, numbering forty-eight guns in its normal establishment. The relationship between battery and regimental commanders of artillery on the opposing sides is thus somewhat confusing to the average reader.

Another source of confusion to English-speaking readers that appears in a number of publications is the designation of the infantry element of a panzer division. Frequently this is translated as "rifle regiment," which in spite of its euphony is nevertheless incorrect. A rifle regiment is a Jäger-Regiment, a unit similar to a British rifle regiment. The infantry of a panzer division belonged to a Schützen Regiment, and, though Schutze may mean rifleman, it also means private, and the unit is a lorried infantry regiment.

The upper echelon of the German command organization often referred to in this book was reorganized by Hitler on two occasions during the war, and was as shown below:

Supreme Commander: Adolf Hitler[1]

Combined Staff of the Armed Forces

[Oberkommando der Wehrmacht—O.K.W.]

The Führer and Commander in Chief of the Armed Forces: Hitler

Chief of Combined Staff: Field Marshal Wilhelm Keitel

Chief of Armed Forces Command Staff: General Alfred Jodl

Chief of Home Defense Staff: General Warlimont

Counter-espionage (Canaris) Armaments (Thomas) Etc.	Land Forces Army High Command (OKH)	Navy	Air Force
	Commander in Chief of Army: Field Marshal Walther von Brauchitsch		
	Chief of Army Staff: General Franz Halder		
	Army group commanders		
	Army commanders Corps commanders		
	Divisional commanders		

On 19 December 1941, Hitler himself took over as commander in chief of the army, and the army staff thereafter retained authority only over the Russian Front, all other theaters being placed directly under the Combined Staff of the Armed Forces.

The final stage, giving Hitler complete control, was reached after the spring of 1942, when further changes were made that eventually led to this organization:

---

[1] The Waffen-S.S. was directly subordinate to Hitler.

Supreme Commander of the Armed Forces and Commander
in Chief of the Army: Hitler
Chief of Combined Staff: Field Marshal Keitel

Armed Forces Command Staff	Army General Staff
(Dealing with all theaters other than the Russian Front)	(Dealing with the Russian Front)
Chief of Staff: General Jodl Deputy CGS: General Warlimont (from November, 1944)	Chief of Staff: General Kurt Zeitzler (from July, 1944, General Heinz Guderian)

Inspectorate of Armored Troops	Army Groups Armies Corps Divisions	Air Force Navy Training Army

CONTENTS

ILLUSTRATIONS

MAPS

(In chronological order by theater of war)

GERMAN GENERALS
OF WORLD WAR II

Chapter 1

GENERAL WERNER BARON VON FRITSCH

The Man Who Built up the Prewar German Army

"For good or evil this man Hitler is Germany's destiny. If he plunges into the abyss, he will drag us all with him. There is nothing we can do about it."

General Fritsch spoke to this effect when, shortly before the moment for the proposed march into the Sudentenland on 1 October 1938, he refused to join a conspiracy to arrest Hitler. As it turned out, the Munich Agreement of 28 September not only spelled the end for Czechoslovakia but also saved Hitler by making the very idea of apprehending him seem ridiculous. In fact, justification for Fritsch's contention that the fate of Germany was inextricably tied up with that of the Führer may be found in tracing the fortunes of the generals discussed in this book.

If one rightly considers General Hans von Seeckt the creator of the 100,000-man Reichswehr, which was all that Germany was permitted by the Treaty of Versailles, then on the same grounds General von Fritsch may be regarded as the man who built up the German Army that waxed immensely powerful from the application of conscription.

Werner Baron von Fritsch was born in Benrath near Düsseldorf, in the Rhineland, on 4 August 1880. On the paternal side he was descended from a line of noted scholars, but his own father was a cavalry officer and ended his military career as a general. Werner was brought up in a strictly Protestant Christian atmosphere.

On 21 September 1898 the young Fritsch joined the Hessian 25th Field Artillery Regiment as a candidate for a commission, or ensign. For any understanding of his attitude toward life and German history up to the end of World War II, it is important to realize that at the time the German Officer Corps constituted a particularly exclusive and elite group of professional soldiers, dedicated to their calling and devoted in loyalty to the Kaiser as commander in chief and to Germany as their Fatherland. Not only in Germany but throughout Europe patriotism, strict Christian morality, dignity, and respect for one's superiors were virtues that commanded admiration among people of all classes. War, as England at the height of her imperial power was finding even in distant South Africa at the time, was still an occupation for "gentlemen."

On 27 January 1900, Fritsch was promoted to second lieutenant. Passionately fond of riding and extremely talented in the military sense, he was soon posted to the Kriegsakademie, or Staff College, where he was very highly regarded. During World War I he served on the General Staff, including a long period as General Staff officer (Operations) of the First Guards Division under Prince Eitel-Friedrich of Prussia, the second son of the emperor.

After the war, with Germany allowed to retain only seven infantry and three cavalry divisions under two corps headquarters, and with a total strength of not more than 100,000 men, apart from 10,000 in the Navy, Fritsch became chief of staff at Northern Frontier Defense Headquarters with the rank of major under Major General von Seeckt, who had returned to Berlin from Turkey in 1919 before being appointed commander in chief of the army in June 1920. It was Seeckt's idea of a "Führerheer"—an army of leaders—that was to lay the foundation of Germany's future military power and especially to endow it with a first-class cadre of highly trained, professional noncommissioned officers, who were—like their officers—invariably capable of filling a post at least one higher than their own.

Seeckt soon learned to appreciate Fritsch's worth and later promoted him to fill particularly important posts. In Ulm he commanded an artillery "Abteilung"—the equivalent of a twelve-gun British artillery brigade of the years before World War II—and in Schwerin he became commanding officer of the Second Artillery Regiment. Then he was appointed chief of operations on the staff of General Wilhelm Heye in Königsberg, where his new general officer commanding (GOC) was senior army commander in East Prussia, which had been separated from the rest of Germany and remained of vital strategic importance. Heye, at the age of fifty-eight, succeeded Seeckt as commander in chief of the army when Field Marshal Paul von Hindenburg became president in 1926. By that time Fritsch was a lieutenant colonel and head of the Army Department of the Truppenamt, a thinly disguised German General Staff whose revival had been forbidden by the peace treaties. Fritsch was probably the only member of Seeckt's staff bold enough to advise him to resist dismissal at the time, but his attitude does not appear to have had any harmful effects on his future career.

On 1 March 1930, Fritsch took over command of the 1st Cavalry Division and subsequently became commander of the Third Military District in Berlin as GOC of the 3d Infantry Division. In view of the vital role played by the capital in the life of Germany, it was a very important appointment.

Hitler, who had legally become chancellor on 30 January 1933, actually wanted as commander in chief of the army General Walther von Reichenau, who was very close to the Nazi party and the only general other than War Minister Werner von Blomberg, favorably inclined toward the party. The aged and greatly revered president, Hindenburg—himself the embodiment of the old, aristocratic officer corps ideal—declined to agree to such a proposal and nominated Fritsch to fill the post on 1 February 1934.

One might ask how we junior officers saw our new commander in chief. Fritsch was of medium height, a wiry man who had been an enthusiastic horseman almost from birth. He was always immaculately dressed in uniform and also sported a large monocle. As with General von Seeckt, one could hardly imagine him without it. In a crowd or in front of the troops, Fritsch was usually somewhat withdrawn, but it was a cloak that was immediately discarded when he found himself in an intimate group. He was then remarkably cordial and invariably showed great understanding when approached with any sort of personal trouble, which encouraged him to act more like an elderly friend than a superior officer.

When he was to carry out an inspection of troops, there was no nervous anticipation of his arrival, and he was gladly welcomed. He was never harsh, and his criticisms were usually very brief and to the point. His personal behavior and example, which were faultless by the strict, high standards of the German Officer Corps, was the key to the widespread respect he commanded.

During the four years of Fritsch's service as commander in chief of the army, he left his stamp on the force in every respect—in training, in equipping, and particularly in building up morale, which has always been one of the most important considerations in any first-class army. He was certainly not what one could call a "political" general but was rather a soldier by nature and in addition a well-endowed staff officer.

If Fritsch deliberately kept aloof from politics, his attitude can hardly be considered exceptional for a truly professional soldier. In the days before the world had become so clearly divided into conflicting ideologies, professional soldiers were expected to steer well clear of politics. Yet the question arises whether, in the circumstances that developed in Hitler's Germany, such aloofness might have been prejudicial to Fritsch's own command. Considering the interests of the army which was placed under him, and risking the accusation that it is easy to be wise after the event, one might say yes.

Though he conscientiously steered clear of politics, it is certain that Fritsch was well informed about foreign countries and their affairs. Similarly, he was fully aware of political developments within Germany itself, though he played no active part in shaping them. To Fritsch, a born nobleman, the often dubious and particularly crude methods employed by Nazi party members were so distasteful that he had as little as possible to do with them. Though not possessing a particular charisma for the rank and file, his influence on the officers of the army was greater than that of anyone after Seeckt. Remarkable though it may seem, though Fritsch was no tribune of the masses, yet the working classes recognized him— exclusive general though he was—as a counterweight to Hitler.

At the time of his appointment as commander in chief, Fritsch received from Hitler the following directive: "You are to create an army of the greatest possible strength, inner determination and uniformity, and to bring it to the highest conceivable pitch of training." Fritsch tackled this instruction and its related task of building up the little 100,000-man Reichswehr into an army of the greatest possible strength in a singularly soldierly manner, brooking no interference from the Nazi party nor allowing himself to be influenced in any way by politically conservative circles.

On 11 April 1934 the cruiser *Deutschland* set out from Kiel for Königsberg carrying Hitler, Blomberg, and the commanders in chief of the army (Fritsch) and navy (Admiral Erich Raeder) to attend the spring maneuvers in East Prussia. With the aged President Hindenburg's days obviously numbered, and with Nazi party Sturmabteilungen (SA) under Ernst Röhm increasingly threatening to usurp the authority of the armed forces, it was not surprising that these two subjects should be discussed between the chancellor and his military advisers, and it appears that it was proposed that the Reichswehr should support the appointment of Hitler himself to succeed Hindenburg, in return for undertaking to put a clamp on the ambitions of the SA as rivals to the legitimate armed forces. Admiral Erich Raeder readily agreed, but Fritsch insisted on first consulting his senior generals.

The senior army commanders met at Bad Nauheim on May 16, and the proposal was put to them. Any decision they took in such a matter was clearly a political, as opposed to a purely military, one, but it was a unanimous decision of professional soldiers whose intention was to serve the best interests of the army. They apparently agreed to support Hitler as Hindenburg's successor, but they were not gifted with the clairvoyance or prophetic insight to foresee where Hitler would lead them. Meanwhile, they set about building up for Germany the most powerful army attainable with the means at their disposal. It was a task they understood and they spared no pains to do their best.

Within the Nazi party itself, however, there occurred an upheaval that vitally affected the future not only of Fritsch himself but also of the whole army he was charged to build up. This was the notorious "Blood Purge" of 30 June 1934, the details of which have not been—and can never be—completely explained, since none of those who knew the full truth survived long enough to feel inclined to divulge the facts. Some details are known, however. Ernst Röhm, one of the founders of the Nazi party and one of Hitler's closest early associates, had become chief of staff of the SA, the so-called Storm Troopers, a purely party-political, uniformed organization whose methods had become increasingly brutal over the years. Systematically enlarging and developing his SA, Röhm had already begun to sabotage the Frontier Defense Force established by the Reichswehr in collaboration with the Prussian government, and his clear aim was to bring the Frontier formations under his own orders. It was his overriding intention to obtain arms for his own Storm Troopers, and in this goal he had reached a point at which civilians who were called up for exercises with the Frontier Defense Force found themselves simultaneously summoned to attend SA parades. Röhm hoped that this sort of thing would paralyze the legitimate frontier defense organization, and it was these attempts at rendering the Frontier Defense Force useless that resulted in the first clash between the army and the SA.

Fritsch had no intention of fighting the SA as such, but he resisted any encroachment from that quarter so far as it impinged on his personal responsibility for national defense. The extent to which the SA's ideas about their own self-importance had grown was well illustrated by a printed list of equivalent SA and army ranks, in which Röhm, as chief of staff of the SA, claimed for himself the seniority of a field marshal. When Fritsch was shown the list, he commented that the SA leader must be out of his mind.

The Army High Command now had no doubt that the SA intended using every means at its disposal to take over the Wehrmacht, as the Reichswehr had become, including its responsibility for defense. The role of professional army officers would be restricted to that of military technicians.

When the sabotage of the Frontier Defense Force by the SA began to make headway and Hitler did nothing about it, Fritsch himself lodged complaints with the chancellor, and he was in a position to offer Hitler proof of the SA's illegal activities. He implicitly believed Hitler's assurances that the Wehrmacht was and would always remain the nation's sole armed force.

Fritsch's attitude toward the SA undoubtedly aroused the displeasure of Minister for War Blomberg, who had been brought back from the disarmament talks in Geneva to join the cabinet on Hitler's assumption of the chancellorship in early 1933. Blomberg already enjoyed Hitler's confidence at the time, and was strongly influenced by Colonel Walter von Reichenau, a confirmed Nazi, who had been his own chief of staff. Blomberg either could not see through the machinations of the SA or had no desire to do so.

Fritsch had never asked Hitler for any drastic solution to the differences of opinion about jurisdiction over the forces. He certainly never demanded the dismissal or liquidation of the SA leaders responsible for the conflict. My brother Horst von Mellenthin, who was personal aide-de-camp to General von Fritsch at the time, is firmly convinced that Hitler intentionally kept his plans for disposing of the SA leaders to himself and never mentioned them to Fritsch. In any event, when Himmler in turn stepped into Röhm's shoes as rival to the Reichswehr with his black-uniformed SS, he and his troops were a far greater danger to the army than the SA had ever been. Had he been aware of what was about to happen, Fritsch would have been fully alive to this unpalatable fact.

On 27 June 1934, Fritsch received a summons from President Hindenburg to report to his estate near Neudeck, in East Prussia. My brother Horst accompanied him. Both men were greatly shocked by the president's state of health. He hardly seemed to understand what was happening and was living only in the past. During the day Hindenburg's son, who was also his father's aide-de-camp, told Fritsch that the SA appeared to have in mind some sort of action that would most likely be directed against the Reichswehr. As a precaution orders were issued for the president's residence to be protected by troops and barbed wire.

My brother Horst then tried to learn over the telephone whether there was any news in Neudeck about events, but only rumors had been heard there. He suggested to Hindenburg's son that the garrison nearest the Neudeck estate should be alerted, to act protectively if necessary in the event the SA had any plans to seize the president.

On 30 June 1934 the Army High Command received a telephone call from the Munich Military District Command reporting that Hitler had unexpectedly arrived there and had spoken to a number of senior officers in a reassuring tone. He had then left immediately for Bad Wiessee, a resort not far from Munich. The report went on to say that Hitler intended to "liquidate" several highly placed SA leaders.

This report was soon confirmed by events. SA Chief of Staff Röhm and other SA leaders were shot on Hitler's personal orders, in Stadelheim Prison, under the direction of Gruppenführer Sepp Dietrich, the commander of the Führer's SS bodyguard. In fact, Röhm—a World War I army captain who had entered the Nazi party in its earliest days and become a fanatical disciple—was but one of many who died sudden deaths that weekend of 30 June to 2 July 1934. General Kurt von Schleicher, Hitler's predecessor as chancellor, was shot in cold blood by SS men in Berlin, as was his wife. His close friend, General Kurt von Bredow, met a similar fate, and dozens of others were killed in a bloody purge.

When General von Fritsch was informed about what had occurred, my brother has said, he was profoundly shocked, particularly in regard to the manner in which the murders had been committed. At the same time, it must be confessed that a great many officers appeared to be much relieved that Hitler had at last taken vigorous action and established control over the SA, the most dangerous enemy of the Wehrmacht.

So tangled was the web of intrigue that had led up to the assassinations that it is doubtful that it could ever be unraveled by anyone outside the small circle of archconspirators, in the forefront of whom were the SS leaders Heinrich Himmler and Reinhard Heydrich, and also Hermann Göring, with General Walter von Reichenau, Blomberg's former chief of staff, well informed about what was going on. It was Reichenau who warned the Reichswehr that something was afoot as early as 22 June, by which time the SS Security Service (Sicherheitsdienst), under the sadistic Heydrich, was already preparing to play its role beside the Gestapo, which until a few months previously had been almost a personal tool in the hands of Göring.

The rumor that the SA intended to act against the Reichswehr was so near the truth as to be easily spread. On June 24 it appeared to be confirmed, and Fritsch alerted the army. When General Ewald von Kleist made his own inquiries and suspected that the SS was playing off the Reichswehr against the SA, his suspicions were brushed aside in Fritsch's presence by Reichenau. One or two fabricated documents, well placed by the Gestapo, quickly confirmed the existence of a dire plot by the SA. While Dietrich's SS bodyguard for Adolf Hitler collected the arms necessary for its part in action planned by his bosses, Röhm was struck off the rolls of the Officers' Corps. By late on Thursday, 28 June, the Reichswehr was so firmly convinced that a "putsch" was imminent that all military districts were placed on the alert. Within forty-eight hours the SS firing squads began shooting, and the SA leadership was wiped out.

In relation to the army, Hitler exploited the elimination of the SA leaders with great skill, as he once again indicated to the public in general that the Reichswehr was the sole dependable support of the state. This had not stopped him from having Generals Schleicher and Bredow murdered, but he explained that the two of them, especially Schleicher, had conspired with a foreign country and were thus guilty of high treason.

It may seem incomprehensible that the Army High Command

did not immediately appeal to President von Hindenburg, but the chain of command within the German Army would never have permitted such a step. My brother believes that, instead, General von Fritsch may have approached the war minister, General von Blomberg, but there is no proof that he did so. Fritsch was always reluctant to deal with his superior, whose readiness to hand over the army to the Nazis was never understood by the commander in chief. Cooperation between the minister and Fritsch was never good.

Since the president was not involved, Blomberg found it easy to play along with Hitler in spite of the obvious murder of the two generals. To the Officer Corps he excused the murders as a necessary measure in the interests of the state. My brother recalls that none of the officers accepted the version that was enunciated by Blomberg.

But Hitler had again been successful. Since he had thwarted the power-hungry SA, the assassination of the two generals was soon forgotten. The army continued to believe in Hitler and to trust his word.

The war minister supported Hitler's policy for the rapid buildup of the army, though Fritsch and the chief of the General Staff, Beck, who committed suicide after the Hitler bomb plot in July 1944, tried to put a brake on developments.

During 1935 and 1936, Hitler gave Fritsch a completely free hand in the formation and training of the forces, as well as in the matter of personnel selection. He did not concern himself in any way with the General Staff's operational schemes during those years. Free from interference, and thanks to his own excellent strength of character and extensive knowledge, Fritsch was able to mold the army to match his own spirit and ideals without hindrance, ably supported by his outstanding chief of staff, Beck. He showed no preference for any particular arm of the service but appreciated the future important role of the armored forces, in whose development he assisted whenever possible. It was from 1935 that we were taught tank tactics in the framework of Panzer armies—an almost revolutionary idea in military circles at that time. Fritsch's views of grand strategy, however, were strongly opposed to Hitler's. He wanted to avoid war against the Western Powers and to prepare the army for defense of Germany's frontiers, even by brief offensive action if necessary.

The points of discussion at one of Fritsch's conferences are illuminating:

Officers should avoid criticism at all costs. We cannot alter government policy but must do our duty. Officers must not only lecture but also train their men. Company commanders and subalterns must treat their men as human beings. Attendance at church is compulsory. Officers must participate. Religious disputes are to be totally avoided. Resignation from the church is forbidden.

Fritsch also tried to put the brake on the reoccupation of the Rhineland, for the French Army was far superior to the German on 7 March 1936, the day on which three army battalions crossed the Rhine at Aachen. But by adhering to his idea of occupying the Rhineland, Hitler managed to carry off one of his greatest bluffs. Once again acting against the advice of his generals, he proved right. The French did nothing, other than moving some divisions to reinforce those in the Maginot Line, and the British simply looked the other way.

On 5 November 1937, a fateful conference took place in the Chancellery in Berlin. Besides Hitler and his aide-de-camp, Colonel Hossbach, those who took part were minister for war, Blomberg; the commanders in chief of the three services, Fritsch, Göring, and Raeder; and the foreign minister, Neurath. So literally did the participants take Hitler's instructions about secrecy as regards the discussion that Fritsch's and Beck's successors, General Walter von Brauchitsch and Franz Halder, first heard about the conference during the Nuremberg Trials (when it became known as the Hossbach File), from which it appeared that Hitler intended to incorporate Austria and Czechoslovakia in the German Reich by force, by 1943 to 1945 at the latest.

Blomberg and Fritsch both expressed concern lest England and France should react as enemies of Germany. In addition, they drew attention to the strength of Czechoslovakian fortifications that compared with the Maginot Line and could render any German attack considerably more difficult. Hitler reckoned that England would not get involved for the sake of Czechoslovakia and neither would France go to war over such an issue. He named the summer of 1938 as the earliest date for the project.

It also appears from the Hossbach File that especially Fritsch, but also Blomberg, as the responsible military authorities, raised fundamental objections to Hitler's proposals. The objections may well have been the real grounds for Hitler's subsequent action against both of them that led to their replacement.

Fritsch's stand was straightforward and clear. Though agreeing to the country's rearming, he wished to place Germany's military leadership in the position where the country could effectively defend itself against attack from any side. His outspoken objections to Hitler's plans, when considered in this light, were understandable. From the time of this discussion, in striking contrast to his attitude in former years, and for the slightest reason, Hitler began to show clear distrust of the army and its supposed "reactionaries" and "monarchists." During a trip to Egypt, which began on 10 November 1937, Fritsch was shadowed by Gestapo agents who were attempting to gather incriminating evidence against him.

Little more than two months after the secret discussions with Hitler, Blomberg, who had committed the indiscretion of marrying a girl of bad reputation (whose morally dubious earlier life was quickly revealed), was sacked as war minister and commander in chief of the Armed Forces—both of which posts disappeared with the establishment of the Oberkommando der Wehrmacht as the Combined Staff of the Armed Forces headed by Hitler in person.

In the following month, February 1936, Fritsch's turn came. Being a confirmed bachelor, he was an easy target for the archschemers Himmler and Heydrich. They had provided Göring with a document to place before Hitler purporting to prove that Fritsch was a homosexual and had been paying blackmail for three years to keep it secret. Homosexual practices in Germany, as elsewhere at the time, were punishable by law, and the accusation was a serious one. Colonel Hossbach, Hitler's aide-de-camp, was flabbergasted at such a suggestion, and—at the cost of his own job, as things turned out—he warned Fritsch, who was summoned to the Chancellery the next evening to face the outrageous charge before Hitler, Göring, and Himmler.

As part of what Chicago gangsters might have termed a "frameup," a decrepit jailbird and blackmailer was produced to corroborate the trumped-up charge, which left the unfortunate Fritsch almost speechless. A demand for trial by a military court of honor, as was customary in Germany when a man's character was impugned, was passed over, and Hitler ordered Fritsch to go on indefinite leave, which was tantamount to dismissal.

When the accusations were made known, we were all deeply shocked and angered. Everyone who knew the general considered the charge absolutely untrue. Immediately we suspected that party intrigue lay behind the whole thing, but it never entered our heads that Hitler could have welcomed such an intrigue or could in fact have engineered it himself.

The trial that Fritsch had demanded before a court of honor was actually granted, but on the very day that it opened, Hitler marched into Austria. Proceedings were suspended for some days, and by the time Fritsch was declared exonerated, momentous events on an international plane had completely overshadowed the news.

We naturally took it for granted that our commander in chief would be reinstated in his post. In fact, we even hoped that he would be appointed commander in chief of the armed forces in Blomberg's place. Hitler never even considered such a thing. Several generals, especially General von Brauchitsch, spoke up on Fritsch's behalf, but all they achieved was his rehabilitation as commander of an artillery regiment, which passed almost unnoticed by the general public. In any event, Fritsch handed in his resignation and retired to Neumünster, a training center from which he kept in touch with his old gunnery regiment in Schwerin. He remained honorary colonel, and the officers made a collection to buy him a house in Berlin. Our disgust at Hitler's attitude and at the behavior of our generals, who to our way of thinking had not done enough for Fritsch, was not diminished when we received an order from the Combined Staff of the Armed Forces to the effect that we were forthwith forbidden even to discuss the "Fritsch case."

From Hitler's point of view, the moment at which to rid himself of Fritsch had been well chosen. The invasion of Austria, the occupation of the Sudetenland and Czechoslovakia, and the increased work involved in expanding the army all tended to push the Fritsch case quickly into the background. Hitler had accurately summed up the attitude of the generals and of the old Officer Corps which sprang from the Imperial Army and the Reichswehr. We had been trained as "soldiers" and well understood our trade. During the days of the 100,000-man army we had been deliberately kept apart from politics. Had we—to quote Liddell-Hart—possessed a "wider horizon," our generals would probably have recognised the intentions and objectives of the Hitler regime as early as 1934, when he ordered the two generals and several SA leaders murdered.

Both during and after the war the question has occasionally been raised whether Fritsch, had he remained commander in chief of the army, would have been able to stand up to Hitler better than his successor, General von Brauchitsch. It is doubtful. Brauchitsch also enjoyed the confidence of the generals who served under him. Among us younger staff officers and the men in the ranks, he was not as well known as Fritsch nor as highly respected, but the two were somewhat alike in manner and appearance. They were both aristocrats with the highest principles. Neither of them could cope with the intrigue and loutish behavior that was the accepted thing in the Nazi party. Even political generals—such as Generals von Blomberg, von Schleicher, and to a certain extent von Reichenau—were outmaneuvered by Hitler, cold-shouldered, or butchered. In the same way, sooner or later, Fritsch would have been broken by Hitler.

The impression that he left upon those who knew him and the manner of his death were recorded by young Lieutenant Werner Rosenhagen in a letter to a friend more than four years before he himself was killed in action on the Russian Front. From 22 August to 22 September 1939, Rosenhagen had had what he himself termed the good fortune to act as escorting officer to General von Fritsch. In Rosenhagen's view one could only describe the general as an accomplished man, inspired by courtesy and good breeding. His memory for people was extraordinary, and he was perpetually active. It was impossible for him to let his mind wander, and his process of thought was extraordinarily well disciplined. He would often make a remark, remain quiet for half an hour, and then comment on the same subject from an entirely new point of view. Fritsch also had a puckish sense of humor, as he displayed on one occasion shortly before the outbreak of the war. Rosenhagen asked him whether he had any orders. They were forty-eight kilometers from the young subaltern's wife and family in Allenstein. Fritsch considered the matter carefully before replying, "I have no orders whatever for you, my dear Rosenhagen, only a request. Please drive to Allenstein and buy me a packet of special candles.

In wartime it is always dark, especially in bivouac. I don't expect you back before eleven o'clock." He looked at Rosenhagen for a few moments before adding, "And please give my very best compliments to your wife."

During the Polish campaign, when Rozan, on the Narev, was occupied by the German infantry spearheads, General von Fritsch—who was with his old regiment as honorary colonel—went forward on foot with Rosenhagen, who had his loaded pistol in his hand as they entered the shattered, burning town, which was in a state of chaos. Suddenly Fritsch looked at Rosenhagen in his quiet way and asked, "Don't you also find Rozan a bit of a disappointment? I had always imagined it a much more pleasant place."

On the morning of 22 September a raiding party from 1/48 Infantry Regiment was to go out to test enemy resistance at Sochaczew (Zazicze), near Warsaw. Light signals were laid on for cooperation between the infantry and artillery, who were to put down supporting fire, and Fritsch and Rosenhagen went forward with the first wave on the left flank. Within about two hundred meters of the start line the attack came to a halt in heavy Polish machine-gun fire, mostly from the flank. The general was in sparkling form, but Rosenhagen felt understandably concerned that Fritsch, in general's uniform, including cap—without steel helmet—was resting on his elbows in a slight depression, with the upper part of his body exposed. Just then Rosenhagen spotted a machine gun in the vicinity and opened up on it with his pistol. The general, whose eyesight was very poor, accompanied this attack with skeptical but good-natured remarks, and it took a great effort on Rosenhagen's part to persuade him eventually to pull back.

By then the situation was really becoming serious. Carefully checking on everything every twenty paces or so, they crawled the first fifty meters, crossed a road, and ran past some houses to a field of turnips. As they ran across the field, machine guns opened fire on them from houses at a crossroad behind them. The two of them jumped into a roadside ditch and had taken only a couple more paces when the general was hit. Within a moment he was dead. It was perhaps a fitting death for a soldier who could not bear to remain at home while others fought.

General Jodl, by no means one who would lightly risk the displeasure of the Führer, announced Fritsch's death with the words, "I have to report that the Armed Forces have today lost their finest soldier, General Baron von Fritsch was killed this afternoon while leading a reconnaissance patrol."

Chapter 2

FIELD MARSHAL ERICH VON (LEWINSKI) MANSTEIN

A General's General and Germany's Greatest Military Strategist of World War II

Field Marshal von Manstein was tall and slim, and a fine figure of a man. To those who did not know him well he gave the impression of being cool, or even standoffish, but those who served under him appreciated his studied discretion and recognizable shrewdness, his quick and sure grasp of the most complex situations, and his pronounced sense of fairness.

Erich von Lewinski was born on 24 November 1887, the tenth child of Artillery General Eduard von Lewinski, a member of an old aristocratic military family that produced seven generals during the twentieth century. His maternal grandfather, Oskar von Sperling, was also a general, and so was his mother's brother. Immediately after Erich's christening, he was adopted by the von Mansteins, who had no children of their own. His foster mother, Hedwig von Manstein, whose maiden name was von Sperling, was his mother's younger sister, and from the day of his baptism he took the name Manstein.

As a child, Erich von Manstein was delicate, but his training in the Royal Prussian Cadet Corps, which he entered in 1900, developed him physically to such an extent that on his entry into the army in 1906 he was declared provisionally fit for active service.

The Cadet Corps, which exercised an enormous influence on the "Old Army" of Germany, dated back even before 1717, when Frederick William of Prussia first combined the various military academies in Berlin into a single cadet corps for boys aged eleven to eighteen, with the five-year-old crown prince—the future Frederick the Great—as nominal commander. Entrance was originally permitted only to the nobility. The cadet institutions could be traced back to the old academies of the seventeenth century, which provided the necessary education for younger members of the nobility, who were destined to be officers with a broad academic background and a highly developed sense of duty in which military training played only a part.

A cadet corps was founded in Dresden in 1692, and the Bavarian Cadet Corps was established in Munich about 1756. Both continued until World War I, as did the Royal Prussian Cadet Corps, whose headquarters moved to imposing new buildings at Lichterfelde in 1878. There ten companies of senior cadets under a colonel received a very high standard of education that did not aim solely at producing officers but rather emphasized building character and creating a harmonious blend of the best aspects of physical, academic, and religious education. This training inevitably included loyalty to the person of the emperor and a highly developed sense of that admirably selfless devotion to ethical and moral perfection which, right up to the birth of the permissive age, was understood by reference to honor.

Such then was the atmosphere in which young Erich von Manstein and his contemporaries were brought up—in an aura of chivalrous and dutiful loyalty to Germany, especially personified in the monarch, who was the supreme warlord.

Von Manstein was bright and able to master a subject very quickly. But his school reports nevertheless stated that with greater application of his talents he could attain better results. He sat for his matriculation examinations at the Senior Cadet School at Lichterfelde and in 1906 joined the Third Foot Guards as an ensign. During 1913 he was posted to the Kriegsakademie on a staff course, and at the outbreak of World War I he was lieutenant and adjutant of the 2d Reserve Regiment of the Guards. In a guards reserve unit he took part in the capture of Namur and (in the east) in the decisive Battle of the Masurian Lakes, which, together with the victory of Tannenberg, halted the Russian advance in East Prussia and brought lasting fame to Hindenburg as commander in chief of the Eighth Army. In the autumn campaign in Poland, Manstein was seriously wounded, but after his recovery he served in various staff appointments, and, even at that early stage as a captain he showed exceptional tactical skill. In the offensives in northern Poland and in Serbia in 1915 and at the attack on the great French fortress Verdun in 1916, he was able to gain a clear insight into the requirements of higher command in the offensive.

After the German collapse of 1918 he was taken into the 100,000-man Reichswehr, which was all that Germany was allowed under the terms of the peace treaties, and at the end of September 1929 he was appointed to a post in the Reichswehr Ministry and took over as head of Group 1 of the TI Section, as the Operations Section of the General Staff was called. Theoretically, under the terms of the Treaty of Versailles, Germany had no general staff, but in fact the Truppenamt served the same purpose. Under Manstein's direction Group 1 controlled the actual operations staff of the commander in chief of the army and allocated tasks to all troops. He also had to arrange the more important war games and instructional tours that were part of the operational training of senior commanders and staff officers.

The German Army—consisting in those days of seven infantry divisions and three cavalry divisions (totaling 100,000 in accordance with the Treaty of Versailles)—faced as potential enemies the French Army, which in very short time could mobilize thirty divisions; the Polish Army with its twenty-five peacetime divisions, which could be doubled under threat of war; and the Czech Army, which had about fifteen infantry divisions and several cavalry brigades.

Since Germany's neighbors had taken only the smallest of steps toward disarmament, though they should have done far more in conformity with the Treaty of Versailles, it had been decided even before Manstein joined the Operations Section of TI that preparations should be made for the mobilization of the 100,000-man Reichswehr. Manstein proposed the immediate trebling of the infantry divisions, from seven to twenty. The main problem in such an increase was the shortage of weapons. No one could take the limitations of Versailles really seriously, in light of the numerical strength of other European armies, but with the treaty's terms in mind Manstein directed his thoughtful endeavors toward training the field army's other ranks to such degree that in a crisis most of the men could command a section, most section commanders would be capable of taking over a platoon, and a qualified platoon commander could command a company or even a battalion. Every officer was trained to fill the next higher post.

Any plan to treble the army in event of war had to have the approval of the minister, to whom Manstein was himself accountable, and the object of German military measures certainly did not consist of preparing for war on Germany's initiative, which would in any event have been totally unrealistic in view of the five-to-one superiority of her possible enemies. Such measures aimed solely at creating the most elementary form of security against a sudden *coup de main* by one of her eastern neighbors.

For this specific purpose the Frontier Defense Force was also established, consisting of volunteers drawn from among the people living along the Polish and Czechoslovakian borders. It comprised some thirty Frontier Defense formations, each with a fighting strength of about one infantry regiment, the equivalent of a British infantry brigade, with its own light brigade of up to twelve guns.

At the end of the 1920's, Poland had "embodied" Wilna, and to prevent her from doing the same with East Prussia (in the so-called Heilsberger Triangle, the only area of East Prussia in which Germany was permitted to build fortifications under the Treaty of Versailles) Manstein extended the old Köningsberg fortress to turn it into a sort of East Prussian redoubt, consisting of barbed-wire entanglements and tank traps, as well as thick concrete bunkers.

Normally, as on all general staffs, it would be part of Manstein's job to prepare concentration schemes in advance. He had to forget about that, since the Reich in 1930 had to reckon with at least three possible enemies, each one of whom was militarily far superior to Germany. In view of the capacity of the German railway network, the army could be concentrated rapidly in any desired direction according to the demands of a particular situation.

On Hitler's seizure of power Manstein was in command of the rifle battalion of the 4th Infantry Regiment at Kolberg, in Pomerania. On 1 February 1934, the day on which Fritsch became commander in chief of the army, Manstein was appointed chief of staff of Military District No. 3 in Berlin, and on 1 July 1935 he became chief of operations at Army Headquarters, a particularly responsible and prestigious post for any staff officer.

In October 1936 he was promoted to major general and appointed quartermaster general of the army, which, in the setup of the German forces at the time, meant that he also became deputy chief of the Army General Staff under General Ludwig

Beck, who had already begun to fall afoul of Hitler by disagreeing with the Führer's successful gamble in reoccupying the Rhineland a few months earlier. Manstein's most important task, in the first instance as chief of operations and now as deputy chief of the General Staff, was to formulate a concentration scheme on the basis of reequipment of the forces from 1936. The first of these schemes was the so-called Strategic Concentration, Case Red (which presupposed war on two fronts, with the main struggle in the west). Basically, this plan covered a hypothetical attack on the Reich by France, and was therefore a purely defensive one.

General von Blomberg, designated minister of war and commander in chief of the armed forces after Hitler's reinstitution of conscription, also foresaw a second possibility, which would again mean war on two fronts, but this time with the main struggle in the southeast, which might force Germany into preemptive attack to forestall an offensive by a superior hostile coalition. For this contingency Case Green was worked out during 1937. It envisaged the employment of the main German forces against the Czechs, to eliminate any threat from the rear during a later decisive battle against the French Army. Both Case Red and Case Green were developed for use solely in the event that Germany was faced with an actual attack by her enemies.

Special preparations were also to be made for three other cases. One was Case Otto, named for the pretender to the Austrian throne. Its object was armed intervention to prevent a restoration of the Austrian monarchy, by means of a march on Vienna. Very few German staff officers heard of it, and it was never mentioned to me. On 5 November 1937, at a top-secret meeting carefully recorded by Hitler's military adjutant, Colonel Hossbach, the Führer divulged to his four senior military commanders and to his foreign minister his determination to gain Lebensraum by attacks on Czechoslovakia and Austria. This was something new, for talk of Lebensraum, we had always understood, referred exclusively to Poland and the western Soviet Union. As William L. Shirer has recorded, the Wehrmacht chiefs were stunned by the idea of provoking a war for which Germany was not prepared. Within three months, for various reasons, Blomberg as minister of war, Fritsch, the commander in chief of the army, and Foreign Minister von Neurath had lost their jobs.

At the time Manstein firmly opposed precipitous rearmament as was envisaged in Hitler's defiant establishment of universal military service in March 1935, with a peacetime army of thirty-six divisions. His opposition was almost certainly one of the main grounds for his removal from the General Staff and his appointment as commander of the Eighteenth Infantry Division at Liegnitz, in Silesia, in the wake of the dismissal of Fritsch and several other high-ranking officers early in 1938. Nevertheless, at Liegnitz as elsewhere, everyone who had not already got to know Manstein well was impressed by his great ability in directing operations. The headquarters of Eighth Corps, to which Manstein's division belonged, often conducted war games and tactical exercises without troops, and on such occasions as a rule divisional commanders would act as commanders of higher formations. They would then have to give their own evaluation of the situation, reach decisions on their own, and issue the necessary orders.

The director of these war games, Infantry General Ernst Busch— later earmarked to command one of the two armies for the invasion of England—would prepare in advance a "Staff College" solution to the problem, and the general selected as commander for the exercise was expected to work out the "correct" answer himself and to act according to the intentions of the directing staff. Manstein was almost invariably nominated army commander of the "German side," and younger staff officers who knew his capabilities would lay bets whether or not he would once again confidently produce the "Staff College" solution. Those who managed to find takers for their bets always won. He summed up any situation with such self-assurance that one got the impression that he must have taken part in planning the exercise. In addition it was invariably clear that he formulated his own moves and tactics to fit in a wider framework with the bigger picture always in mind. His superior officers acknowledged him as a superb tactician.

Case Otto, meanwhile, had been conveniently forgotten by the headquarters of the army, and when Hitler suddenly decided to march into Austria and summoned Beck to the Reich Chancellery, Manstein was about to leave Berlin to take up another divisional post. He was frantically pulled back and in five hours drafted the orders necessary to mobilize three corps. With war imminent Hitler could not afford to let such surpassing talent go to waste.

Shortly before the Polish Campaign of 1939, Hitler appointed Manstein chief of staff, Army Group South, which was commanded by General Gerd von Rundstedt. The plan for the conquest of Poland was virtually the brainchild of these two and Colonel Günther Blumentritt. During the campaign Manstein interceded asking that due consideration be shown to the Polish civilian population. He was strongly supported in this by his GOC. With Rundstedt he also tried to dissuade Hitler from bombing Warsaw, but in vain.

The way Manstein went about things and the source of his tactical decisions were quite different from those of most of his fellow staff officers. Colonel Heusinger, who was chief of operations, expresses this very clearly in the preface to *Aufstand und Gehorsam (Rebellion and Submission):*

From 1930 onward, I served immediately under Manstein, Jodl and then for four years under [Franz] Halder [successor to Beck as chief of the General Staff]. The methods of the Prussian [Manstein] and the two Bavarians [Halder and Jodl] were fundamentally different. Manstein's tactical decisions sprang largely from intuition. The task of his assistants was to determine to what extent this intuition could be put into practice. Halder and Jodl, on the other hand, spent long hours of work at night on the military groundwork, before they managed to reach a decision.

After the Polish Campaign had ended, Manstein remained chief of staff to Rundstedt, who became Commander of Army Group A on the left of Colonel General Fedor von Bock's Army Group B for the offensive against France in 1940. Under a plan worked out by the General Staff of the Army under Halder, the main attack was to be made through Holland and northern Belgium, with Army Group B in the major role, seeking by this flank attack to inflict a decisive defeat not only on the Dutch and Belgian forces but also on the British and French. The left would be covered by Army Group A, which was assigned a secondary role through the wooded Ardennes hill country, setting out from the area of the southern Eifel and the Hunsrück.

An officer carrying a copy of the plan was force-landed in Belgium on 10 January 1940, and the Allies were forewarned. Regarding the whole episode as a put-up show, they benefited little from the incident, but Hitler was left with sound reason to seek a new plan.

Manstein's objection to the original plan was that it was merely a repetition of the famous Schlieffen Plan of 1914. But Schlieffen then aimed at encircling the enemy from the north with what one might call a sweeping embrace, so as to drive west of Paris and force the Allied armies into capitulation with their backs to the Swiss frontier.

In the 1939 plan of operations, in Manstein's opinion, there would be no final decision but merely a partial victory, with a territorial advance to the Channel Coast. As an alternative he proposed to the High Command of the Army that the "Schwerpunkt," or main weight, of the German offensive should rest on Army Group A and that it should cut off the enemy forces that had been thrown into Belgium by launching a surprise thrust through the Ardennes in the direction of the lower Somme. On this line of advance the Allies would never expect the use of armored units because of the terrain. In fact, as early as 1933 Sir Basil Liddell-Hart had suggested to the British War Office that in any future war fast tank formations should be employed in a rapid counterstroke through the Ardennes and had been told that the region was impassable. Manstein regarded such an advance as the only way in which the whole of the Allied north flank in Belgium could be destroyed, as a prerequisite for attaining a final decision in France. The purely frontal attack envisaged by the Army High Command, in his view, offered no real foundation on which to build an annihilating victory.

Manstein's plan, known as "Sichelschnitt" ("Cut of a Sickle") was turned down by Halder, because the latter had been instructed by Hitler to reserve the creation of the Schwerpunkt with Army Group B, though keeping open the possibility of shifting the main weight of the attack during the offensive.

On 25 January 1940, Manstein learned that he was to be given command of the 38th Infantry Corps with headquarters in Stettin in eastern Germany, well removed from any likely offensive. The high command wanted to rid itself of a troublemaker, and on February 17 he was received by Hitler, to whom he had to report as general officer commanding a corps. At their meeting Hitler encouraged him to express his ideas about the coming offensive in the West and fully supported Manstein's Sichelschnitt plan, which he was later to claim as his own.

The attack on France began on 10 May 1940, when Manstein's corps was instructed to move to Braunschweig before being placed

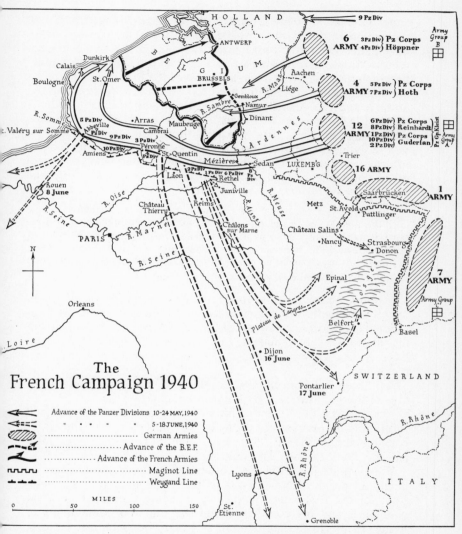

The
French Campaign 1940

Advance of the Panzer Divisions 10-24 MAY, 1940
     "   "   "   "   5-18 JUNE, 1940
German Armies
Advance of the B.E.F.
Advance of the French Armies
Maginot Line
Weugand Line

MILES

0   50   100   150

From Major General F. W. von Mellenthin, *Panzer Battles* (Norman: University of Oklahoma Press, 1956).

27

under Command Army Group A on 16 May. Manstein did not receive operation orders for his corps until 25 May. He was to relieve Paul von Kleist's 14th Panzer Corps in the Abbeville-Amiens sector. Manstein's divisions attacked across the Somme on 5 June, by which time the French had lost most of their mechanized forces and could gather only 49 divisions to cover a new front along the Somme and the Aisne, with 17 in the Maginot Line—hardly a match for Germany's 10 Panzer divisions and 130 infantry divisions. As is so often true in war, information about the enemy was sadly lacking, but Manstein was never the man to let lack of information delay him in making decisions. He described his method of command in such a situation in his own book, *Verlorene Siege (Lost Victories):*

> The military commander who in such circumstances delays action until the position is completely clarified by unquestionable situation reports is hardly likely even to touch the hem of the mantle of Bellona, goddess of war. The hour of destiny will pass him by. For that very reason, at first light I myself went up to the most advanced tactical headquarters of 46th Division on the south bank of the Somme.

In short, on this as on so many other occasions, Manstein made his own evaluation of the situation and then acted without hesitation. He always seized the initiative and expected the same from his subordinate commanders, and it was this fact that formed the basis of his own success and that of the troops placed under his command.

At the end of February, when Hitler was already planning to invade Russia, Manstein took over command of the 56th Panzer Corps. It was a fulfillment of his wish to command a mechanized formation, in this case consisting of the 8th Panzer Division under Brandenberger, the 3d Motorized Infantry Division under Jahn and the 290th Infantry Division, with a total of 570 tanks.

When Hitler, in March 1941, ordered that the forthcoming campaign against the Russians was to be waged unmercifully, Manstein for the first time found himself facing a conflict between obedience and his conscience, and he told the commander of Army Group North that he could not carry out such instructions, which were against his sense of honor as a soldier.

As part of Wilhelm von Leeb's Army Group (whose route was to run through the Baltic States from East Prussia), Manstein's

Panzer Corps began its advance on Leningrad on 22 June 1941, the day that the German attack was launched on Russia. He was quite clear in his own mind that the Russian Campaign could achieve success only if the mechanized formations thrust forward at top speed, regardless of any threat to flanks or rear. The Russians should not be allowed any time for organized resistance.

The first objective of his own corps was to seize the bridges over the River Dvina near Dvinsk, in Latvia. In accordance with his plan the corps rolled forward relentlessly. In common British parlance of the Desert War, they "pressed on regardless" and by 26 June held the Dvina crossing. Manstein's acute sense of time and space urged him to exploit this success immediately by continuing his advance, even at considerable risk, for his infantry had been unable to keep pace with his armored spearhead. Hitler got cold feet and ordered the corps to halt. By the time the infantry had caught up with the mechanized units, six most valuable days had been lost.

Many persons may be inclined to the view that a senior officer, holding a high command, must need both quiet and time to cogitate over a problem, and it would not have been surprising if Manstein had kept clear of the immediate turmoil of battle and, like many another commander, led from the rear. In his case exactly the opposite was invariably so. He led his troops exclusively from the front and turned up at all critical points during action among the most forward elements so as to see the situation at first hand. He then usually gave any necessary orders on the spot, which frequently interfered ruthlessly in the normal chain of command within individual units. Since the steps he took invariably turned out to be right, his subordinate commanders and the troops themselves learned to place absolute trust in him and in his orders, even when at first sight they hardly seemed to make sense.

On one occasion in the sector southeast of Leningrad, where his corps was held up by strong enemy resistance, he ordered one of his divisions pulled out during the night. His idea was to throw in this and another division the next day in an outflanking attack on the Russians.

In the divisional positions thus vacated, he left a single company of military police, consisting of about 150 men armed only with rifles and intended for police duties in occupied Russian towns. The company commander concerned was hardly delighted with such a task, which not only he but also divisional headquarters thought to be more than hazardous. The attack by Manstein's two divisions the next day was a success; the Russians were taken completely by surprise and overrun. He was then able to continue his advance.

This and similar episodes gave Manstein a reputation among the troops. He was admired, and faith in his leadership was unbounded. Had he been able to unbend more and to be a little more cordial in his day-to-day dealings with others, he would undoubtedly have ranked among the most popular of German military commanders.

Manstein was generous and just. A Colonel H. R. Dingler, GSO 1 of one of Manstein's divisions, once heard him say some very harsh and unjustified things about the division, in which certain action by the Divisional Command did not fit in with Manstein's ideas. It was a particularly hot day, and tempers were somewhat frayed. In the absence of his divisional commander, Dingler was not prepared to take Manstein's criticisms lying down. He immediately lodged a complaint against his corps commander, who was informed accordingly, in the normal procedure.

Summoning Dingler to report to him, Manstein asked for a factual account of the situation and divisional headquarters' opinion about it. On the strength of what Dingler told him he unreservedly withdrew his derogatory and critical comments and made his peace over a glass of wine.

On 12 September 1941, Manstein was unexpectedly called away from his post and appointed to command the Eleventh Army. Some three weeks earlier Hitler had issued his directive to the German forces in the east to turn aside from their drive on Moscow, to occupy the Crimea and the Donetz Basin, and to cut the supply route to the oil fields in the Caucasus. A giant pincer trapped some 600,000 Russians around Kiev, but winter was fast approaching before the German advance renewed at the end of September, and another 600,000 or so Russians were trapped in the Vyasma sector. Now, with their troops worn out and the deteriorating weather turning the limitless countryside into a morass of slush, the specter of Napoleon's retreat from Moscow haunted more than one German general. Yet, in the hope of de-

THE GERMAN ATTACK ON RUSSIA

From *The War, 1939–1945* (London: Cassell & Collier Macmillan, Ltd., 1957).

livering a final knockout blow on 15 November the big push toward Moscow was renewed. Barely twenty miles from its objective the great offensive was halted in the snow.

On his arrival at the headquarters of Gerdvon Rundstedt's Army Group South, two major tasks confronted Manstein's army. He was expected to throw back the Russians north of the Sea of Asov and to follow up by occupying the Crimean Peninsula, where some 50,000 British and French troops had landed 87 years before to besiege the great fortress of Sebastopol for a full year, with the support of 15,000 Piedmontese. Thanks to Manstein's outstanding military ability, the Crimea was almost totally in German hands as early as 16 November 1941, the day after the drive on Moscow had been resumed. Only the important fortress of Sebastopol still held out.

On 1 February 1942, Hitler promoted Manstein to colonel general in recognition of his great achievements. Meanwhile, a particularly difficult situation had built up for the Eleventh Army, since the Russians had attacked from the direction of Kerch, at the very eastern tip of the Crimea, where the straits from the Black Sea lead into the Sea of Asov. The German corps holding the vital sector had pulled back on its own initiative, and as an immediate result the assault on Sebastopol had to be postponed.

What mattered most to Manstein was to destroy the enemy at Kerch before he could turn his attention again to Sebastopol. For the Eleventh Army there followed a most critical period, during which Manstein never lost sight of the over-all situation. On 18 May the Russians were finally defeated at Kerch, and the Eleventh Army rounded up 170,000 prisoners.

In spite of the impending final assault on Sebastopol, Manstein could still find time to concern himself with things that affected him not merely as a soldier but also as a human being. He was particularly interested in the accommodation and feeding of the enormous numbers of prisoners of war, he worried about the needy civilian population of the Crimea, and whenever possible he visited his own troops and hospitals.

Before the attack on Sebastopol he remained true to his precept: "Do your own reconnaissance. See for yourself and then get down to the job without delay." He reconnoitered possible points of attack on the fortress not only from landward but also from the sea, by investigating the whole of the southern coast of the Crimea in an Italian torpedo boat which was attacked by Russian aircraft. A number of the crew were killed, including Sergeant Friedrich Nagel, who had been Manstein's personal driver for years. How closely the commander felt bound to his men and how deeply he was affected by the death of a single one of them may be seen from the words he spoke at Nagel's graveside and quoted in *Verlorene Siege:*

"We are taking leave of a very dear friend, Sergeant Friedrich Nagel. In life he was a keen soldier. The military profession was a vocation to him, and soldierliness, inherited from his father, shaped his thoughts and conduct. He was, for that very reason, not only very brave but also loyal, full of energy, and conscious of his duty, an exemplary soldier who would have been destined for greater things had Fate not decreed otherwise. He was a good friend, always cheerful and helpful, and with a place in the heart of each one of us as a result. He went through life a happy man."

Further laudatory remarks followed, and then Manstein concluded:

"For more than five years, he sat beside me at the wheel of our vehicle as my driver and companion. His keen eye and steady hand guided us through many countries and over thousands of kilometers. There was never a single argument between us. During these years together, we saw much that was beautiful, and together we experienced great events which are part of history and of victory. Last year he was wounded at my side, and now he has been mortally struck. In the shared years of our daily lives we had become friends, and such a bond of friendship cannot be broken by the bullet that struck him down. My gratitude and constant friendship, and the thoughts of all of us, follow him beyond the grave and to eternity. My dear friend, may you rest in peace."

The final assault on Sebastopol began on 7 June 1942. It was to free the whole of the Eleventh Army as a necessary preliminary to Hitler's intended push toward Stalingrad and the Caucasus, which would represent an advance in depth on one flank with no corresponding threat to the Russians' center. The idea went against all the strategic tenets of the German General Staff. The culminating attack on the Crimean fortress was a particularly grim affair in which every inch of ground was bitterly contested by General I. E. Petrov's Coastal Army of more than 100,000 men with some 600 guns and more than 100 mortars, but only 38 tanks.

Manstein delivered his main blow against the northeastern side of the fortifications, employing 54th Corps, supported by 120 batteries of guns, including a battery of superheavy 615-mm mortars and an 800-mm railway gun. Some 204,000 men were concentrated for the operation, which included a secondary thrust on the general axis of the Yalta road, which comes in from the southeast. More than 100 bombers and a number of MTB's and other craft blockaded the fortress from seaward, and H Hour followed five days of aerial and artillery bombardment.

Desperate hand-to-hand fighting ensued, and the last Soviet reinforcements managed to land from warships on 26 June, but on the night of 28/29 June Manstein's forces crossed North Bay and dug in. The next day they broke into the heart of Sebastopol, and Red Army remnants began evacuation by sea after a siege that had lasted 250 days. On 1 July the German radio announced the fall of the historic fortress, and Hitler promoted Manstein to field marshal.

The army commander's first thought after his great victory was to shake hands with as many of his comrades-in-arms as possible. Since that was possible on only a limited scale, he invited all unit commanders, as well as all officers, noncommissioned officers, and men who had been awarded the Knight's Cross or the German Cross to a victory celebration at which all fallen comrades were solemnly remembered.

After the conquest of the Crimea it was Hitler's intention to push on toward Stalingrad and the Caucasus, but in the midst of preparations for this new offensive, Manstein suddenly received orders from Hitler to move to the northern flank of the Russian Front with his Eleventh Army and capture Leningrad.

He was aghast at the order which went against one of the most crucial and time-proven dictates of strategy: that all available forces should be concentrated on the main sector of an offensive. And this main sector now lay clearly along the southern front in Russia. There Hitler's disregard of well-established principles was to lead to unmitigated disaster at Stalingrad, ultimate withdrawal from the Caucasus, and failure to take Leningrad in the north.

As it turned out, the thrust on Leningrad by Manstein's army never materialized. The Russians broke through the German lines along the River Volkov, and the Eleventh Army had to be thrown in there to stop them. Then, on 20 November 1942, Manstein

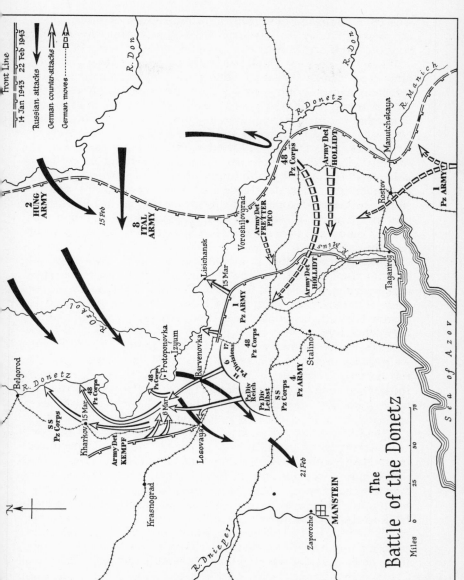

The

Battle of the Donetz

Miles

0   25   50   75

MANSTEIN

Krasnograd

Zaporozhe

R. Dnieper

R. Donetz

Belgorod

SS Pz Corps

Kharkov

15 Mar

48 Pz Corps

Army Det KEMPF

6 Mar

48 Pz Corps

Protoponovka

Izyum

Barvenovka

Losovaya

Pz Div Reich

Pz Div Leibst

SS Pz Corps

4 Pz ARMY

Stalino

21 Feb

11 Divisions

6 17

48 Pz Corps

I Pz ARMY

15 Mar

Lisichansk

Voroshilovgrad

Army Det FRETTER PICO

8 ITAL ARMY

15 Feb

2 HUNG ARMY

R. Oskol

R. Don

R. Donetz

Army Det HOLLIDT

R. Mius

Army Det HOLLIDT

48 Pz Corps

Stalino

Taganrog

Sea of Azov

Rostov

I Pz ARMY

R. Manich

R. Don

Manutchskaya

Front Line

14 Jan 1943   22 Feb 1943

Russian attacks

German counter-attacks

German moves

was given command of a newly constituted Army Group Don in the Stalingrad sector. The part he played during the ensuing tragedy is told in Chapter 6.

When the Russians poured down both sides of the River Don after the German defeat of Stalingrad, they presented a grave threat to Army Group A as it pulled back desperately from the Caucasus before the trap closed behind it. It was due to Manstein alone that his Army Group Don, fighting in the white desolation of the Russian winter, could still inflict defeat on the enemy in battles along the Donetz and the Dnieper and at Kharkov on 15 March 1943. Kleist's forces from the Caucasus had barely been able to slip through, and Manstein averted full-scale disaster by a counterstroke that developed into a counteroffensive and restored the German front. The performance dramatically illustrated that in a country as vast as Russia it is not militarily important to hold onto fixed lines or even localities merely for the sake of holding territory. Here Manstein—like Rommel in the desert of Cyrenaica—showed that in mobile warfare inflexibility does not pay. He also demonstrated that it is possible to turn a withdrawal into a victory by inspired use of mobile units in suitable terrain such as the vast, level steppes of Russia. As February turned to March 1943, Manstein had once more regained the initiative for the Wehrmacht.

He then tried to convince the army high command that the full weight of Germany's military effort should be concentrated on the Eastern Front during 1943. All available forces from other theaters of war should be transferred to the Russian Front to force a decisive showdown. Only then, with victory in the east achieved, could one turn one's attention to other enemies, before they had time to become active in western and southern Europe.

However, Hitler would not make up his mind to concentrate his military effort in the east, nor was he willing to give up the industrially important Donetz Basin, which Manstein's countermeasures had regained. The Führer was faced with an irresistible temptation to ignore suggestions that the whole line be pulled back to shorten the front and allow refitting and regrouping beyond the reach of the Russians, whose lines of communication were already heavily overtaxed. Unwilling ever to let go of anything he held, Hitler was eventually to be left with nothing.

OPERATIONS IN RUSSIA, JULY–DEC. 1943

From *The War, 1939–1945.*

37

In order at least to straighten out the German line, Manstein suggested that an attack be mounted on Kursk as soon as possible. The date he set for the offensive was the beginning of May, but Hitler kept postponing the attack, and it was the beginning of July before operations could begin. Meanwhile, the Russians had developed the whole area into a veritable fortress, and the element of surprise on which Manstein had been counting was lost. The offensive did not succeed, and the initiative passed to the Russians.

On 27 January 1944, Hitler summoned all commanders in chief from the Russian Front to his headquarters. With diminishing forces available to hold a length of front that in terms of space presented few problems to the Red Army's almost limitless reservoir of manpower, Manstein was all for withdrawing, but he had been expressly forbidden by Hitler to give up ground. Already suffering from eye trouble, Manstein became involved in serious clashes with Hitler and, as usual, displayed considerable personal courage in his dealings with the dictator. Hitler would not budge, and nothing that Manstein could say would make him change his mind.

On 30 March 1944, Hitler informed the field marshal that the time for large-scale operations, for which Manstein was particularly suited, had passed. What was needed now was determined hanging on, for which Manstein's talents were less well suited than those of Field Marshal Walter Model, whom Hitler wished to appoint in Manstein's place.

Manstein was relieved of his command and awarded the Crossed Swords, to add to his Knight's Cross of the Iron Cross. After his sight was restored by an operation, the man whom many consider to have been the greatest strategist Germany produced during World War II, lived out the rest of the war in retirement at Celle, was captured by the British, and—as a sad reflection of the times— was sentenced to eighteen years imprisonment at the Nuremberg Trials. He was released in May 1953.

All who knew Field Marshal von Manstein, or had any dealings with him in war or peace, admired his rare ability, and that was especially the feeling of those who served under him. Certainly good fortune often smiled on him, but it is well to remember that fortune favors only the most capable in the long run. And without doubt Manstein was among the most capable of soldiers. He was truly a great general. And that was what his subordinates considered him to be.

Chapter 4

FIELD MARSHAL
ERWIN ROMMEL

The Most Popular German Soldier of World War II

It is rewarding to take a good look at Erwin Rommel's childhood and youth, since the key to so much in his later life lies in characteristics that were already strongly evident in his younger days. Rommel did not come from a family traditionally military. He was born on 15 November 1891 in Heidenheim in Württemberg. His father, like his grandfather, was a schoolmaster and became principal of the Realgymnasium at Aalen. His mother, Helene, was from the von Lutz family, who were prominent civil servants of Württemberg.

As a child Erwin was of delicate health, but he had a good disposition and was shy of no one. Even then he displayed one characteristic that was to be particularly conspicuous later on, especially during the two world wars: he never showed any sign of anxiety or fear. When other children would run away from the chimney sweep with his soot-blackened face, Erwin would go up to him without a qualm and shake him by the hand.

At school young Rommel liked mathematics and was an outstanding sportsman, with a preference for skiing, athletics, and cycling. He was interested in mechanical work: when his motorcycle needed repair, he would not rest until he had completely stripped his motorcycle and then carefully reassembled it himself. Later, as a senior commander, he would often demonstrate this practical skill by personally putting a broken-down tank in running order.

Even while he was at school, Rommel's dream was to be a soldier. In 1909 he joined the 126th Württemberg Infantry Regiment, and in 1911, while at the Military College in Danzig, he met his future wife, Lucie-Maria Mollin. She was the only woman ever to play a role in his life. The trust and affection between them may be gauged from the letters Rommel wrote her almost daily throughout World War II (preserved for posterity in *The Rommel Papers,* thanks to the efforts of Sir Basil Liddell-Hart. Every sentence of Rommel's letters rings with honesty, decency, and clarity of thought.

Rommel became a second lieutenant in 1910 and went on active service in 1914. His very first engagements and fighting patrols demonstrated his ability to exploit successfully any given situation in spite of danger. His greatest achievement during World War I was the storming of Monte Matajur, southwest of Caporretto on the Isonzo Front, on 26 October 1917. The Austrians had suffered a reverse on the Italian Front and had asked for German help. Among the formations sent to support the Austrians happened to be the Württemberg Mountain Battalion, in which Lieutenant Rommel commanded a company. The battalion was to act as flank protection for the regiment forming the spearhead of the German attack, and Rommel's handling of the situation was typical of him.

When he realized that the German assault was coming to a standstill, he launched an attack with his company on his own initiative and without orders. Taken completely unaware, the Italians in his sector surrendered without a fight, and he immediately continued his advance. With his men he clambered up a steep mountain path toward Monte Matajur and decided that an attack on the heights was bound to succeed. And it did. When Rommel rushed the Italian positions in the early morning hours of 10 December 1917, the enemy was so taken by surprise that 43 officers and about 1,500 men surrendered. For this deliberate and daring undertaking, Rommel was awarded Germany's highest decoration for valor, the Pour le Mérite, an order instituted by King Frederick II of Prussia in 1740.

After the war Rommel remained a soldier, and in 1929 he became an instructor at the Infantry School in Dresden. There he wrote a book, *Infanterie greift an,* which contains graphic accounts of battles of World War I and the lessons to be learned from them. It is common knowledge that Hitler read the book and spoke of it approvingly, which is probably one of the reasons why he took some notice of Rommel later.

Rommel was promoted to major and commanding officer of the Rifle Battalion in Goslar in 1933—the year Hitler came to power. When he arrived to take over the battalion, the officers thought they would have a little joke by putting their new CO through a "field-service fitness test." They invited Rommel to a ski run, and when they arrived at the summit they planned to have a rest and something to drink. But they did not know Rommel. He immediately challenged them to a ski race down the slopes, which was followed by several further runs down the lower foothills without a single stop for breath. The officers were astounded at their sporting commanding officer, whose physical fitness left them all outclassed.

By 1935 Rommel was a lieutenant colonel. Without doubt he was in favor of the political developments of those years. Though by nature and by training of the "Seeckt school" of the Reichswehr, he was not politically inclined, but like many other officers of the day, he could see that Hitler was destined to free Germany from the shackles of the Treaty of Versailles. On the other hand, he had no time for the undisciplined rowdies of the Nazi party "Sturmabteilungen," and he was certainly not pleased when Hitler entrusted him with the task of acting as liaison officer for the Hitler Jugend, the party youth organization, to improve their discipline.

It was when Rommel was serving in this new capacity that I first met him in Berlin, in 1938. I was at the time third General Staff officer of the Third Corps in the city. Bursting with energy and good health, Rommel came into my office to discuss his activities in the Berlin area.

He said that it was obvious to him that one could not turn thirteen-year-old boys into Napoleons. He would do his best to instill in them some idea of order and discipline, but he was continually having difficulty with the Hitler Jugend leader, Baldur von Schirach. Barely three years after this conversation I was in North Africa, and for nearly fifteen months I was one of Rommel's closest associates.

During the Polish Campaign he had been commandant of the Führer's headquarters. He then asked Hitler for a command more in keeping with his abilities and was appointed to command the 7th Panzer Division. With this formation—which soon earned the name "Ghost Division" because of its sudden and unexpected appearances—he fought in the French Campaign.

At the beginning of the offensive Rommel's 218-tank division, which formed part of Hermann Hoth's 15th Panzer Corps in the Fourth Army under Gunther von Kluge, crossed the Belgian frontier on 10 May 1940 and headed for Dinant, quickly overcoming roadblocks and obstructions but slowed down by demolished bridges and spirited defense by Belgian Chasseurs Ardennais at Chabrehez in the evening. By 4 P.M. on 12 May, however, the French had had to pull back, and all Meuse bridges on the Ninth' Army front from Dinant to the River Bar had been blown up. Rommel was in hot pursuit, and by early afternoon his leading reconnaissance armored cars had reached the Meuse. That very day his division had been reinforced with the 31st Panzer Regiment from the 5th Panzer Division, which was sent to join his own 25th Panzer Regiment. Under the divisional commander's personal guidance the newcomers drove back the French rear guards and rumbled down to the Meuse at Yvoir, where demolition charges were ignited just in time to halt the advance.

But at Houx, Rommel's motorcyclists made a daring crossing at an old weir during the night. He had gained a foothold across the river and, characteristically, was about to exploit his opportunity to the full. With resistance mounting on the opposite bank, at one stage Rommel took personal command of a battalion of the 7th Lorried Infantry Regiment and crossed in one of the first boats, a dangerous journey he was to repeat more than once. Determined to get part of a Panzer regiment across, he stood waist-deep in water himself and lent a hand at bridge building. By nightfall on 13 May, Corap's Ninth Army had lost its chance to stop him. It had been the sort of action Rommel took for granted. For the further advance of his division, Rommel used nights of the full moon to the utmost, a tactic he would later employ frequently with success in North Africa.

The main thrust was to be delivered by Heinz Guderian's Panzer Corps further south, but Rommel pushed on. By 16 May he was concentrating forces to smash through the hastily constructed extension of the Maginot Line. He fought his way across the French border and pursued the enemy through the night. He cleared Avesnes and, having no further orders, pushed on and only halted just east of Le Cateau when ammunition and petrol were almost exhausted. The French Ninth Army was finished. Just after midnight on 19 May, Rommel was off on yet another dash. He was himself surrounded for a while but by evening was hammering Major General R. L. Petre's British forces at Arras. That night Guderian's men reached the sea at Noyelles. Only on 23 May did Lord Gort order the abandonment of Arras, just in time to avoid encirclement. But an order halting the Panzers came from Hitler and put a temporary end to pursuit. When the order was rescinded, Rommel drove forward once more and on 27 May broke through the British line, captured Armentières, and was then pulled out for six days' rest at the end of Phase 1 of Operation Sichelschnitt. No sooner were Rommel's Panzers back in the fray than they precipitated disaster for the French by breaking through west of Amiens and driving southward fifty miles in two days.

The division's objective was now the village Saint-Valéry-en-Caux. It split the French Tenth Army in two, with the British 51st Highland Division on its coastal flank. On 8 May, Rommel sealed off Rouen and then captured it as General von Manstein's 38th Infantry Corps came up on his left. Another sixty-mile advance brought Rommel to the sea. At Saint-Valéry, where the Fifty-first Highland Division was trying to form a bridgehead for evacuation, he forced them to surrender on June 12. His bag of prisoners that day totaled 40,000, including the whole of the Highland Division, with its commander, Major General V. M. Fortune. Britain had lost one of its finest fighting formations.

The African Campaign, in which Rommel was to play such a significant role, was regarded by Hitler as a mere sideshow. His main objective was, of course, Russia. But when the Italian commander in chief, Graziani, was roundly defeated, lost the important forward position Sidi Barrani, and was driven back all the way through Cyrenaica, Hitler decided that he should provide the Italians with a "blocking force" as a barrier against further British advance. Originally this force consisted of only the 5th Light Division, to which the 15th Panzer Division was later added. The task was purely defensive and consisted of holding Tripolitania by preventing any enemy advance beyond a line from Buerat southward. In command was Major General Erwin Rommel.

Before leaving for North Africa, Rommel reported to the commander in chief of the army, Field Marshal von Brauchitsch, and to the chief of the army staff, General Halder. The latter was not much impressed by Rommel, to whom it was made quite clear that there was only one real objective for the German army, and that lay in Russia.

"We cannot spare more than two—and at the very most three—divisions for North Africa," Rommel was told. His immediate situation and the scope of his future operations were thus exactly defined.

In February the officer commanding the newly constituted Deutsches Afrika Korps, now Lieutenant General Rommel, arrived in the theater of war that was to bring him much honor and renown. Dynamic go-getter and aggressive field commander that he was, Rommel saw neither future nor stability for the war in Africa through a defensive strategy based on a defensive line at El Agheila. He quickly decided to go over to the offensive as soon as possible, before the British—who had withdrawn men and aircraft for Greece at Churchill's behest—could deploy sufficient forces to attack again in a drive on Tripoli.

On 1 March 1941, Rommel's mobile forces took the enemy completely by surprise, and by 4 April, Bengasi was in German hands and Rommel was laying siege to Tobruk. With their last drop of fuel his troops reached Bardia, on the Libyan-Egyptian frontier.

For a general and troops with no previous experience of desert warfare, with its extraordinary demands on the supply services and on men's physical endurance under unaccustomed conditions, the Afrika Korps' achievement was all the more remarkable for the fact that the Fifteenth Panzer Division was still arriving in dribs and drabs at the time it was ordered to attack Tobruk.

A staff officer naturally faces the question whether Rommel did the right thing in disregarding explicit instructions to stand and defend Tripoli. Should he have resisted the temptation to pursue a fleeing enemy all the way to the Egyptian border? I believe that under the circumstances he did the only sensible thing. Why did the High Command not stop him once he had retaken Jebel el Akdar, between Bengasi and Derna, if they disagreed with his decision? He had to exploit his opportunities as they presented themselves.

It is the responsibility of the High Command to match a psychologically suitable commander to a specific task, and in Rommel's case the Army Personnel Branch must have known what kind of man they were sending to Africa to fight a purely defensive action,

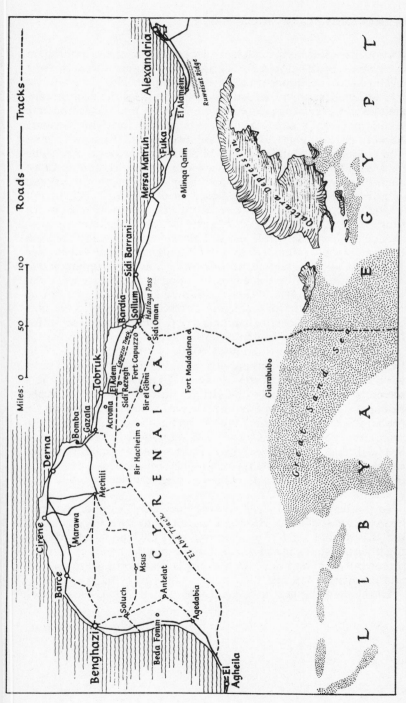

NORTH AFRICA – The Swaying Battle, 1940–42

From *The War, 1939–1945.*

particularly after his spectacular successes in offensive operations at the head of the Ghost Division on the Western Front in 1940.

The British reaction to their first encounter with Rommel was interesting. The advance reconnaissance units of the British commander in Cyrenaica, Lieutenant General Sir Philip Neame, were resting peacefully at El Agheila while he was fortifying Bengasi. Nobody gave thought to the possibility of a German offensive. The commander in chief of the Middle East, General Sir Archibald Wavell took the orthodox view (though not shared by Churchill) that any German force would have to be built up to at least two divisions before it could hazard an offensive.

On 24 March 1941, Neame received the usual report from the front: "All quiet. Nothing to report." At the same time an intelligence officer on his staff showed him a report saying that fresh German troops, estimated at about one division, had just arrived at Tripoli and containing information about their commander. Rommel was described as aggressive, and his military career was set down in detail. However, British Intelligence sources reported confidently from Berlin that there was no prospect of a German offensive and that Rommel and his troops had been sent to stiffen the backbone of the Italian defense.

What actually happened was contrary to expectations. The British were caught unprepared and either fled in confusion or were taken prisoner. In the whole of Cyrenaica, in fact, there seems to have been only one British officer who fully grasped Rommel's conduct of operations. He was Lieutenant General Sir Richard O'Connor, a lean, wiry, energetic Irishman, whose Western Desert Force of 30,000 men had soundly defeated Graziani's 80,000 Italians and driven them all the way from Sidi Barrani to the gates of Tripolitania before his advance was halted on instructions from Churchill cabled to General Wavell on 12 February.

At the beginning of April, Wavell had sent O'Connor out from Cairo to assist Neame. He was determined to save Cyrenaica for the British, but on 6 April, Neame and O'Connor left Mataua together in a staff car and drove straight into the hands of German motorcyclists. The brains of Western Desert Force were bagged, and the British had lost their battle.

Of the many battles subsequently fought in Africa, I shall touch on only three, which, in my opinion, typify Rommel's character and his conduct of operations. His very daring decision to set out on a headlong chase toward Egypt on 24 November 1941, was, in my view, a grave mistake. The situation was as follows:

The newly established British Eighth Army under General Sir Alan Cunningham and consisting of the 13th Corps (which had been the Western Desert Force) and the 30th Corps, planned to launch its offensive, called on "Crusader," 18 November 1941, the day before Panzergruppe Afrika (as Rommel's command was now called) intended assaulting Tobruk, which the British had doggedly held for nine months. In every respect the Eighth Army was superior to Rommel's forces, especially in armor, which dominated the fighting in the open desert, where mobility and firepower were of vital importance. The Germans and Italians together had only about 390 tanks, of which 139 were Mark III's and 35 Mark IV's. The rest were light Mark II's, of little use for anything but reconnaissance, and 146 Italian M13/40's, which were far too thinly armored to stand up to the British. Against these the British could muster no fewer than 500 tanks of cruiser class, in addition to 132 infantry tanks in the Thirteenth Corps and another 69 within the Tobruk fortress.

The British intention, after crossing the Egyptian frontier south of the Trigh el Abd, was for the 7th Armored Division and the 4th Armored Brigde Group to advance northwest and destroy Rommel's armor, while the 1st South African Division and the 22d Guards Brigade protected the lines of communication and later captured Sidi Rezegh ridge, overlooking the Trigh Capuzzo, as part of an operation to link up with forces breaking out of Tobruk. The German-Italian forces in the frontier positions at Bardia, Sidi Omar, and Halfaya dnd Sollum were to be cut off and captured by 13th Corps.

By the afternoon of 19 November part of the British 7th Armored Division and the reconnaissance vehicles of the South African 4th Armored Car Regiment had occupied Sidi Rezeg landing ground only 15 kilometers from the positions encircling Tobruk. The rest of the 7th Armored Division, however, was scattered at Bir el Gubi, 40 kilometers south, and at Gabr Saleh, about 60 kilometers southeast of Sidi Rezeg. Even before meeting the Afrika Korps in strength, confusion between the British Army

Corps and divisional commanders had led to dispersal of their armor, which, when concentrated, was numerically far superior to anything at Rommel's disposal.

Rommel at once recognized the danger posed by the British armored forces that had thrust forward to Sidi Rezeg, and he concentrated all his own armor in the area at the right moment. Then he attacked and on 23 November smashed the British forces at Sidi Rezeg. The British suffered heavily, losing some 4,000 of 5,700 men of the 5th South African Infantry Brigade and part of the 22d Armored Brigade and suffering many other casualties. The Afrika Korps itself was by no means unscathed and lost more tanks on that day than on any other during those winter battles.

This last fact was not fully appreciated, and, acting on what was perhaps too optimistic a report from General Ludwig Crüwell's tactical headquarters of the Afrika Korps—whose main headquarters was itself captured that evening—Rommel decided to thrust forward the next day with all available mobile units, in the direction of Sidi Omar on the Egyptian frontier. His intention was to attack the enemy on the Sollum Front and then to throw the Eighth Army supply lines into confusion.

This decision, which differed from Crüwell's wish to complete the destruction of the British forces still in the 23 November battle area, appeared to me to be based, first, on an overestimation of the extent of our local success at Sidi Rezeg and, second, on an underestimation of our own losses in men and material. I tried to warn Rommel and drew his attention particularly to the rapid advance of the New Zealand Division along both sides of the Trigh Capuzzo toward Tobruk. Rommel's staff officer for operations, Colonel Siegfried Westphal, also tried to make it quite clear that it was dangerous to move our mobile forces so far from Tobruk at this particular time.

Rommel was not to be convinced. He undoubtedly sometimes allowed himself to be unduly influenced by the flush of a local success or setback, and he would let such occurrences cloud his judgment on broader issues. That is precisely what happened then.

On 24 November he took personal command of the force heading for the Egyptian frontier, accompanied by his chief of staff, General Alfred Gause. Colonel Westphal was left to hold the position before Tobruk. All motorized units of the 15th and 21st Panzer divisions and the Italian Ariete Armored Division followed

Rommel at top speed toward Sidi Omar. Only a small German force under Major General Karl Boettcher, the army artillery commander, was left south of Tobruk.

Rommel, heading east at great speed with the 21st Panzer Division Headquarters, crossed the frontier at Gasr el Abid and reached the area south of Sollum with the leading elements of the division late on the afternoon of 24 November. His daring stroke had almost smashed the Eighth Army's 30th Corps, and General Alan Gordon Cunningham was ready to break off the battle and retreat into Egypt with whatever troops he had left. General Sir Claude Auchinleck, now commander in chief, Middle East—who was to match his wits against Rommel more than once—had already spent some time at Eighth Army Advanced Headquarters. He sensed that Rommel had dispersed his forces and gave General Cunningham unequivocal orders "to continue to press our offensive with every means in our power." There was no possible doubt, he added, that that was the right and only course for the Eighth Army to follow, and General Cunningham accepted his commander's decision loyally.

On his way back to Cairo, however, General Auchinleck had misgivings about Cunningham's defensive attitude and decided to relieve him. To avoid upsetting arrangements at corps level in the midst of battle, on 20 November he temporarily appointed his own chief of staff, Major General Neil Ritchie, to exercise command over the Eighth Army, to ensure that his orders for a stern offensive would be carried out. His action saved Operation Crusader.

While Auchinleck pondered the problem of who should command the Eighth Army, Rommel charged the 21st Panzer Division with the task of attacking the New Zealand Division, which he took to be near Sollum. Having destroyed this division, 21st Panzer was to thrust deep into Egypt. During the night of 24/25 November he drove to the 15th Panzer Division, who had been attacking the 4th Indian Division, which was well dug in at Sidi Omar, and had been repulsed with severe losses. During the journey in the dark, Rommel's car broke down, and while it was being repaired, he and General Gause had the good luck to meet General Crüwell and his chief of staff, Colonel Fritz Bayerlein. The four German officers, upon whom so much now depended, spent the night on Egyptian soil, in the midst of British gun positions.

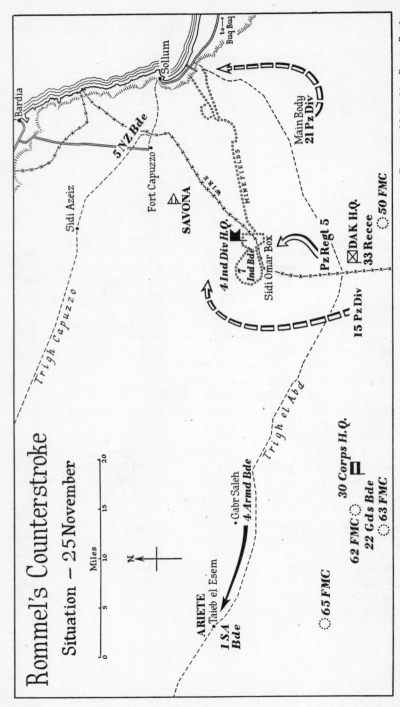

Rommel's Counterstroke
Situation — 25 November

Bardia

5 NZ Bde

Sidi Azeiz

Sollum

to → Buq Buq

Main Body
21 Pz Div

Trigh Capuzzo

Fort Capuzzo

SAVONA

WIRE

MINEFIELDS

4 Ind Div H.Q.

7 Ind Bde

Sidi Omar Box

Pz Regt 5

DAK H.Q.

33 Recce

50 FMC

15 Pz Div

Trigh el Abd

N

Miles

0   5   10   15   20

Gabr Saleh
4 Armd Bde

30 Corps H.Q.

62 FMC

22 Gds Bde

63 FMC

65 FMC

ARIETE
Taieb el Esem

1 S.A
Bde

From von Mellenthin, *Panzer Battles.*

Meanwhile, at Tobruk, where only weak German forces had been left, the situation had seriously deteriorated. The British garrison at the fortress had managed to break out and penetrate the German line at several points, and the 2d New Zealand Division was rapidly approaching to relieve the fortress. At that critical moment Rommel was nowhere to be found.

Military common sense demands that an army commander in chief should not absent himself from his own headquarters for days on end, but Rommel liked to lead his troops "from the front," which gave him firsthand knowledge of the situation and an intuitive "feel" that led to daring and usually successful decisions and to the dashing style of leadership that earned him so many laurels. But these long absences from battle headquarters were at times extremely dangerous and put an additional burden on the shoulders of his staff.

Five times Colonel Westphal sent out a Storch reconnaissance aircraft to search for Rommel and pass on the information about Tobruk, but he could not be found. True to German General Staff tradition, Colonel Westphal then decided to act on his own, and at midday on November 26—the day General Auchinleck sent Ritchie to relieve Cunningham—the following order went out by radio to the Afrika Korps: "All previous orders to pursue the enemy are canceled forthwith. The Afrika Korps shall turn about toward Tobruk and attack the enemy advancing on Tobruk from the rear."

While the 21st Panzer Division was retracing its steps in accordance with its orders, Rommel, who had turned up again and made contact with his headquarters, led the 15th Panzer Division south of Bardia into an attack against the 5th New Zealand Brigade between Musa'id and Menasti and destroyed their headquarters group at Sidi Azeiz.

On his return Rommel was at first very angry about Westphal's decision to recall the Afrika Korps from their pursuit of the enemy. When he had had time to consider the situation in detail, however, he withdrew his objections and gave his unreserved approval to Westphal's action.

The battle that Rommel had sparked off on the Egyptian frontier now developed into a battle for Tobruk. During the night of 26/27 November the New Zealanders took Sidi Rezeg after the British fortress troops from Tobruk had occupied Ed Duda during the afternoon. Thus the Eighth Army reestablished direct communication with the Tobruk garrison. But Rommel would not give up. Returning from the east, the 15th and 21st Panzer divisions attacked and drove the New Zealanders back from Sidi Rezeg.

To Ritchie it was now clear that Rommel's forces were almost exhausted. They were too weak to maintain the Tobruk siege. After some further reverses, partly caused by the inactivity of the completely exhausted Italian 20th Corps, Rommel decided to break off the battle for Tobruk and to make a fighting withdrawal onto the Gazala positions. And so his daring plan to invade Egypt ended in a "lost victory." Brilliant though it was to plan to throw the enemy rear into confusion, in this particular instance Rommel lost his sense of reality. His motorized units were far too weak for such a wide-ranging operation, particularly after their heavy losses at Sidi Rezeg on 23 November.

In January 1942, after a withdrawal of 500 miles, Rommel again made one of his daring decisions to smash the enemy and retake Cyrenaica. Though the Eighth Army was overextended along hundreds of miles of tenuous communications, Rommel had wisely withdrawn from the Agedabia area to the El Agheila bottleneck to reorganize. By 11 January 1942, the German-Italian Panzergruppe—which was to become the Panzerarmee Afrika on 22 January—was established in the Mersa Brega positions, and, in spite of heavy losses during the past seven weeks, Rommel was not unfavorably placed strategically.

Luftflotte II had been transferred from the Russian Front to Sicily and southern Italy, and the British no longer enjoyed unchallenged air superiority. The supply situation had improved considerably on the Axis side. Two large convoys had reached Africa on 18 December and 5 January, escorted by Italian battleships. They brought not only the longed-for ammunition and fuel but four fully equipped and fresh companies of tanks.

By contrast, the Eighth Army's situation was by no means rosy. The British forces were now stretched to the limit from the Egyptian Frontier, where fighting continued for Bardia, Halfaya, and Sollum, which blocked the only good road. Though Bardia fell in the new year, the garrison at Halfaya only capitulated on 27 January. Until then the 2d South African Division was fully engaged in that sector.

Meanwhile, on 12 January a conference was held at Rommel's

battle headquarters where I—as staff officer (intelligence)—was able to present a detailed account of Eighth Army dispositions. Our air reconnaissance and our Wireless Interception Unit (Horchkompagnie) had done their work well. It had been established that the 7th Armored Division was so worn out after the fighting of the past few weeks that it had been withdrawn to the area south of Tobruk. In the vicinity of Agedabia its place had been taken by the 1st Armored Division, which had just arrived from England and had absolutely no experience of desert warfare.

The 4th Indian Division was still in the Bengasi area, and it was also known that the 1st South African Division, the 2d New Zealand Division, and the 50th British Division had not yet been brought forward into the battle area. This meant that the German forces would enjoy a definite superiority over the Eighth Army troops facing them in the forward areas until about January 25. After that, relative strengths would quickly alter to our disadvantage.

Rommel had flown over the Mersa Brega positions himself and had become convinced that it would be dangerous to wait there until the enemy had brought up sufficient forces for a renewed attack. It was also obvious that our Italian allies would not be able to stand another defensive battle.

Colonel Westphal, Rommel's chief operations officer, was able to convince him that we had sufficient transport to sustain a counteroffensive. Rommel was full of enthusiasm and all set to rejoin battle, but he insisted that the operation had to be a complete surprise to the enemy. He ordered absolute secrecy. Nothing of his plans was to be divulged to subordinate commands until the latest possible moment, nor, in fact, was higher authority to be let into the secret.

It might well be asked whether Rommel was right in counterattacking without consulting his superiors. His characteristic self-confidence and courage led him to act according to what he judged to be right, without regard to conventions, precedent, military protocol, or personal interest. Had he followed normal procedure and asked his superiors for permission to renew the offensive after a five-hundred-mile retreat, the Italian High Command's answer would have been a foregone conclusion. They—or, for that matter, the German High Command—would never have dared to sanction such a step. But time was Rommel's greatest enemy.

He had to act, and act quickly, before the British had finished licking their wounds and were ready to bring their superior strength to bear against our small band. If the gamble did not come off, he and he alone would face the consequences of disregarding the accepted chain of command.

To simulate preparations for further retreat, he ordered the burning of some old ships, sly "Desert Fox" that he was. He sent convoys of vehicles toward the west to reinforce the pretense of abandoning Mersa Brega, and to add a further touch of realism he even set fire to some old staging camps. The commander of the Afrika Korps, General Crüwell, did not know about the Panzergruppe commander's true intentions until 16 January, and the divisional commanders were told only on 19 January, with the attack scheduled for 6:30 P.M. on the 21st.

There were two attacking formations. Mobile units of the 90th Light Division, supported by a few tanks from 21st Panzer Division and under command of Colonel Werner Marcks, were to advance along both sides of the Via Balbia—which runs some way inland between Mersa Brega and Agadabia. The Afrika Korps proper was to swing farther south through the desert and thrust as quickly as possible northward beyond Wadi el Faregh.

The attack went well right from the start, with Group Marcks pushing back weak British detachments. The Afrika Korps captured a large number of guns and vehicles from the completely surprised British. Reconnaissance on the evening of 21 January revealed that the British were withdrawing northwest and that the 1st Armored Division was concentrating at Agedabia.

Because the Afrika Korps was making only slow headway over difficult going in the open desert and was short of fuel, Rommel personally took over the lead of Group Marcks, urging it on at utmost speed so as to prevent the British from becoming firmly established at Agedabia.

Now Rommel was in his element, a man of quick decisions, adaptable and bold. Brushing aside weak enemy resistance, Group Marcks occupied Agedabia at 11:00 A.M. on 22 January. Rommel ordered an immediate follow-through to Antelat and Saunnu (further northeast on the two tracks that converge on Msus). In carrying out these orders, the group drove clean through British supply columns and created indescribable chaos. By 3:30 P.M. they had reached Antelat, and regardless of approaching darkness they

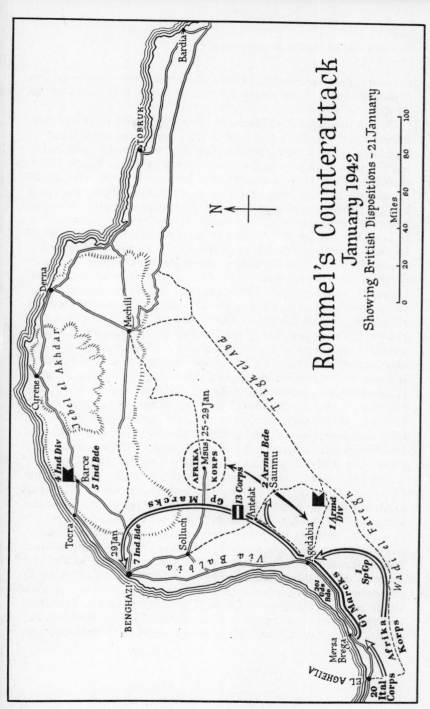

Rommel's Counterattack
January 1942
Showing British Dispositions – 21 January

From von Mellenthin, *Panzer Battles*.

Miles

0   20   40   60   80   100

N

pressed on toward Saunnu. By shortly after 9:00 P.M. it was also captured after a short engagement against the B Echelon of the 2d Armored Brigade.

During the night 22/23 January, Rommel issued orders for the encirclement of the 1st Armored Division in the area south of Agedabia. It was an ambitious plan and only partly successful. In fact, through a rare failure of staff work at Afrika Korps Headquarters, when Group Marcks left Saunnu at 5:00 A.M. on 23 January to fulfill its task, the region was not promptly occupied by 21st Panzer Division, and the 200th Guards Brigade managed to escape. Rommel had lost valuable time.

To make up for it he decided to wipe out the 1st Armored Division by a thrust on Msus by the Afrika Korps on 25 January. The 15th Panzer Division struck strong British armored units well supported by British and South African field and antitank guns about six miles northwest of Saunnu, but German superiority over the inexperienced British was quickly established, and the enemy withdrew in great haste. At 11:00 A.M. on 25 January the 15th Panzer Division reached Msus landing ground and captured 12 aircraft that were about to take off and a great quantity of stores and equipment, including 96 tanks, 38 guns, and 190 vehicles. It was a success that underlined a difference of opinion between General Ritchie, commanding the Eighth Army and General Godwin-Austen, the commander of the 30th Corps, whom Auchinleck had originally wished to appoint as army commander during the Crusader offensive but had passed over so as not to disturb the 30th Corps. The corps commander's request for discretion to withdraw toward Mekili was now refused by General Ritchie.

Rommel had to make up his mind whether to try to cut off the 4th Indian Division in the Bengasi area and eastward by a thrust to Mekili, but he had to let the opportunity pass, for the Afrika Korps had insufficient fuel for further mobile operations. He ordered both German Panzer divisions to make a feint toward Mekili, and while it was in progress, he once again did something unique. Putting himself at the head of Group Marcks and the 3d and 33d Armored Reconnaissance units, he led a forced march in pouring rain over extremely difficult hilly terrain and launched a sudden attack on Bengasi from the east. The British were taken completely by surprise in the town, which General Ritchie had ordered to be held despite formal objections by General Godwin-Austen.

Some 4,000 men of Major General F. I. S. Tuker's 4th Indian Division were captured, and on 29 January 1942, Rommel entered Bengasi at the head of his battle group. In recognition of the achievement Hitler promoted him to colonel general.

Meanwhile, the Italian High Command, to whom Rommel was nominally subordinate, were doing everything in their power to stop his counteroffensive. With Bengazi already reoccupied, they decided to grant Rommel permission to advance on the town!

On the British side, two decisions of singular importance for the future — both unknown beyond the highest circles at the time — were made at this juncture. On 4 February 1942 the three British commanders in chief in the Middle East unanimously agreed that in the event of a further withdrawal Tobruk would *not* be held. And General Godwin-Austen, whom General Auchinleck had already specifically mentioned for command in Libya, with General Ritchie in charge of GHQ Reserve of three or four divisions, asked to be relieved of his command. Differences of opinion between him and General Ritchie about the conduct of operations convinced Godwin-Austen that he could no longer conscientiously exercise command of his corps, and the commander in chief had no option but to accept his resignation and leave the Eighth Army in the hands of a staff officer who, fine man though he was, could not match Rommel as a field commander. At the same time Tobruk was stripped of mines, and no preparations were made for its defense.

General Ritchie was forced to give up almost all of Cyrenaica west of Tobruk and pull back to the Gazala positions, before which Rommel's offensive came to a halt on 6 February 1942. Only Marmarica, or eastern Libya, remained in British hands.

Rommel's clear-headed strategic objective had been to launch a counteroffensive to prevent the British from concentrating powerful superior forces that he and his Italian allies could never have withstood successfully. Tripoli would certainly have been lost, and the German-Italian Panzerarmee would have been destroyed. It was only by means of this preemptive counteroffensive that Rommel had been able to defeat British forces that had not yet been concentrated.

Now for an example that shows Rommel not as the daring Panzer commander but as the tough, tenacious commander of collectively weak formations, as was the case during the summer offensive of the Axis motorized forces against Tobruk. The situation was so desperate from the very earliest days of the battle that it is a miracle the British did not wipe out the virtually surrounded German-Italian forces. Part of the explanation may lie in General Ritchie's inability to react with anything like the rapidity of his opponent and, to some degree, in his too-great dependence on advice from General "Strafer" Gott, who had succeeded Godwin-Austen as corps commander. Though junior to the Australian Morshead, the New Zealander Freyberg, and the South African Brink, he was English and experienced in armor and the desert.

Rommel's plan of battle provided that the two Italian infantry corps were to tie down the Eighth Army in the north by a frontal attack on the Gazala Line. The German Afrika Korps, the 90th Light, and the Italian 20th Motorized Corps were to turn the flank of the enemy in the south at Bir Hakeim and then thrust northward behind the British lines toward Tobruk. On 26 May 1942, the attack began, ill-starred from the start. Tactical surprise, so important in any major operation, was not achieved. British Intelligence had not only give warning of impending attack but even predicted the date to within a couple of days and suggested that it would probably take the form of a right hook in a wide southward sweep. The presence of 150th Brigade between the Trigh Capuzzo and the Trigh el Abd well to the south of the South Africans and the British 151 and 69th brigades, came as an unpleasant surprise to Rommel, and he had no previous knowledge of the position of the Guards Brigade near Knightsbridge. *Crisis in the Desert* records how the southward movement of the German-Italian forces was sighted and reported by a screen of British and South African armored cars from as early as 3:00 on the afternoon of the opening day of the battle. Around midnight, with the 4th South African Armored Car Regiment constantly passing back information—the movement of the German armor round Bir Hakeim was reported, even though the Afrika Korps had not yet sighted the enemy.

The British simply failed to appreciate the urgent need for swift, concentrated retaliation, and the 7th Armor Division's reaction was so sluggish that its advance headquarters was captured before battle had been joined. It was some time before uncoordinated British armored attacks went in, as the 4th Armored Brigade struck the rearmost units of the 15th Panzer Division.

The 1st Armored Division joined in, and the newly arrived Grant tanks, well armored and with a 75-mm gun, took the Germans by surprise. The rear supply units of the 15th Panzer gave ground toward the south and southwest, and in the meantime the attack of the Afrika Korps was wearing itself out against the brave and obstinate resistance of the guards at Knightsbridge.

The frontal attack by the Italian infantry on the Gazala Line in the north was a complete failure, and the German armored force had placed itself in a dangerous trap at the very beginning of the battle. Had the British launched their armor in a properly coordinated and concentrated attack, our total destruction would have been inevitable and swift. The German armor's supply lines were wide-open to interference at Bir Hakeim and in the Bir el Gubi area, with the Panzer units fighting against a superior enemy behind the Gazala Line and cut off from their own supports.

The Eighth Army was in a far more favorable position. Up in the north behind the 1st South African Division, General Ritchie had the 32d Army Tank Brigade with two regiments of Valentines and one of Matildas, and south of it lay the 1st Army Tank Brigade with two more regiments of Matildas—all tough infantry tanks. All the commander of the Eighth Army had to do was send them in a concentrated attack against our lines of communication. But the Eighth Army's cumbersome machinery of command, which seems to have tolerated much discussion and argument, all of which consumed valuable time, was apparently incapable of ordering decisive action.

Rommel's staff advised retreat through the minefields between the 150th Brigade and Bir Hakeim as the only salvation. By all the rules and logic of war, annihilation seemed to be the only alternative. Yet the British hesitated, and Rommel, seeing his chance, acted at once. He gave no thought to withdrawal but decided to pull back all his mobile forces into a hedgehog position against the minefields and assault the enemy's main strongpoint at Got el Ualeb, where the presence of the 150th Brigade box had been such an unpleasant surprise. By smashing this box, a wide, direct line of communications would be established through the minefields.

By midday on 1 June, Rommel had achieved his objective. Once again he had assessed his enemy correctly. During the next few days uncoordinated attacks were launched against the Afrika

Korps's hedgehog position in what the British called The "Cauldron," but they were all repulsed with heavy loss to the enemy. Then Rommel was again ready to go over to the attack.

Having regained the initiative, he launched an assault on what turned out to be a singularly hard nut to crack, the Bir Hakeim box, obstinately defended by the Free French Brigade under Brigadier General M. P. Koenig. That miniature fortress fell on 11 June, after one crisis had followed another. Rommel was always master of the situation, and by his tenacity and steadfastness, which contrasted with the indecisiveness of the opposing army command, he crowned his outstanding career as a military commander with the taking of the stronghold of Tobruk on 21 June 1942. Major General H. B. Klopper, in the mistaken belief that the Eighth Army was still in condition to protect his eastern perimenter, had placed all his fresh troops on the western and southwestern sectors. With his unfulfilled 1941 plan of attack— and even old ammunition dumps—to hand, Rommel broke through rapidly on the southeast of Tobruk perimeter, and while the Eighth Army lay helpless on the Egyptian frontier, he quickly subdued the fortress. Hitler promoted him to field marshal, but Rommel wrote to tell his wife that he would rather the Führer had presented him with a single fresh division.

Flushed with victory and with a disorganized Eighth Army on the run even before the loss of Tobruk, Rommel now understandably pressed for the chance to pursue the defeated enemy into Egypt, though he knew that the capture of Malta was the next item on the strategic program. The capture of Malta would eliminate the constant threat to his supply line from Europe. Against the advice of Field Marshal Albert Kesselring, of the German Naval Staff and of the Italian Commando Supremo, Hitler let Rommel have his way, and the German-Italian forces—as often as not in captured British vehicles—chased the Eighth Army all the way past Mersa Matruh.

But Rommel's move was a fateful one. General Auchinleck, faced with the danger of losing Egypt and the Suez Canal, personally relieved General Ritchie and took command of the Eighth Army. At El Alamein, he halted Rommel's exhausted forces on 4 July 1942. "Resistance is too great," Rommel wrote that day to his wife "and our strength is exhausted. However, I still hope to find a way to achieve our goal. I'm rather tired and fagged out." It

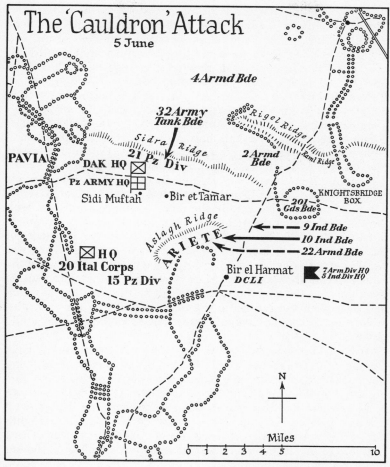

The 'Cauldron' Attack
5 June

4. Armd Bde

32 Army Tank Bde

Sidra Ridge

Rigel Ridge

PAVIA

21 Pz Div

2 Armd Bde

Raml Ridge

DAK HQ

Pz ARMY HQ

Sidi Muftah

•Bir et Tamar

KNIGHTSBRIDGE BOX

201 Gds Bde

Aslagh Ridge

ARIETE

← 9 Ind Bde

← 10 Ind Bde

← 22 Armd Bde

HQ
20 Ital Corps
15 Pz Div

Bir el Harmat
DCLI

7 Arm Div HQ
5 Ind Div HQ

N

Miles

0   1   2   3   4   5   10

From von Mellenthin, *Panzer Battles.*

was the turning point in Africa, for overwhelming reinforcements in tanks and guns were already on their way to the Eighth Army, and before the end of July plans were afoot for a British-American landing hundreds of miles behind Rommel's depleted forces.

During August 1942 the Panzerarmee stood at the crossroads. The possibility of a breakthrough to Alexandria and the Suez Canal and the specter of a link-up between Rommel's forces and the Wehrmacht divisions already threatening to drive southward over the Caucasus were a nightmare to defeatists on the Allied side. But even before the Panzerarmee had come within sight of El Alamein, the Anglo-American war machine had been speeded up to nullify Rommel's successes. As early as 25 June, four days after Rommel's triumph at Tobruk, the American chief of staff, General George C. Marshall, had proposed to send 300 Sherman tanks and 100 self-propelled guns to the Middle East by the fastest possible means as part of a gigantic reinforcement drive.

Convoy after convoy was sighted in the gulf of Suez by our reconnaissance aircraft, and it was clear that the Eighth Army was gaining a decisive lead in the race to build up supplies, with the Panzerarmee at the end of overextended lines of communication stretching all the way back to Tripoli and the British right on the doorstep of their main base. Our own supply position was causing grave concern. We were now paying the penalty for the failure to capture Malta. The Mare Nostrum was completely under the control of the Commonwealth's Middle East air forces, which had overtaken the Luftwaffe not only numerically but now also technically. Most of our supplies were destroyed before they could reach us.

At the end of August 1942 we were ordered by the Army High Command to try another breakthrough effort at Alam Halfa, and the Panzerarmee staff gave Rommel a sober appraisal. We did not believe that we could break through to the Nile, and we pointed out to Rommel that in armored strength the British, with General Bernard L. Montgomery now commanding the Eighth Army, had a superiority of three to one, and in airpower of five to one. On our side the greatest handicap was lack of sufficient fuel for a major battle. In fact, we could not even affort to stand and wait at El Alamein for the Eighth Army to attack; the enormous superiority enjoyed by the British could result only in defeat for the Panzerarmee.

We of Rommel's staff suggested the withdrawal of all nonmobile formations to Libya, leaving only armored and motorized divisions in the forward area. Rommel agreed, but Hitler ordered him to launch an attack. Though ill and in the doctor's hands, at the end of August 1942, Rommel began the attack, which failed completely. We could then do nothing but stand and wait for Montgomery's offensive. Contrary to all the rules for good generalship in desert warfare, which may be compared with a battle at sea, our nonmotorized forces had to dig in on a rigid defense line.

Had our own plans been adopted, Montgomery's great attack with enormous superiority of all arms would have fallen on barren ground, for there would have been no nonmobile troops at the front. All of them—especially the foot-slogging Italian Infantry—would have been withdrawn well in advance to the area of Tobruk. Our mobile forces would then have gracefully pulled back some twenty miles west and once again forced the Eighth Army into mobile warfare, at which Rommel and the Afrika Korps of course excelled. As it was, Rommel was recalled from sick leave after battle had already been joined, and even belated withdrawal was forbidden by Hitler at a most critical stage, with disaster the inevitable result.

Yet this Second Battle of Alamein must, in my opinion, go down in history as unnecessary, even from the British point of view, for it began only about three weeks after the first ships had left the United Kingdom as part of the plan for an ambitious Anglo-American landing in North Africa, considerably nearer Rommel's unprotected main base at Tripoli. "Operation Torch" would in any event have forced Rommel to fall back before being cut off and crushed between two armies each infinitely superior to his own. The Battle of Alamein, which cost the Commonwealth forces 13,560 casualties in killed, wounded and missing, could have been fought with a minimum of loss if it had been postponed for a matter of a few days, until the Torch landings, which spelled the end of Panzerarmee Afrika. It was the Allied forces in his rear that made Rommel evacuate his defenses at El Agheila, as they would have also done at El Alamein.

It is of some interest to compare the personalities of Montgomery and Rommel, both of whom were real "leaders" in their respective armies. We Germans felt that Montgomery brought a new spirit to the Eighth Army, thus illustrating once again the vital importance of personal leadership in war. Both he and Rommel were ruthless and swift in dealing with the incompetent, and both were publicity minded, always in the fore when press photographers were about. Each had a self-conscious, even egoistical manner, and each had written a book on infantry before World War II: Montgomery, *The Current Infantry Training Regulations,* and Rommel, *Infanterie greift an.* But in directing a battle they differed greatly.

Montgomery was undoubtedly a great tactician, circumspect and thorough in making his plans and utterly ruthless in carrying them out. He was inflexible, preferred the "slugging match" of a frontal assault, and would delay action until he was assured of absolute superiority of all arms—something that Rommel never once had during all the time he was in the desert. Rommel summed up the British general as "a very careful man, who will take no risks."

Rommel was, in my opinion, the ideal commander for mobile desert warfare, even though his custom of "leading from the front" occasionally worked against him. By going to danger spots himself, he was always able to adapt his plans to the changing situation. In planning an operation, he was painstaking and thorough, but in making decisions, he was swift and audacious.

It was not Montgomery who stopped Rommel at El Alamein, however, but General Auchinleck, and the Panzerarmee commander had been immediately aware of the change in the Eighth Army from the moment Auchinleck personally took over. Rommel wrote:

General Auchinleck, who had meanwhile taken command in the Alamein positions himself, was handling his forces with considerable skill, and tactically better than Ritchie. He seemed to view the situation with remarkable calm, and never allowed himself to be so influenced by any of our measures as to accept a "second-rate" solution. This would manifest itself particularly in what followed.

General Auchinleck is worthy of mention for the greatness of his personality and his generalship. For it was he who saved Crusader in November 1941, when he arrived at Cunningham's Eighth Army headquarters and categorically forbade withdrawal while insisting on an immediate and determined attack, which ultimately drove the German-Italian forces right back to El Agheila. And it was he who saved Egypt at First Alamein in July 1942, when he took over an army in full retreat and stopped Rommel long before the flood of reinforcements that were to back Montgomery had reached the front. His ideas of forming a Schwerpunkt corresponded closely with our own, and his tactics compared very well with ours.

In September 1943, Hitler appointed Rommel commander in chief of Army Group B in France. He was given the task of checking the defenses of the whole of the Western Front from Denmark to the south of France.

The Allied invasion of France followed on 6 June 1944, when Germany had nothing to challenge the powerful Anglo-American air forces. The Allied landing could not be stopped, particularly since Hitler held the Panzer divisions farther back in reserve under his personal orders. Their release for battle came far too late.

Rommel was highly incensed over Hitler's interference in the conduct of the war. Even before the invasion he had made contact with the German resistance movement, and he became a determined opponent of Hitler, his policies, and above all his conduct of military operations.

On 1 July 1944, Hitler dismissed Field Marshal von Rundstedt and entrusted the command of the whole of the Western Front to Field Marshal Günther von Kluge. On 15 July, with Kluge's consent Rommel wrote a remarkable memorandum that he dispatched to Hitler. It ended with the following words: "I feel compelled to ask you to take immediate note of the political consequences of the present situation. As commander of an Army Group, I feel it my duty to make this perfectly clear." To a confidant, Rommel said, "I have given him [Hitler] his last chance. If he does not take the hint, we will act."

He had no intention of assassinating Hitler but would have arrested him and brought him to trial before a German court, before negotiating an armistice with the Western Powers. But it turned out quite differently.

On 17 July 1944, Rommel's staff car was strafed by an American fighter-bomber. The driver was killed, and Rommel suffered a serious head injury. At his own request he was taken to a hospital in Ulm.

At the end of October, I heard from von Rundstedt that Rommel had died of his wounds and that the field marshal was to represent Hitler at a state funeral. It was only in Allied captivity that I first learned that Rommel had not died from his head wounds but had taken poison on Hitler's orders to avoid being brought to trial before a "people's court" for taking part in the plot against Hitler.

In conclusion, I would like to add a few personal remarks about Rommel. In my mind, there is no doubt whatever that it was because of Rommel's personality that the fighting in North Africa turned out to be "the last gentlemen's war." Both the British and the Germans at all times observed the decencies of civilized warfare. The Afrika Korps had Rommel constantly before them as an example, and his soldiers fought accordingly.

The British once issued an order that prisoners of war were not to be given anything to eat or drink until they had been interrogated, and this incensed Rommel. By sending an appropriate message to the other side by wireless, he had the order rescinded. One interrogation that I conducted myself is worth recalling. It took place during the Crusader offensive at our battle headquarters near El Adem in November 1941, when a brigadier of the 2d New Zealand Division was captured. I received him with beer and sausages in the hope that he might tell me something about "the other side," but I very soon realized that this most honorable man was utterly uncommunicative about military matters. Nevertheless, I did discover that we had both been cavalrymen and were still enthusiastic horsemen. A lively and interesting discussion on horse breeding and racing ensued. When I finally dismissed the brigadier, Rommel hurried in, eager to hear something about the enemy's troop dispositions. When I told him that I had only spoken to the prisoner about horse breeding and racing, he laughed heartily and remarked, "What a pity that people with so much in common have to fight one another."

It was not easy to satisfy Rommel, and yet the men of the Afrika Korps practically worshiped him. He demanded much of his staff and those who worked with him, but he never spared himself. From early in the morning till late at night he was on his feet.

He had an extraordinary sense of direction and an almost uncanny sixth sense for what was in the wind. He never sent his troops into action without careful thought. Meticulous collection of information and reconnaissance, often carried out personally, always preceded an operation. On his frequent visits to the front he quickly spotted anything worrying the men in the line, and he not only issued orders for something to be done immediately to rectify the situation, but also took care to see that his instructions had been promptly carried out. He had extraordinary vitality and was Spartan in the simplicity of all his habits, his food, and his drink. His men knew that he would expect nothing from them that he would spare himself. He was always among them, a born leader.

Since I served with Rommel for more than a year through all the ups and downs of the African Campaign as one of his closest associates, I am at a loss to explain the broadcast in November 1971 on German television of "The Rommel Myth—The Glory and the Passing of a Soldier." The theme of this broadcast was that Rommel had been built up as a national hero and acclaimed by Hitler through Goebbels' propaganda machine. I was profoundly shocked by this tactlessness and insensitivity, since I have lived in foreign countries for the past twenty-five years and know in what high regard the British and Americans held Rommel both during the war and to this day. I quote two examples: During the North African Campaign, General Auchinleck issued the following order:

TO: All Commanders and Chief of Staff

FROM: Headquarters, British Troops in Egypt and Middle East Forces

There exists a real danger that our friend Rommel is becoming a kind of magician or bogey-man to our troops, who are talking far too much about him. He is by no means a superman, although he is undoubtedly very energetic and able. Even if he were a superman, it would be highly undesirable that our men should credit him with supernatural powers.

I wish you to dispel by all possible means the idea that Rommel represents something more than an ordinary German general. The important thing now is to see to it that we do not always talk of Rommel when we mean the enemy in Libya. We must refer to "the Germans" of "the Axis powers," or "the enemy" and not always keep harping on Rommel.

Please ensure that this order is put into immediate effect, and impress upon all Commanders that, from a psychological point of view, it is a matter of the highest importance.

[Signed] C. J. Auchinleck, General,
Commander-in-Chief, M.E.F.

A second example is this comment made by Sir Winston Churchill in his speech to the British Parliament on 27 January 1942: "We have a very daring and skillful opponent against us and, may I say across the havoc of war, a great general."

It would be difficult to find a man who fought on either side in the tumultuous desert battles who does not agree with that characterization.

Chapter 5

GENERAL HEINZ GUDERIAN

The Creator and Architect of the German Armored Forces

Armored fighting vehicles went into action on a number of occasions during World War I. On 15 September 1916, at the Battle of the Somme, the British employed their first "tanks," so called after the code name under which they had been secretly developed. In April 1917 the French followed the British example by employing the new weapon, and in a surprise attack on 20 November 1917, 378 British tanks at Cambrai made a deep penetration into the German defenses, but the success was not fully exploited. Then again in July 1918 the French used 600 *chars d'assault* at Soissons, and a short time later on 8 August 1918, a combined force of 462 British and French tanks overran the German front at Amiens and drove a wedge into the German positions 30 kilometers wide and 15 kilometers deep on the first day of the attack.

At that time the tank did not have a decisive influence on the outcome of a battle. It restored mobility to forces locked in trench warfare, but with only local success. Tactical exploitation of such success was still lacking, and the tank was considered merely a support weapon for the infantry.

After World War I all armies began, more or less hesitantly, to explore the tactical possibilities of this new arm of the service. In England, General J. F. C. Fuller and Captain Liddell-Hart especially worked on the potentialities of the tank. In France it was General Étienne and later Colonel Georges de Gaulle who concentrated on the subject.

By the Treaty of Versailles, Germany was forbidden to have an armored corps of any sort or to manufacture or import tanks.

Yet in spite of that prohibition, at the beginning of World War II she possessed the most modern Panzer force in the world, and it was that force which enabled her to mount her shattering Blitzkrieg against Poland and France and, initially with similar success, against Russia. The creator of this Panzer force was General Heinz Guderian.

Heinz's father was an officer of the Pomeranian Rifles, and Heinz was born on 17 June 1888 in Kulm on the Vistula River, in what was then East Prussia. His grandfathers on both sides were gentlemen-farmers, but through a great-grandmother he sprang from one Brandenburg and three Prussian generals, as well as being descended from the defender of East Prussia in the Seven Years' War, Field Marshal Hans von Lehwald. Both Heinz and his brother Fritz wanted to become army officers, and they joined the Cadet Corps at the Cadet School in Karlsruhe on 1 April 1901. Two years later Heinz went on to the Senior Cadet School at Gross-Lichterfelde in Berlin, and in February 1907 he took his final examinations and was appointed an ensign in the 10th Rifle Battalion in Bitsch, in Lorraine, where his father was battalion commander until December 1908.

By the time the battalion returned to its original garrison town of Goslar, Guderian was a second lieutenant. In Goslar he met his future wife, Margarete Goerne, to whom he had been married almost a year when World War I broke out in 1914.

On active service as a lieutenant, Guderian was a signals officer with the 5th Cavalry Division, in charge of a main radio station. He became familiar with all the advantages and disadvantages of operating with mounted troops, which in those days provided the only mobile arm of an army consisting mainly of masses of slow-marching infantry. During the Marne retreat, his signals station was left without orders and was lost when the division prematurely withdrew in great haste. Guderian sent in a report to his superior signals station at Divisional Headquarters, accusing his divisional commander of cowardice and failure in exercising command. He himself admitted the report to be "perhaps a little too sharp." General Balck's father, who passed on this story to Balck, was a major general and director of signals services at Army Headquarters. He quickly intervened and posted Guderian to the Fourth Army to save him from the consequences. The divisional commander was relieved of his command. Guderian was later transferred to the General Staff, on which he served after February 1918.

Guderian was of medium height, lightly but athletically built, and carried himself with a military bearing. He had a lively disposition, was mentally active, and was always full of new ideas. In the field he was always well up with the forward troops, where his personal bravery and daring came to the fore, earning him the Iron Cross, both First and Second Class. He was very decisive and his opinions were often dogmatic, with the result that many of his seniors thought of him as a "difficult subordinate."

Shortly after the war he served in the Eastern Frontier Defense Command, before being transferred to Northern Command. He then became a company commander in the 10th Rifle Battalion— his old unit—of the Reichswehr in Goslar, to which he returned on 1 January 1921. That he had a sense of humor is apparent from his correspondence as a company commander. He received the following letter from a civilian:

Dear Captain,

When I went in to my maid's bedroom last night, I found two riflemen of your company in her bed, sir! In former days of the Kaiser such a thing was impossible. I urgently demand redress. I ask you, is my house a brothel?

Yours faithfully,

Guderian promptly replied:

Dear Sir,

Even in the days of the Kaiser, it happened that riflemen were found in servant girls' beds, and it will happen again. As regards your final query, as to whether your house is a brothel, I am not able to give an answer. You are in the best position to judge this for yourself.

Yours faithfully,
H. Guderian.

This correspondence found its way through the local member of the Reichstag to the Ministry of War, and Guderian was officially asked for an explanation. "I gave an objective answer to an objective question," he explained. The ministry accepted the explanation, and the matter was dropped.

A year or so later Guderian was transferred to the 7th (Bavarian) Mechanical Transport Battalion, and on 1 April 1922 he was posted to the Reichswehr Ministry Department "In 6," the Directorate of Mechanical Transport. While in this post he began seriously to study the works of Liddell-Hart, John F. C. Fuller, and Sir Gifford Martel, all of whom were forceful advocates of the potentialities of armored fighting vehicles.

In 1924, Guderian was transferred to the staff of the 2d Division in Stettin as an instructor, and there he became closely associated with Major Oswald Lutz, an enthusiastic supporter of the still-novel idea of using motorized troops as combat units and not merely as transport for stores, equipment, and personnel. On 1 February 1927, at the age of thirty-nine, Guderian was promoted to major, and by October 1928 he was lecturing on tank tactics, of which he as yet had had no practical experience.

In developing the new German Panzer force, he had often to face difficulties with the authorities, for his ideas about the creation of a new combat arm did not always meet with the approval of the higher command. On 9 December 1926, however, Germany and Russia agreed to the establishment of a tank training school at Kama, near Kazan in the Soviet Union—which overcame the limitations of the Versailles Treaty. Since Germany had no tanks of her own, the school did not open until 1929, but Guderian had already clearly recognized the potential value of highly mobile forces and armor. He was determined to make the most of the operational mobility and speed that mechanization offered. It was no easy matter to persuade superiors steeped in the traditions of infantry and cavalry, to whom things mechanical were often anathema, especially if they appeared to replace the horse.

After briefly commanding another mechanized-transport unit early in 1930, Guderian returned to the inspectorate as chief of staff to Lutz, who was now a major general. Together they fought for the creation of a Panzer corps and for mechanization of the army. Many were skeptical, but General von Fritsch supported their ideas. In 1932, Guderian—now a colonel—accompanied his chief on a visit to the school at Kama, where the first German prototype Panzers were being tested. Future Panzer officers continued training in Russia until 1933, with mutual advantage to the Red Army and the Reichswehr. Germany built up a cadre of first-class officers and instructors.

With thinly disguised mechanized-transport units as a basis, the foundations were laid for a Panzer force, and cavalry units were converted. On 15 October 1935, with the Wehrmacht expanding under Hitler's regime, the Dresden Cavalry Regiment became Panzer Regiment 3 as part of the 2d Panzer Division, commanded by Colonel Guderian. Only light tanks, Mark I's and Mark II's, were available, but three Panzer divisions were established, with General Lutz as the first general of Panzer troops. By 1937 the famous Mark III's and Mark IV's were coming off the production line for the new Panzer regiments. Guderian's ideas had taken firm root.

In the crisis created by Hitler's dismissal of Blomberg and Fritsch early in 1938 General Lutz was among those who also lost their posts for political reasons. Guderian was bitter at the turn of events, but one result was that he was promoted to lieutenant general and appointed Lutz's successor as commander of the 16th Panzer Corps. The corps then consisted of three divisions and was later expanded to two Panzer and two motorized divisions.

Guderian had been demanding, and at last was getting, complete formations built up around tanks, instead of using tanks merely in support of infantry. He looked for basic weapons, combined with armor, antitank guns, mobile vehicles (some tracked) to carry artillery, and independent means of communication. The whole was to be an independent formation, and he became not only the creator of the Panzer force but also its tutor and instructor.

His oft-repeated precept was, "Nicht kleckern, sondern klotzen" ("Not a drizzle, but a downpour"). By that he meant that in battle the need was to reinforce the hard core of armor—in other words, to keep the tanks, their firepower, and their mobility concentrated, never to disperse them. Panzers and all their support weapons should be thrown in at the crucial moment so as to drive irresistibly deep into the enemy's defense system.

Guderian thus created not only a new combat arm of the service but simultaneously a new technique of command, in which success depended on the greatest possible speed and on orders that were brief but clear. He was by no means a theorist, but a decidedly practical officer highly versed in all aspects of active soldiering. He had mastered military technology as far as it had been developed at this stage, without letting himself get lost in details. He placed consideration for his men above all else, and they were devoted to him. They knew that he would never demand of them more than he was prepared to give of himself. In addition, he never let slip an opportunity to thank his men on the spot for any special services. He offered praise more often than criticism, but his subordinate commanders did not always have an easy time, for if he sensed lack of drive or decisiveness, he could speak pretty plainly.

How little appreciation the topmost echelons of the military command had of the significance of a man like Guderian even shortly before the outbreak of war is indicated by his designation under mobilization plans: GOC of a reserve infantry corps. Only after his own vigorous protests was this designation altered and he became GOC, 19th Corps, with undercommand the 3d Panzer Division (commanded by Freiherr Geyr von Schweppenburg), the 2d Motorized Division (under Lieutenant General Bader) and the 20th Motorized Division (under Lieutenant General Wiktorin), to which the 10th Panzer Division (under Major General Schaal) was later added. It was with this corps that he went into action in the Polish Campaign, when he had the satisfaction of putting his own teaching to the test for the first time. Also for the first time the world learned what "Blitzkrieg" tactics meant, with bombers smashing and demoralizing the defense ahead of concentrated Panzer and mechanized forces, which drove deeply into the enemy rear, with the slower-moving infantry following them to mop up and consolidate.

When Manstein was working out his Sichelschnitt plan, which was to lead to overwhelming success in France in 1940, it was Guderian whom he consulted about the feasibility of sending Panzer divisions driving through the Ardennes, which so-called experts on both sides considered impenetrable to armored units. When the campaign opened, Guderian's 19th Panzer Corps had three Panzer divisions under command: the 1st, under Major General Kirchner: the 2d, under Lieutenant General Veiel; and the 10th, under Lieutenant General Schaal.

Guderian crossed the Luxembourg border with the 1st Panzer Division on 10 May 1940. In the words of Liddell-Hart, "The decisive act of the world-shaking drama began on the 13th, when Guderian's Panzer Corps crossed the Meuse at Sedan." He launched his assault at 4:00 P.M. after preparatory dive-bombing, and by the following afternoon he had all three of his Panzer divisions across the river, with the roads to the channel ports open to his exultant troops. Had his Panzers not been halted by

Hitler at a critical stage, there might never have been a British "miracle of Dunkirk."

The following episode provides insight into Guderian's character and the nature of his leadership.

During the campaign in France, Colonel Dingler was detached by the Army High Command to Guderian's Panzer Corps as a liaison officer. In searching for the general's command post, Dingler ran into artillery fire and got the impression that the German attack in that sector was not going according to plan. In a ditch at the roadside he spotted a divisional commander taking cover with one of his staff officers. He joined them and asked where he could find General Guderian. With a laugh they told him, "If you want to speak to the general, grab a rifle and inch your way up to the crest in front of us. He's up there among the men, taking potshots at the French!"

After the breakthrough at Sedan at the beginning of the French Campaign and the successful crossing of the Meuse, Guderian concluded that the Supreme Command should order the breakthrough to be exploited and that the pursuit should not be halted until the English Channel was reached. Of all the senior German commanders, he alone sensed that Hitler might suddenly panic at his own daring, halt the Panzer formations, and order them to wait for the infantry to arrive and close up. And that is what happened.

On 17 May 1940, General von Kleist, commanding Guderian's superior Panzergruppe, suddenly appeared at Guderian's battle headquarters and bitterly reproached him for having departed from the Supreme Command instructions and continuing his advance. The discussion between the two generals became extremely stormy. Guderian curtly demanded to be relieved of command of his Panzer Corps, to which General von Kleist astonishingly agreed, effective immediately.

On orders from the commander in chief of the Army Group, General von Rundstedt, General von List immediately went to see Guderian and told him that the order to halt the advance had been given by Hitler personally, but the Army Group would have nothing against Guderian's pushing forward a "reconnaissance in force." Guderian resumed command of his Panzer Corps forthwith. "Reconnaissance in force" was a procedure that, within the over-all framework of operational plans for a breakthrough, allowed one to initiate almost anything. Guderian did not need to be told twice. He himself remained at his command post so as to be accessible to higher command at all times, but he made his reconnaissance in force so strong that it was able to prevent the enemy from building up a defensive front.

Ordered to form a Panzer Group under his own command for Phase 2 of the campaign in France, he had under him a complete Panzergruppe, an armored body of divisions that was an entirely new concept, consisting of two Panzer Corps—the 39th, under General Schmidt; and the 41st, under General Reinhardt. Both had two Panzer divisions and a motorized division.

During the attack across the Aisne and the Aisne Canal in early June 1940, after the infantry had established bridgeheads, Guderian's Panzergruppe was to advance through the infantry formations and, according to how the situation developed, head in the direction of Paris or the Longres Plateau. Guderian asked the commander in chief of the Twelfth Army, General Siegmund List, for permission to take his tanks straight forward, so that he could establish bridgeheads with them instead of with the infantry. The request was refused, but Guderian was by no means satisfied. He sent the Army High Command's liaison officer, Colonel Dingler, to the chief of staff of the army, General Halder, to get a definite order about who was to attack across the Aisne first, the tanks or the infantry.

Halder gave Dingler the partly ominous, partly humorous reply: "Tell the tin god of tanks [as he called Guderian] that whoever is closest to the enemy should attack first."

For Guderian the order said nothing and everything. When Dingler flew back to him in a Fieseler Storch, Guderian's Panzers were already crossing the river. In spite of vigorous protests from the infantry, the general had cleared them away from the bridge and taken possession of it exclusively for his Panzer units. It was not exactly considerate, but the resultant success once again proved him right.

If Guderian was a "difficult subordinate," he was so only in respect to operations under his own command and in the interest of their success. Any accusation that he was blind to the wider aspects of a question was certainly not justified.

On 9 June, Guderian's tanks thrust south and then east and

rapidly drove to the Swiss frontier behind the Maginot Line, cutting off all the French forces east of them. On the night of 16 June the French asked for an armistice.

Guderian was open to any logical and pertinent suggestions, but Hitler's order for a pause in May 1940 was not logical, nor did it take into account the realities of the situation. To Hitler, Guderian certainly was a "difficult subordinate," but he was not so to those who, like himself, were practical men.

Guderian's almost frenetic urge to advance was certainly somewhat disconcerting to his superiors, but he never acted without due reflection. In spite of his temperament, he was a thoughtful staff officer who always made due allowance for his own capabilities and the potential of his own troops. General Halder once remarked to him, "Your operations always hang on a thread." That may well have seemed to be the case to a very deliberative chief of staff. But success was Guderian's justification, and his troops followed him with enthusiasm and without hesitation.

In the Russian Campaign he commanded Panzergruppe 2, which was part of Field Marshal von Bock's Army Group Center. The Panzergruppe was to rip open the Russian front on both sides of the fortress of Brest-Litovsk on the first day of the attack and to reach the area round Smolensk, thus preventing the establishment of a new enemy defense line and setting the stage for a victorious campaign before the end of 1941. The main objective for Army Group Center was now clearly Moscow. At least so it seemed to all the German formation commanders.

On 29 July 1941, Hitler's senior aide-de-camp, Colonel Rudolf Schmundt, invested Guderian with the Oak Leaves to his Iron Cross. During the discussion that followed, Guderian learned to his astonishment that Hitler had not yet decided whether he should continue the advance on Moscow or occupy the Ukraine.

Guderian pressed Schmundt urgently to impress upon Hitler that Moscow must be regarded as the vital main objective. On 4 August 1941, Generals Guderian and Hoth told Hitler, who was on a visit to battle headquarters of Army Group Center, that their two Panzergruppen would be ready for the decisive thrust on Moscow between August 15 and 20. But Hitler still made no decision.

On 23 August, General Halder deeply shaken, informed the commander in chief of Army Group Center that Hitler had decided not to advance on Moscow but to occupy the Ukraine and the Crimea. Guderian immediately strongly protested the decision. In his opinion as regards both personnel and equipment, the Panzer formations could not undertake the long trek to the Ukraine and then a winter campaign against Moscow. Halder fully agreed, and it was decided to send Guderian himself to Hitler's headquarters so that he, as an experienced front-line commander, could personally put the case to the Führer.

Neither the commander in chief of the army, Field Marshal von Brauchitsch, nor his chief of staff, Halder, was present at the discussion between Hitler and Guderian. It is astonishing that these two responsible officers were absent from the meeting and even more astounding that Brauchitsch had ordered Guderian on no account to mention Moscow to Hitler, since his decision to take the Ukraine was irrevocable.

At the interview Hitler asked Guderian whether he felt that his Panzer formations were still fit for another great effort after all they had already accomplished. Guderian affirmed that they were, provided they were set a really worthwhile objective, to which Hitler replied, "You mean Moscow, of course!"

Guderian agreed and unfolded his own ideas to Hitler. After the fall of Moscow and the destruction of the Russian forces in that area, the Ukraine would drop into German hands like a ripe plum. To attack the Ukraine first and have to travel those enormous distances would greatly deplete the forces in both men and material—so much so, asserted Guderian, that an attack on Moscow so late in the year would be drastically lacking in power and impact.

Hitler, with his mind on the wheat of the Ukraine and the oil of the Caucasus, answered, "My generals understand nothing of the economics of war." He immediately gave orders for an advance on Kiev and the Ukraine.

It was not until 26 September that the battle for Kiev was brought to a conclusion. About 665,000 Russians were captured in a terrible encircling battle. Yet in spite of that one could not seriously consider it a success of strategic significance. The great strategic target was still Moscow, which had not been reached. In October the dreaded Russian winter began, with mud and slush followed by bitter cold and snow. The German offensive ground to a halt, even though another great encircling movement, this time round Vyasma, brought in another 600,000 Russian prisoners. Fresh Russian troops, terrible weather, and their own exhaustion could not fail to remind the Germans of the disaster that had overtaken Napoleon, but the die was cast, and they struggled on, only to be stopped in the very outskirts of the city. The Germans could go no farther, and the Panzer units that had been sent to the Ukraine were not there.

At the beginning of November 1941, Guderian flew to the Moscow front, and the impressions he gained there are set down in his memoirs *(Errinerungen eines Soldaten)*:

This is sheer torture for the troops, and for our cause it is a tragedy, for the enemy is gaining time, and in spite of all our plans we are being carried deeper into the winter. It really makes me sad. The best of intentions are wrecked by the weather. The unique opportunity to launch a really great offensive recedes further and further, and I doubt if it will ever recur. God alone knows how things will turn out. One must just hope and keep one's spirits up, but at the moment it is a great test.

It was at this time, about the middle of November, that General Balck, then general commanding mobile troops, visited Guderian himself to get a clear picture of the situation before Moscow. One could not fail to see that the men were at the end of their tether. Because of their numerical weakness they were constantly facing a serious crisis, and Guderian reckoned that at best they might capture Tula, but no more. A halt to further attacks seemed called for, with a switch to the defensive, but Hitler continued to demand attacks.

By the middle of December 1941 it was quite clear that the capture of Moscow was no longer feasible. In the presence of the commander in chief of the army group, Field Marshal von Kluge, Guderian described the situation to the commander in chief of the army, Field Marshal von Brauchitsch (who was to be dismissed a few days later when Hitler himself took over direct command of the army) and asked for the Moscow front to be pulled back. His dispatch was immediately forwarded to Hitler, who forbade any withdrawals. But they had already been partly initiated by Guderian, acting involuntarily under enemy pressure.

He now decided to fly to see Hitler personally and to put before him the almost impossible situation. The five-hour discussion was not merely lively but, on Hitler's part, downright antagonistic.

During the interview Guderian suggested among other things a change in the structure of supreme military command through replacement of the men at the top by generals with frontline experience, which was not among the qualifications of Field Marshal Keitel, whom Hitler had selected as his chief of staff when he himself took over direct command of the armed forces in 1939, or of General Alfred Jodl, who headed the army section of the Combined Staff of the Armed Forces.

Guderian was putting into words what we staff officers at the front had frequently discussed among ourselves, with Field Marshal von Manstein and General Marcks in mind. This proposal of Guderian's was indignantly turned down by Hitler, and up to 25 December 1941, Guderian did everything humanly possible to maintain his front unbroken. His leadership and the courage and toughness of his troops partly succeeded in achieving the impossible.

After some very unpleasant arguments between the army group commander, Field Marshal von Kluge, and Guderian—during which Kluge accused Guderian of misleading him—Guderian decided to ask to be relieved of command of Panzergruppe 2. Hitler favored Kluge, and on 26 December 1941 he relieved Guderian of his post. But he did not actually dismiss him; Guderian was posted to the Reserve of Officers. In other words, Hitler did not want to lose touch with him completely, just in case the time might come when he could again use so capable a commander of armor.

General Balck, who had served under Guderian for years, had this to say about the affair:

Guderian's dismissal was a heavy blow to us all, especially the Panzer troops. Kluge discussed the matter with me at length. He said he was forced into taking this step, as Guderian had not been completely frank with him. In carrying out his orders, he had promised to hold a definite line, although his troops were already withdrawing from it. I think the explanation may be found in Guderian's autocratic and self-willed nature, particularly in his hostile attitude to virtually all his superiors, and especially towards Kluge.

And what of Guderian himself? On his last visit to Guderian, Balck noted in his diary:

From the psychological point of view Guderian's manner of command is masterly, and he is all the more successful when his decisions are dependent upon the morale and relative weakness of his own troops. The men look up to him, and feel he understands them, for he displays none of the harshness of a general demanding the very utmost effort from his troops. Any such thought one can brush aside, as he actually achieved what he set out to do through his masterly handling of people.

Even Hitler admitted as much. On 20 December 1941—less than a week before dismissing Guderian—he told him, "You stand too close to things. You let yourself be influenced too much by the hardships of your men. You sympathize too deeply with the other ranks, when you should cut yourself off from them more."

Guderian was, in my view, a noble, kind-hearted man. His innermost nature was warm and sympathetic, but in the knowledge of the problems into which such characteristics could lead him, he often forced himself to be harsh and plain-speaking, with all the compulsion of his own hot temperament and his love for and sense of responsibility toward Germany, which would stop at nothing. Both militarily and in civil life he had the courage of his convictions, and he naturally made many enemies, who were always ready to criticize him.

After a year "on ice" Guderian was summoned by Hitler. He realized that only necessity had forced the Führer to recall him. The African Campaign had gone badly, and Stalingrad had been retaken by the Russians. Guderian, who was not in the best of health, was also aware that, as a result of the increasing superiority of the Russians, the armored forces he had created were in such a bad state that a fundamental reorganization was urgently needed. Hitler appointed him inspector general of all German Panzer forces, and as such he was responsible directly to Hitler and was given very broad powers.

In the Reichsminister for War Supplies, Albert Speer, Guderian found an understanding, knowledgeable, and energetic coworker. Tank production was given priority over all other demands for equipment. New types were conceived—the Panther and the Tiger II, later the King Tiger.

Hitler intended to mount a new offensive in the Kursk area in the middle of July 1943, and the Panther tanks were to be used there in great numbers, though Guderian was not in favor of the premature employment of the new tanks. They were still suffering from "teething troubles," which meant that losses might occur that would not be easy to replace. His concern proved correct, and the offensive against Kursk was a failure, and many German tanks were lost.

On 21 July 1944, immediately after the unsuccessful attempt on Hitler's life, Guderian was entrusted with the duties of chief of staff of the army, in addition to his other responsibilities. He had had nothing whatever to do with the conspiracy of 20 July and was never what one might call a "political soldier." In fact, he was respected within the party solely for his military successes. The task he had now been set was perhaps the most thankless imaginable, and he undertook it only because he wished to save the Eastern Army and his own East German homeland from the Russians.

By December 1944 it was clear that the offensive against the Americans in the Ardennes had failed. On the 24th, Guderian drove to Hitler's headquarters at Giessen (Ziegenberg) and asked that every available division be transferred to the east to face a big Russian attack expected on the Vistula on 12 January 1945. Supported by accurate information from the Foreign Armies East Intelligence Section, he told Hitler that the superiority of the Russians over the Germans on the Vistula Front was: tanks 7 to 1, guns 20 to 1, and aircraft 20 to 1. Every available man, he thought, should be sent to the Eastern Front to stop the Russians from flooding Germany. Considering the Reich's over-all situation after the failure of the Ardennes offensive and the threat of a major Russian attack on Berlin itself, his demands were more stringent than ever: "Halt all initiative in the West; ruthless disengagement on the Western, Italian, and Norwegian fronts, to form a powerful, mobile battle group east of Berlin to smash any Russian advance across the Vistula, by counterattack in mobile warfare."

Hitler saw things differently. He believed that the picture painted by Reinhard Gehlen's Foreign Armies East was "pure bluff" and that the Russians had hardly any tanks. He reckoned that enemy rifle divisions had at most 7,000 men on strength. Most dangerous of all was opposition of Jodl, then chief of operations, to the release of any troops for the Eastern Front. Although Hitler had lost the Ardennes offensive, he did not want to give up the initiative he had regained in the west, and he intended to carry on by going over to the offensive at Zebern (Saverne) and later at Strasbourg. Even the 26 divisions under Schörner, isolated by the Russians in the Courland Peninsula west of the Baltic port Riga, were being left to their fate rather than evacuated by sea to help defend Germany itself.

In the meantime, behind Guderian's back, Hitler ordered the transfer of the SS Corps Gille with its two SS divisions from the area north of Warsaw, where a major Russian attack was expected within a few days, down to Budapest to free the city from the Russians. On New Year's Eve, 1944/45, Guderian again reported the catastrophic situation on the Eastern Front, after obtaining three divisions from the Western Front and one from Italy, magnanimously offered by the commander in chief West, Von Rundstedt and his chief of staff, General Siegfried Westphal. The four allotted divisions were released for the Eastern Front, but on Hitler's orders they were sent to Budapest, while the bulk of the reserves were held in the west in an attempt to retain the initiative there.

I feel the deepest sympathy for Guderian, for, had Hitler accepted his advice to establish a powerful attacking force east of Berlin, though he might not have prevented the ultimate downfall of the German Reich, he could have avoided the overrunning of eastern Germany by the Russian hordes. That Guderian, born in eastern Germany, was unable to overcome the opposition of Hitler and Jodl to assembling sufficient troops east of Berlin to save his homeland from the Russians was the greatest tragedy of his life.

General Guderian enjoyed immense popularity throughout the army and was most highly regarded by everyone not only as a great Panzer commander but particularly as a man. He set a fine example as a soldier, and the extent to which his military doctrine and principles of training were approved among all ranks is illustrated by the following amusing anecdote related to me by his son, also named Heinz Guderian and later a major general in the Bundeswehr.

Guderian the elder was known among his troops by the nicknames "Hasty Heinz" and "Heinz the Hustler." One day during the war some trainees were set a task as a test of their ability to make decisions. In front, according to the test, there are enemy tanks; on the right is a minefield; on the left is a precipice. Behind you is Heinz the Hustler. What would you do? "Obviously I'd attack," came the answer. "Advance!"

Near the end of March 1945, after heated argument about the

evacuation of Courland and again about General Wenck replacing Himmler as commander in chief on the Vistula, the final break between Guderian and Hitler came. Speaking the truth, Hitler made his parting shot, "General Guderian, your health demands immediate sick leave of six weeks."

The general was captured by the Americans on 10 May 1945 with his inspectorate staff in the Tyrol, and was released on his sixtieth birthday. He died on 14 May 1954, and was buried in his old garrison town, Goslar, to be remembered as one of Germany's greatest military commanders.

Chapter 6

FIELD MARSHAL FRIEDRICH PAULUS

Fabius Cuncator — the Temporizer?

To understand the behavior of Field Marshal Paulus at the catastrophe of Stalingrad, one needs to know something of his background, personality, and character.

Born in 1890 at Breitenau, in Hesse, Friedrich Paulus came from the so-called middle class. His father who had served as a soldier, was an administrative official in a reform school. His grandfather, like his great-grandfather, was a builder, and his mother was the daughter of the principal of the school where his father worked. After passing his matriculation examinations, Paulus' dearest wish was to join the Imperial German Navy, but his application for a commission was rejected because he did not come from the upper class, a fact that probably had some influence on the development of his nature, even if only subconsciously.

He began studying law, but then joined the 3d Baden Infantry Regiment in Rastatt, close to the River Rhine below Karlsruhe, as an ensign. A year later he was promoted to second lieutenant, and soon afterward he married Elena Rosetti-Solescu, a Rumanian aristocrat. That marriage, his own tall, elegant appearance, and his always immaculately correct uniform counted for a lot in his later life.

In World War I, Paulus' superior officers soon realized that he was cut out for the General Staff, and in 1917 he was transferred to Headquarters of the Alpine Corps. This appointment particularly suited his methodical way of doing things. After the war he was transferred to the Reichswehr, and in 1920 he became regimental adjutant of the 14th Baden Infantry Regiment at Constance.

Paulus gained a reputation for studying every situation minutely and drawing up his orders in the most explicit detail. It took him hours to work out the orders, but then they were given out in classic form. During maneuvers in the 1920's he was unexpectedly placed in command of the regiment and found it tough going, for he had to make rapid decisions. The directing staff of the exercise reported, "This officer lacks decisiveness." A personal report by his commanding officer at the time read as follows:

A typical staff officer of the old school. Tall, and in outward appearance painstakingly well groomed. Modest, perhaps too modest, amiable, with extremely courteous manners, and a good comrade, anxious not to offend anyone. Exceptionally talented and interested in military matters, and a meticulous desk worker, with a passion for war games and formulating plans on the mapboard or sand table. At this he displays considerable talent, considering every decision at length and with careful deliberation before giving the appropriate orders.

From 1923 to 1927, Paulus was general staff officer of the 5th Infantry Command at Stuttgart, where he also lectured on staff courses for some years. His pupils declared him the best turned out of all the officers and nicknamed him "Der Cunctator," after the Roman Consul Fabius, who tried to exhaust Hannibal by everlastingly refusing to give battle.

For one year Paulus was a company commander in the 13th Infantry Regiment in Stuttgart, where he and Rommel were together—Rommel one of the most enthusiastic and successful regimental officers, Paulus leaning more toward dispassionate, impersonal staff work.

When Hitler was appointed chancellor, Paulus was a lieutenant colonel, but, unlike Generals von Blomberg and von Reichenau, he was not among the Führer's devoted followers. He had a very conservative outlook, but, like so many of his associates, he was naturally impressed by Hitler's promises and political achievements. He also welcomed the introduction of conscription, and was especially pleased by his own appointment as chief of staff to the newly established Panzer Headquarters in Berlin, all the more because in the development of this new branch of the service he met with considerable understanding on Hitler's side.

During the Polish Campaign, Paulus was chief of staff in the Tenth (later the Sixth) Army, and his commander in chief as later

in France, was General von Richenau. These two men complemented one another perfectly, something vitally important to
smooth-running command. Reichenau was ruthless and could even
be brutal. He was impulsive, wrapped up in himself, and vain,
and he loved to be in the limelight. He was very good at sports,
always commanded his troops from well to the front, and made
quick decisions. In addition, he was interested and active in politics. Paulus, on the other hand, preferred to keep in the background. He relieved his commander of all desk work, to such an
extent that Reichenau seldom bothered to read orders drafted by
Paulus, who was thus the ideal chief of staff upon whom Reichenau
could rely completely.

My friend Colonel Dingler—himself a staff officer—first served
under Paulus during the fighting round Stalingrad. He had previously met him only briefly during the campaign in France and
at the preparations for "Operation Sea Lion," the planned attack
on England. Dingler was strongly impressed by Paulus' quiet calmness, his constant courtesy, especially to his juniors, and with his
manner, which was businesslike in every respect. From the very
beginning, Paulus inspired confidence.

In the late summer of 1940, Major General Paulus became
Oberquartiermeister, or Director of Operations, at General Headquarters of the Army—which was equivalent to deputy chief of
the general staff in the British or American forces. His senior,
General Halder, chief of the army staff, spoke of him as an excellent and likable man, highly developed intellectually. Halder
needed a specialist in armor on his staff, and he reckoned Paulus
to be a knowledgeable officer, though he was no fighter by nature.

In his capacity as director of operations Paulus was given the
task of preparing a draft plan for the attack on Russia, for Hitler
was not satisfied with the scheme previously worked out by General Marcks, which appeared to him too "contrived." In view of
his operational planning ability, Paulus was particularly suited
to such a task. At the beginning of June 1941 he laid before the
chief of the general staff a detailed map indicating the dispositions
of Soviet forces. It presented a somber picture. According to
Paulus' information, the Russians were fully mobilized and so deployed as to indicate to the experienced eye an immediate offensive capability.

At a discussion with the armed forces commanders in chief,

this serious view of the enemy's preparedness induced Hitler to set the date for the German attack as 22 June 1941, to beat the Russians to it, with the object of forcing them to sue for peace before the end of 1941. Events in Yugoslavia and the Balkans had already caused him to defer the tentative date for the offensive, and time was running out.

When the campaign in the east began, it was Paulus' responsibility to direct operations along general lines from his map board, but keeping in close touch with the army groups. He exercised control very differently from Hitler, who increasingly interfered in direct command, especially when an attack led to a serious crisis.

As a later chief of staff of a Panzer army and of an army group, I should stress that Paulus' ideas on controlling operations were excellent. He allotted a task to an army group and then left it to them to decide on the best method of carrying it out. Hitler, on the other hand, instead of allotting tasks, kept interfering more and more in detail and thus nullified the effect of directives issued by formation staffs on their own initiative.

For the summer of 1942, Hitler ordered a large-scale offensive with far-reaching objectives, and on 5 March 1942 he issued his orders. The new offensive was to take place between the Black Sea and Kursk, with the middle reaches of the Don and the Volga at Stalingrad as objectives. Field Marshal von Bock's Army Group South was ordered to occupy the Caucasus and to break through to the line from Batum to Baku to take possession of the oil fields on the Caspian Sea. A secondary offensive was planned for the capture of Leningrad in the far north, but, with German reserves already dangerously stretched to their limit, Hitler planned no particular pressure on the center of the long Eastern Front, and his generals felt particularly uneasy at the thought that protection of the left flank of their troops advancing toward the Caucasus would have to be entrusted to Rumanian, Hungarian, and Italian allies, in whom they placed no great faith against determined Russian attack. What made matters even worse was that one Italian corps on the endless level steppes consisted of Alpine troops originally intended for mountain fighting in the Caucasus.

Hitler had thus ordered two divergent operations in the south, as well as over the entire front, that would inevitably disperse the already overtaxed German forces still more. Both Halder, as chief of the army staff, and Paulus, as director of operations, suggested that it would be better to adopt the strategic defensive, against which enemy forces would wear themselves out. During the bitter winter battles, with their crises between 1 November 1941 and 1 April 1942, the German forces lost about 900,000 men and enormous quantities of equipment, but Hitler would not admit that they were no longer as battleworthy as they had been at the opening of the campaign on the Eastern Front. He stuck to his utopian orders, which considerably underestimated the Russian forces, whom he thought of as already exhausted. He did not realize that as the Red Army pulled farther east it drew ever nearer to the Soviet Union's immense reserves of manpower and sources of guns, tanks, and other armament.

At the beginning of 1942, Paulus was made commander in chief of the Sixth Army. His predecessor, Von Reichenau, was appointed commander in chief of Army Group South, and Hitler had ordered the former army group commander, Von Rundstedt, home. When Reichenau succumbed to a heart attack, he in turn was followed by Bock early in 1942, but by the time Paulus became deeply involved in the events that were to culminate in the Stalingrad disaster, reorganization in the south had led to the establishment of a special Army Group A under Field Marshal List for the Caucasus thrust, while Bock—followed by Weichs—retained command of Army Group B, which included the Sixth Army and the more mobile Fourth Panzer Army under Hoth.

To appoint as an army commander a highly qualified staff officer such as Paulus was a grave mistake in personnel selection (the British perhaps made the same error in placing Ritchie, who was only deputy chief of staff in Cairo at the time of his appointment, in command of their Eighth Army in the desert, and lost Tobruk). Paulus had never commanded a division or a corps. Every man, no matter how well he may have done in the most senior staff appointments, must have some experience of command of smaller formations to develop the characteristics of inner confidence, independence, and self-assurance necessary for high command. Failure to take due account of this fact was to contribute greatly to the disaster at Stalingrad.

It was coincidental that Paulus, who was really too young to be an army commander, should return to the Sixth Army, with which he had served in Poland and France with such success as a chief of staff. Shortly before the intended German attack on Voronezh could be launched, Marshal S. K. Timoshenko attacked on both flanks toward Kharkov on 12 May 1942, in an attempt to break through the German front to the Dnieper. Paulus, who had meanwhile been promoted general of Panzer troops, imposed a shattering defeat on Timoshenko with his Sixth Army, and for this skillfully directed operation he was awarded the Knight's Cross.

The German Southern Front immediately went over to the offensive, attacking not only toward the Don and Volga but also in the direction of the Caucasus. With the former Army Group now split, Bock's Army Group B was to continue its advance toward the Don and the Volga, with the Sixth Army and the Fourth Panzer Army under command, while Army Group A under Field Marshal List advanced southward toward the Caucasus and its oil fields, without which Hitler believed Germany would not be able to continue the war. In simplest terms, the offensive was to drive down the land corridor between the Don and Donetz; the two army groups were then to part, one continuing south while the other turned east for Stalingrad and the Volga.

When Army Group B reached Voronezh on the Don, von Bock planned to halt and to secure his open flanks before continuing his advance toward the Volga bend where it comes nearest to the Don, a good 300 miles farther southeast. Hitler did not approve. Bock was dismissed and replaced by Field Marshal Baron von Weichs.

Early in July 1942, the 14th Panzer Corps of the Sixth Army thrust forward from the area south of Vorsehilov on the Don, and the Russians fled eastwards before the clenched fist of armor and headed for Stalingrad, toward which further Russian troops also fell back to escape Kleist's southward drive as his armored forces swung down from Chertkovo, past Millerovo and Kamensk to cross the lower Don well west of Stalingrad.

Now a strange thing happened. The German forces could advance no farther. Unknown to the Germans, Stalingrad had been selected as the final point for a Russian stand, and on Stalin's orders the tide was to be turned in this strategically favorable area. Timoshenko, the commander in chief in the sector, was given orders to concentrate all his available forces so as to gain time for the purpose. Since the German armor had not followed up, Major General V. Y. Kolpachi was able to concentrate the full strength of his Sixty-second Army in the Don bend and establish a strong bridgehead near Kalach.

What were the Germans doing meanwhile?

Hitler's cardinal error of trying to drive simultaneously on both Stalingrad and the Caucasus had resulted in a dispersal of forces already too weak for their tasks. Acting on a decision taken by Hitler's headquarters to bolster the thrust to the Caucasus, the Fourth Panzer Army, which should have headed straight for Stalingrad, was diverted to help Kleist cross the Don, where, according to Kleist himself, it simply got in the way and cluttered up the road. Most of the fuel allotted to the Sixth Army was redirected to the Caucasus front, and for eighteen long days the Sixth Army was virtually immobile, thus allowing the Russians valuable time to strengthen their defense of Stalingrad.

Only on 20 July was Paulus able to recommence activities, but with each step farther southward between the Don and the Donetz his strength diminished in proportion to his extending left flank, for the guarding of which he had to detach more and more units. Through a bold pincer movement he managed to destroy the Russian bridgehead at Kalach, which his spearheads reached on 28 July and brought his leading troops 350 miles from their start line and little more than 40 miles from Stalingrad itself, on the bend of the Volga. By 8 August the trap was sprung, and the Germans managed to establish bridgeheads across the Don, but they still lacked real punch for a final drive to the Volga, and Hoth's Fourth Panzer Army was having to fight its way back from the area of the Don-Aksai river junction, while the VIII Fliegerkorps was also transferred back to support an attack.

In Marshal Georgi Zhukov's memoirs one can gather how close to collapse the situation was for the Red Army. After the great losses in these preliminary battles, General Lopatin, now commanding the Sixty-second Army, had decided that, in view of the apparent hopelessness of the situation, Stalingrad should be surrendered. General Krylenko, chief of staff to General A. L. Yeremenko, commander in chief of Stalingrad and the Southeastern Front, refused to permit such a thing and so informed the commander in chief and his political commissar, Nikita Krushchev, of whom the world was to hear much more in the years to come. Lopatin was dismissed, and until 12 September the Sixty-second Army was led by General Krylenko himself.

On 21 August the German Sixth Army attacked across the Don on both sides of Vertyachi. By 23 August tanks of the 14th Panzer Corps had reached the Volga near Rynok in the northern outskirts of Stalingrad. The Russians pulled back, and a desperate battle now began, reminiscent of the inconclusive and wasteful struggle at Verdun in World War I. The Tragedy of Stalingrad had started.

The Red Army defended itself desperately, and from the north made ceaseless attacks against the land corridor being used by the German forces, with the intention of bringing aid to the Russians in Stalingrad. They were fighting with their backs to the two-mile-wide Volga, across which there were no bridges to offer easy escape. In the city itself every house, every building, the factories, and the station were bitterly contested. Stuka attacks and heavy artillery fire left everything in ruins. On 12 September 1942, Yeremenko and Krushchev appointed General V. I. Chuikov, former deputy GOC, Sixty-fourth Army, as commander of the Sixty-second Army and charged him with the defense of Stalingrad.

The battle for Stalingrad, in which thousands of German soldiers were sacrificed, had no particular strategic significance. It became a battle of prestige between Hitler and Stalin, who was determined that the city that bore his name should not fall into enemy hands. Stalin ordered the troops on the west bank of the Volga to dig in and not surrender a foot of ground to the enemy. Anyone who tried to retreat across the Volga was to be shot out of hand.

By midday on 14 September the Germans of the 29th Motorized Division of the Fourth Panzer Army were fighting on the edge of the southern suburbs at Kuporosnoye and threatening the railway stations. The Russians were desperately clinging to the river-port and the ferry landing stage. Every reserve available was thrown in, and that night Major General A. I. Rodimtsev's 13th Guards Rifle Division crossed the Volga and went immediately into action. In the southern city reserves of the 35th Russian Guards Division were ferried across the river to the southern landing stage and immediately entered the battle. By the morning of 16 September it again looked as though the Russians could not possibly hold out. The southern railway station had already fallen to the Germans. Then Stalin released a brigade of marines and an armored brigade from his reserves. Together they helped to prevent collapse, and from that time until 3 October no fewer than six fresh infantry divisions were diverted by the Red Army to defend the ruins of Stalingrad.

At the end of September, General Paulus with all available forces tried to storm the last remaining Russian strongpoints one after the other, but owing to the severe losses his Sixth Army had already suffered, his troops simply could not force the issue. By the middle of October about four-fifths of the city was in German hands, but the Russians still held a few factory buildings and a few kilometers of the steep western banks of the Volga.

In the meantime the situation in the German Army Group B, and that of the Sixth Army in particular, was steadily declining. Paulus' army was the apex of a long salient whose 400-kilometer northern flank along the Don was covered with inadequately equipped troops of Germany's allies—the Second Hungarian Army, the Eighth Italian Army, and the Third Rumanian Army. South of Stalingrad, on the southern flank, was the Fourth Rumanian Army. The general line traced by the front and the known weakness of Germany's allies encouraged the Russians to counterattack with the object of completely surrounding the German and allied formations. With the German position in front of the British Eighth Army at El Alamein in North Africa also steadily deteriorating, the psychological moment for an all-out effort in Russia was fast approaching. A serious reverse for the Germans battling to establish themselves in Stalingrad would inevitably threaten the forces in the Caucasus with an attack in the rear and force their withdrawal, thus removing the one arm of the immense pincers that the British feared might close on the Suez Canal from north and west.

Paulus wanted to halt all attacks on Stalingrad, which, from the over-all operational point of view, were useless. He wanted to withdraw his 14th Panzer Corps from the line for reorganization and hold it as a reserve in the rear, but Hitler—purely for the sake of prestige—wanted Stalingrad at any price and would not agree to what was in fact the only sensible suggestion.

By 21 September, General Chuikov had been forced to move his own headquarters out of the deep gorge of the Tsaritsa River, which cuts through the southern half of Stalingrad, and he was back at Matveyev Kurgan, farther north as his tired men stubbornly resisted, often isolated but fighting till they ran out of ammunition. For their part the Germans were equally feeling the strain of endless battle, and, as they tried to take one pile of ruins after another in the southern suburbs, Hoth's Panzer Army men were perpetually harassed by Russian pockets bypassed in the first armored rush. At street fighting the Russians were more than their equals, and the Russian reserves seemed unlimited.

As early as August the German General Staff had warned Hitler that the long flank on the Don would be untenable in winter after the river froze, but in the long weeks that followed his mind remained concentrated on Stalingrad, where General Chuikov's Sixty-second Army and part of Shumilov's Sixty-fourth Army held on grimly, while the flow of Russian reinforcements mounted.

At the end of October, Paulus informed Army Group B that the Russians were deploying on the flanks of the Sixth Army. Hitler was kept fully informed, but only halfhearted measures were ordered to reinforce the flanks. Only the 48th Panzer Corps, consisting of a weak German Panzer division and a Rumanian Panzer division unable to match the Russian T34 tanks, was put in behind the Third Rumanian Army. To these were added a few blocking units, some flak and some army artillery. Within Stalingrad itself Panzer units totally unsuited for house-to-house fighting among the ruins wore themselves out. When General Gustav von Wietersheim, commanding the armor that had broken through to the Volga at Rynok, suggested that his tanks should be withdrawn and the corridor kept open by infantry, he was sent back to Germany—to end up as a private in the Volksstrum in 1945.

At midnight on 19 November some 3,500 Soviet guns and mortars opened a barrage on the positions held by the Rumanian armies on the northern and southern flanks of Paulus' Sixth Army. It was the greatest weight of artillery fire ever experienced, and at 8:00 the next morning strong Soviet units attacked in accordance with a plan shrewdly devised by Generals Zhukov, A. M. Vasilevsky, and N. N. Voronov, backed by enormous reserves built up over many weeks. The Rumanians defended themselves gallantly, but were overwhelmed by superior Russian strength. Panic crept in and then deteriorated into headlong flight. General Paulus threw all available units of the Sixth Army against the Soviet eastern flank, but he was unable to prevent the junction at Kalach, on the Don, of Russian shock troops thrown in from north and south. The Sixth Army was completely surrounded. The curtain was rising on the Tragedy of Stalingrad.

In Egypt, Montgomery had defeated Panzer Army Afrika at El Alamein, Anglo-American forces had landed in French North Africa, and, on the evening of 12 November, Rommel's crowning triumph, the capture of Tobruk, was wiped out when South African armored cars reentered the fortress. Within less than a fortnight, Paulus' Sixth Army and a corps of Hoth's Fourth Panzer Army, totaling 22 German divisions and about 330,000 men, were ringed by Russian forces in the Stalingrad area. If there was a single psychological turning point of the war, this was it.

Paulus and his chief of staff, General Schmidt, failed to realize the deadly danger of the encirclement of the Sixth Army until 21 November. They came to the same conclusion: that to avoid encirclement they should break out to the southwest after regrouping. But on the same evening orders were received from Hitler to hold their existing positions. Paulus and his chief of staff, by nature alike, obeyed orders. I think that I myself, accustomed to independent decisions by Rommel and Balck, would have advised Paulus urgently to break out even after he had received the order. On the evening of 21 November, Paulus issued the following order: "Stalingrad and the Volga Front are to be held. The 11th and 13th Corps will assemble west of the Don to counterattack the enemy breakthrough." But two corps could not even *hold* the area west of the Don, and in view of the enemy's superiority there could be no thought of counterattack. They had to pull back to the east bank of the Don on 22 November. During that day Paulus received a meaningless radio signal from the Army Group: "Army to hold out, further orders follow." During the evening a radio message from Hitler made any thought of breakout impossible: "Hold your position." No detailed instructions were given.

The Chief of the Army General Staff, Colonel General Zeitzler; the commander in chief of Army Group B, Field Marshal von Weichs, and the Army Commander, General Paulus, all came to the same conclusion: that the Sixth Army should withdraw into a position within the bend bounded by the Don and Chir rivers. There a line should be formed to receive those parts of the Sixth Army cut off east of the Don. The army was holding down tens of thousands of Russian troops, and it was the Sixth Army's continued existence—not Stalingrad—that was of real strategic importance, since every Russian released from the Stalingrad front increased the danger to Rostov and the German forces in the Caucasus.

On 23 November, General Zeitzler did his utmost to get Hitler to agree to a withdrawal into the Don bend as a last resort to save the Sixth Army. On the same day Paulus was urged by the generals under his command, led by General Hans Hube (the one-armed commander whom the Anglo-Americans were to face in Sicily), to abandon Stalingrad forthwith and break out to the southwest.

Paulus immediately sent a radio message requesting Hitler to grant him complete freedom of action regarding movement of his troops. On the morning of 24 November, Hitler's reply came: "Führer decree—Create a pocket. Present Volga front and present northern front to be held at all costs. Supplies coming by air." One is tempted to ask why Paulus did not act independently on 22 or 23 November, as his generals—especially General Walter von Seydlitz-Kurzbach, commanding the 51st Corps and the oldest and most experienced of his formation commanders—had advised him to do.

Manstein, commander in chief of Army Group Don, arrived at the headquarters of Weichs's Army Group B at Starobjelsk on 24 November, and only then was he able to form a clear idea of what had happened during the past few days and realized the actual situation. He described it in *Verlorene Siege:*

Hitler had nailed down the Sixth Army in Stalingrad, when a chance still remained that they could have fought their way out. Operationally, they were now immobile. Without going into detail about the course of the first few days of the Soviet offensive, one may say that the encirclement of the Sixth Army could have been prevented only by challenging the enemy breakthrough at the very start, either to the west across the Don or east of the river toward the southwest. Orders for this were the responsibility of Supreme Headquarters, but Paulus should have taken things into his own hands and retreated from Stalingrad.

Personally I am convinced that Paulus' hesitation was due to his habit of giving the most careful consideration to any subject. He was never one to make quick decisions. Between 21 and 24 November, while events were taking this catastrophic turn, immediate action was required. Not an hour should have been wasted. The watchword should have been "Get out of the trap before it closes." Action should have been made in keeping with the bigger picture, by maintaining the Sixth Army ready for action against the main Russian offensive. But Paulus, a highly trained operations staff officer, was accustomed throughout his life to ponder every decision thoroughly and to weigh every possibility most carefully. It went against the grain to give a snap decision involving what in his opinion amounted to grave risk and foolhardiness. He also steadfastly believed in unquestioning loyalty to his superior officers, and in Hitler's and Göring's promises that his army would be supplied by air, although his own air force advisers had warned him that this was virtually impossible, and he obviously could not have known that Göering's undertaking had been carried to Hitler by his Luftwaffe chief of staff, Major General Hans Jeschonnek with qualifications. Those included the need to hold the necessary airfields and hopes for suitably fine weather. Events in Stalingrad also pose the question whether it is sufficient for a senior military commander, such as the commander in chief of an army, to obey without question orders that are in no way appropriate to a situation.

Colonel Dingler, who was staff officer (operations) of the 3d Motorized Division in General von Wietersheim's 14th Panzer Corps when a breakout was still possible, told Paulus some time later that it was the opinion of the troops themselves that they should fight their way out, with or without orders. Paulus replied: "I expect you as a soldier to carry out the orders of your superior officers. In the same manner the Führer, as my superior, can and must expect that I shall obey his orders." But when an army commander reaches a decision, does it not also involve his responsibility for the lives of some 250,000 German soldiers?

On 25 November, the corps commander of the 51st Corps, General von Seydlitz-Kurbach, sent a memorandum to Paulus urging him to disobey the Führer's orders and break out of the encirclement on his own responsibility. Such a decision offered the chance of smashing the southern sector of the enemy investment and keeping a large part of the Sixth Army intact for further operations. Von Seydlitz had himself fought his way through to free six divisions from the stranglehold of the Demyansk pocket in April. His memorandum read:

Unless the Army High Command immediately rescinds its order to hold out in a hedgehog position, it becomes our inescapable duty before our own conscience, our duty to the army and to the German people to seize that freedom of action that we are being denied by the present order, and to take the opportunity which still exists at this moment to avert catastrophe by ourselves attacking. The complete annihilation of 200,000 fighting men and their entire equipment is at stake. There is no other choice.

This emotional appeal for disobedience carried no weight with Paulus, the cool-headed staff officer. Would generals such as Reichenau, Guderian or Rommel have behaved differently under such circumstances? These three were fundamentally different from Paulus in character. They were much more impulsive and far quicker at making decisions. And that was what mattered in this catastrophic situation.

In the meantime, at Stalingrad, the opportunity of escaping had been allowed to pass. By the end of November the encirclement of the Fortress of Stalingrad was so strong in the south and southwest that the Sixth Army could no longer break out on its own. What mobility its horses had afforded was even lost, for they had to be slaughtered to supplement the meager rations. The immediate solution for relief of the army now was for the Fourth Panzer Army east of the Don to attack from the south. Preparations for such assistance and the actual conduct of operations were under Field Marshal von Manstein as commander in chief of Army Group Don. He gathered various units—the 23d Panzer Division from the Caucasus, the 6th Panzer Division from the Western Front, and, a little later, the 17th Panzer Division—in the area around Kotelnikov. This Panzergruppe, under the command of the Fourth Panzer Army, was to attack east of the Don under the direction of General Hoth. After breaking through the Russian covering forces, it was to attack the southern and western encircling forces in the flank and rear and then roll up the front.

Manstein clearly knew, as did General Zeitzler, that, should the Fourth Panzer Army succeed in reaching the trapped Sixth Army, it would be impossible to hold the northern flank of the penetration thus achieved, or the "Northern Gate," as it was called, or even Stalingrad itself. But Hitler still had to be convinced of the position. It was a struggle for the continued existence not only of the Sixth Army, but of the whole southern German front, especially since reports were received that a major Russian attack was to be expected against the Italian and Hungarian forces covering the northern flank. In other words, the utmost speed was once again essential.

The attack by the Fourth Panzer Army began on 12 December 1942 at a critical juncture when events elsewhere were foreshadowing the total eclipse of Axis forces in Africa. At first the operations in Russia made good progress, and until 19 December the German divisions scored repeated successes. An important stretch of terrain, the Aksay sector at the eastern tip of the Don bend, was crossed, and the German Army spearhead reached the Muschkova Brook, which was only 48 kilometers from the enemy's southern front encircling Stalingrad.

Behind the Fourth Panzer Army were motor-transport columns laden with 3,000 tons of fuel, ammunition, and supplies, as well as towing vehicles to shift the heavy weapons of the Sixth Army, which had by now become more or less immobilized. All these supplies were to flow forward as soon as the Fourth Panzer Army had created a definite line of communication with the Sixth Army.

On 19 December, Manstein sent an urgent message to Hitler asking for full discretion in freeing the Sixth Army from Stalingrad and letting him attack so as to join up with the Fourth Panzer Army. When no reply from Hitler's headquarters had been received by 6:00 P.M. that day, Manstein gave the Sixth Army orders to break through to the southwest and reestablish communication with the Fourth Panzer Army so that all of the heavy equipment could be towed out. His orders included instructions for a complete breakout by the whole of the Sixth Army, which was to join up with the units actually pulling out. On the code word "Thunderbolt" the breakout was to be put into effect by evacuating one sector after another around Stalingrad.

Why, one might ask, did not Paulus seize this opportunity at once? It is almost impossible to find an answer to this question, but what one now knows about the Russian reaction to the situation is interesting. General Yeremenko, commanding the Russian encircling forces, anxiously reported to Stalin: "There is a danger that the German Fourth Panzer Army will strike the rear of our Fifty-first Army, which is holding the southwestern perimeter of the Stalingrad pocket. If Paulus manages to attack to the southwest at this moment, it will be difficult to stop him from breaking

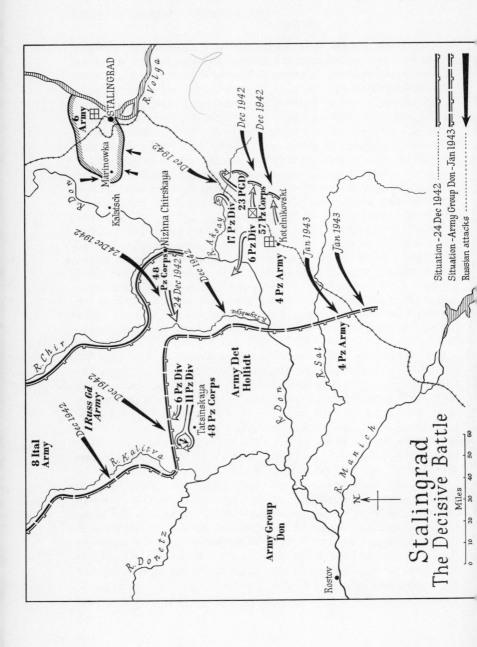

Stalingrad
The Decisive Battle

Situation – 24 Dec 1942 —————
Situation – Army Group Don – Jan 1943 =========
Russian attacks —————

STALINGRAD

R. Volga

6 Army

Marinowka

Kalatsch

R. Don

Nizhna Chirskaya

24 Dec 1942

4·8 Pz Corps

24 Dec 1942

Dec 1942

Dec 1942

R. Aksay

17 Pz Div

23 PGD

6 Pz Div

57 Pz Corps

Kotelnikovski

Dec 1942

Dec 1942

Jan 1943

Jan 1943

4 Pz Army

4 Pz Army

R. Tzimblya

Army Det Hollidt

R. Sal

R. Chir

1 Russ Gd Army

Dec 1942

6 Pz Div
11 Pz Div
Tatsinskaya
4·8 Pz Corps

8 Ital Army

Dec 1942

R. Kalitva

R. Don

R. Donetz

R. Manich

Army Group Don

Rostov

N

Miles
0   10   20   30   40   50   60

through." At the same time General Hoth, commanding the Fourth Panzer Army, radioed Paulus to put in diversionary attacks at once on the southern front to help the Fourth Panzer Army cover the last 20 kilometers needed to reach the encircling defenses.

The situation developed with great speed. On the lower Chir, along which the outstandingly able Colonel Wenck had contributed much to holding back the enemy during the latter part of November to cover Hoth's northern flank, the 48th Panzer Corps was strongly attacked from 10 December onward by powerful Russian armored formations. The corps was forced to withdraw from the attack for the relief of Stalingrad.

I was then chief of staff of this corps, and several times I asked Paulus by radio for more positive action on the southwestern front of Stalingrad, but there was no noticeable result.

On 17 December the situation of Army Group Don—Manstein's group—was critical, not only in the Chir sector but also on the group's left wing, or western flank, which had been stabilized by the drastic efforts of combat groups under Colonel von Pannwitz, Major Sauvant, and others but was now being attacked by the enemy in force. Again Manstein demanded of Hitler immediate preparations for the breakout of the Sixth Army, but again Hitler refused.

Meanwhile, Manstein had Major Eissmann flown to Stalingrad to confer with Paulus and to give him Manstein's own plans for a breakthrough that would undoubtedly be necessary within a very short time. Manstein's suggestions were more or less as follows:

It was debatable whether the Fourth Panzer Army would be able to reach the actual enemy line around the Sixth Army, for the Russians were constantly throwing in fresh forces against them. Therefore, it was high time for the Sixth Army itself to become more active on the southern front, with the object of fighting its way through the enemy lines. This would considerably help the Fourth Panzer Army advance to the north and join hands with the Sixth Army.

Eissman's suggestions greatly impressed Paulus, but the army commander's strong-willed chief of staff, Major General Arthur Schmidt (not the one captured at Bardia in January 1942) declared that a breakthrough by the Sixth Army at that time would be impossible. It would be a "catastrophic solution."

"The Sixth Army," he told Eissmann, "will be able to hold out until Easter. You must just keep it better supplied."

As Colonel Dingler reported, the troops at the front did not share the opinion of Paulus' chief of staff. What *they* thought was impossible was to hold out until Easter, in view of the weather, the shortage of ammunition, and an almost total lack of fuel. General Schmidt was generally regarded as a quiet, serious, reserved, considerate staff officer, but many called him "stubborn," for he stuck uncompromisingly to a decision once it had been reached, and he was not adaptable.

These two senior officers, Paulus and Schmidt, did not complement one another, for their characters were too similar, and the question thus naturally arises whether a younger, more wide-awake chief of staff capable of snap decisions might have been able to make Paulus change his mind. I do not think so. Paulus would have listened to any other chief of staff with the same close attention he gave to every report on the situation. It might have become a little more difficult for him to carry out Hitler's orders, but I am sure that he would have followed his own ideas and intentions, come what may. His whole character, nature, and manner of thought had become so firmly established that he would not act inconsistently once he had reached a decision.

That he did not follow the suggestion to make an all-out attempt at a breakout Paulus explained by the weakness of his troops, the lack of mobility of his divisions, and the great risk involved in any attempt at fighting his way out. He added that his fuel supplies were sufficient only for 30 kilometers at most. That was a point on which he laid too great a stress; in the event of a simultaneous attack by 4th Panzer Army the distance between the two armies would have become considerably less than 30 kilometers.

For six long days von Manstein's army group offered the Sixth Army the chance of saving itself in cooperation with the Fourth Panzer Army, even though the decision involved great risk for the entire German southern front. But during the last days of 1942 the Sixth Army's second chance of escape was also allowed to pass.

The rapidly deteriorating over-all situation demanded of Field Marshal von Manstein the difficult decision to call off the Fourth Panzer Army's attack on Stalingrad, so as to free those forces to cover the threatened flanks of his army group. There was a particular danger that the Russian breakthrough in the Eighth Italian Army's sector toward Rostov on the Don would cut off the German army group in the Caucasus. With this suspension of the Fourth Panzer Army's attack for the relief of the Sixth Army, the final phase of the Battle of Stalingrad began.

It is appropriate at this point to remark upon Göring's assurances of so-called air supply for the fortress of Stalingrad to the extent of 500 tons of supplies a day. A promise of supply by air was just the excuse Hitler needed to justify his unrealistic orders for holding the beleaguered ruins when no other line of communication remained open for essential rations, ammunition, and fuel for the Sixth Army. The Ju52 aircraft used by the regular Luftwaffe transport units of Luftflotte III, which would be responsible for airlifting the supplies, could carry only 2 1/2 tons of freight each. They flew unceasingly, in spite of atrocious weather, including fog and heavy snowstorms. But during the first two days they could land only 65 tons, and on the third day they lifted almost nothing. It was six days before they could get the daily total up to 100 tons, a bare one-fifth of what the Sixth Army needed after slaughtering all their horses to augment the rations. Even HeIII bombers were roped in as extra transports, as well as a complete Gruppe—the equivalent of a British wing—of He177's and another complete heavy transport Gruppe of Fw200's, Ju90's, and Ju290's. In final desperation even aircraft from the advanced flying schools in Germany were sent to Russia in a bid to fly in rations, ammunition, and medical supplies and to bring out the wounded.

Paulus should have realized as early as the beginning of December that the airlift, on which he had based his decision to remain in Stalingrad, was a failure. At most the army received 100 tons a day. One cannot fathom how General Schmidt could talk of holding out until Easter.

On 8 January 1943, the Sixth Army received from the Russians a demand for surrender. Paulus refused, and rightly so, for capitulation at that stage would have led to a total collapse of the southern flank of the German armies in the east. The Russians already had about 90 large formations around Stalingrad, and had they been suddenly released by the surrender of the Sixth Army, a catastrophe of the greatest proportions would have overtaken the German forces on the Eastern Front. By the refusal to surrender, the Sixth Army's heroic stand during the final phase of the Stalingrad disaster still made military sense.

On 16 January 1943, the Pitomnik airfield was lost. Six days later the Russian capture of Gumrak landing ground left the Luftwaffe incapable of any real airlift, and supplies could only be dropped in cannisters, which were often lost in the snow. No fewer than 18,000 wounded men were left helpless, without drugs or dressings. The end could not long be delayed. On 2 February 1943 the 91,000 survivors of what must go down in history as the worst ordeal of World War II surrendered. Not only had the Wehrmacht been dealt a devastating blow, but the Luftwaffe's air-training program had been virtually halted. It had lost aircraft and irreplaceable trained men and had only managed to find enough aviation fuel by cutting down on its operational flying. Any hope of ever regaining air superiority, or even parity, was gone.

One cannot gloss over Hitler's decision, which was, in the final analysis, the cause of the senseless sacrifice of 250,000 men of the Sixth Army. The disaster that he caused began with sending too few troops in divergent directions, the one army group toward Stalingrad and the other to the Caucasus. To this was added Hitler's mania for prestige, which obsessed him with the idea of capturing Stalingrad and made him waste his finest troops in a merciless, long-drawn-out house-to-house battle of attrition, instead of exploiting mobility to the best advantage, as was so well understood by German commanders and German soldiers.

For Field Marshal Paulus, as for General von Fritsch, the saying is particularly appropriate: "For good or evil, this man Hitler is Germany's destiny. If he plunges into the abyss, he will drag us all with him."

General Fellgiebel, senior signals officer at Hitler's headquarters, and a close acquaintance of Paulus, told one of his colleagues who had to fly to Stalingrad on 31 December 1942: "In Paulus you will meet an honorable and chivalrous man in the true sense of the word, and in addition a man who is extraordinarily wise, capable and warmhearted. But he has always been more a man of theory than of action."

On 30 January 1943 the 14th Panzer Corps capitulated. One day later 51st Corps surrendered, and on the same day Paulus—

promoted to field marshal during the death throes of his army—made contact with the Soviets. At the capitulation negotiations, which were conducted on the German side by General Schmidt, the Chief of Staff, Field Marshal Paulus let the Russians know that he could surrender only for himself and his staff and not for the rest of his army, with whom he was no longer in touch.

Paulus was driven out of Stalingrad by car, and in his prisoner-of-war camp he was met by four senior Russian officers, Generals Shumilov, K. K. Rokossovsky, N. N. Voronov, and A. M. Vasilevsky. Their first remark was that they were astounded that a man as valuable as Paulus had not been flown out of Stalingrad in good time. In their organization, such a thing would have been impossible. Paulus answered that in the view of German soldiers the commander in chief was expected to share the fate of his troops.

He remained for a long time in Russian captivity, in several different POW camps, and was always correctly treated. In the summer of 1943 generals of the Sixth Army, led by General von Seydlitz, founded the Bund Deutscher Offiziere (The German Officers' League) as part of the National Committee of Free Germany established by German Communist immigrants. Though the Russians tried in every way to persuade him, Paulus hesitated for a long time before deciding to join this Bund, which he did only after the plot against Hitler on 20 July 1944 and after he had heard that old friends such as Field Marshal von Witzleben, General Hoepner, and General Fellgiebel had been sent to the gallows.

He switched to the Russian side not because he had become converted to Communism but because he had gradually become convinced that it would be better for the reconstruction of post-war Germany that she should be linked with Russia rather than with the West. On release from captivity he chose to reside in Dresden, which lies in Communist East Germany. There he lived on the Weissen Hirsch (the White Stag), and after a long, serious illness, he died on 1 February 1951.

Chapter 7

GENERAL HORST VON MELLENTHIN

A Political-Military Soldier and Superior Commander

Horst von Mellenthin, my brother, was born on 31 July 1898 in Hanover. At the time his father was attached to the Cavalry School there. It was taken for granted that Horst, as a descendant of an old Neumark-Pomeranian noble family, would become an army officer. Educated at home until his twelfth year, he was then sent to the King William High School in Breslau, where he spent every free minute in the barracks with his father, who was at the time a battery commander in the 6th Field Regiment stationed in the area.

From his sixth year, Horst took riding lessons from an artillery sergeant major, and whenever possible he accompanied his father on horseback when he was on duty. Even as a tiny boy, Horst von Mellenthin was outspoken, and my mother once told me how, during the christening of my second brother, at which three-year-old Horst was naturally present, surrounded by many kind aunts, uncles, and cousins, he became irritated by the unfamiliar sight of the parson. During a few moments of solemn silence he demanded loudly, "What is that man in black doing here?"

At the age of twelve Horst entered the Cadet School in Potsdam and later went on to the Senior Cadet School at Lichterfelde. He was supposed to enter the army only after having taken his school-leaving examination, but World War I changed his plans. In December 1914 he took the ensign's examination at the Cadet Corps and passed, classed as "good." On 20 January 1915 he was posted to the 6th Field Artillery Regiment in Breslau as an ensign. All gunner regiments in those days were still mounted, of course, since motor-driven gun tractors had not yet been introduced. Horst was only sixteen years five months old, and I can still recall taking farewell of him. I was just ten years old, and when he spotted tears in my eyes before his train was about to pull out for the front, he said to me curtly, in the Prussian manner, "Pull yourself together."

On 18 June 1915, at the age of only sixteen years ten months, Horst was promoted to second lieutenant, and during the war he saw action on the Western Front as section leader and observation-post officer, then as Section Commander, and later as orderly officer, battery captain and regimental adjutant. In 1918 he was sent to the Balkans as artillery intelligence officer to a corps headquarters.

During the war he was twice wounded, once slightly and once seriously. On the first occasion, on 14 July 1914, during the early stages of the fighting at La Bassee and Arras, heavy French artillery fire scored a direct hit on his observation post and for a while he was buried alive, but fortunately he could remain on duty. Later, during the autumn battles in the same sector, he was at the gun position at La Folie Chateau on Vimy Ridge as gun-position officer when intense gunfire from a number of French batteries was put down on the position, killing or wounding about a fifth of the battery personnel, including von Mellenthin, who was hit by seventeen shell fragments and seriously wounded.

In May 1917, at age eighteen, he was decorated with the Iron Cross, First Class for an outstanding achievement on 2 July, 1916 during the Battle of the Somme. The action was recorded in the regimental history:

As 4th Battery could not engage toward the northwest from its gun positions, both guns on the right were pulled out from under cover and came into action in the open, firing over 1st Battery, which lay to their right rear. The 4th Battery equipment suffered so severely under continuous enemy fire that second lieutenant von Mellenthin was left with only two—and eventually only one—gun with which to hold off the attacks on Estrees. Nevertheless, when the enemy again attacked en masse before dark, he brought them to a halt before they could reach Estrees.

The Iron Cross, First Class, was not lightly awarded in those days before the end of 1917, and young von Mellenthin was only the 25th in the whole regiment who had been so decorated since the beginning of the war in August 1914. He was invested with it by his father, who was at that time his regimental commander. Horst greatly admired and respected his regimental commander, whose most cherished principle was to achieve the utmost with the least possible sacrifice of men under his command. On duty a definite aloofness was maintained between father and son, the latter making a point of always addressing his father as "sir."

After being demobilized in 1918, Horst commanded a battery in the frontier defense of Silesia and Posnań, fighting against the Poles. It was at this juncture that the name von Mellenthin first appeared in the Silesian newspapers, which reported the dashing advance of his guns in action to repulse a Polish attack by firing over open sights while under intense enemy machine-gun fire.

On 1 January 1921, it was announced that only one second lieutenant of the 6th Field Regiment would be accepted into the 100,000-man army of the Reichswehr, allowed under the Treaty of Versailles. The one selected was Second Lieutenant von Mellenthin.

It was typical of Horst that he did not immediately accept the appointment. As a former officer of the Royal Prussian forces, he had qualms about serving under a socialist republic after the dissolution of the monarchy. He could no longer consult his father, who had been killed in action in 1918, and he turned to the senior member of the von Mellenthin family for his views and advice. Only after he had been told that he should go ahead did he join the army, and from 1921 to 1923 he was attached to the Cavalry School.

On 1 March 1925 he was promoted to lieutenant, and for four years he was battery captain of the Horse Artillery Battery of the 3d Artillery Regiment at Potsdam. For two years he was at a training school for formation commanders' assistants (later the Kriegsakademie, or Staff College). Then for a year he acted as staff officer for press and internal political affairs in the East Prussian Command.

On 1 April 1932 he was promoted captain, and until 30 September 1934—about six weeks after Hitler's assumption of the presidency was confirmed by an overwhelming majority at the polls—he served as aide-de-camp, or personal staff officer,[1] to the commander

---

[1]In German the post is referred to as adjutant, of which there appears to be no exact equivalent in English in this sense, which covers the duties of a fully competent aide-de-camp.

in chief of the army, at first under General Kurt von Hammerstein-Equord and later under his successor, General von Fritsch.

Mellenthin has noted a number of interesting details about General Baron von Hammerstein. An officer of the 3d Foot Guards, in 1929 he found himself appointed head of the Truppenamt, which was the equivalent of the old General Staff. He was thus virtually second in command of the army, largely through the influence of his friend General Kurt von Schleicher, the right-hand man to the minister of defense and, by coincidence, also from the 3d Foot Guards, which was President Hindenburg's old regiment. In 1930, Hammerstein succeeded Heye as commander in chief of the army at the age of only fifty-two. He quite clearly rejected Hitler's brand of national socialism. His voice was one of very few in high circles that was raised in protest when Generals von Schleicher and von Bredow were among those murdered by the Nazis at the end of June 1934, when Hitler disposed of Ernst Röhm and his cronies. But by that time Hammerstein had already been succeeded by General von Fritsch.

Hammerstein, noted Mellenthin, was usually very sloppily dressed, a most unusual trait for a senior German officer. His youthful aide-de-camp told him politely but firmly that as commander in chief of the army he could not afford to be untidily turned out, and from that time on Hammerstein's lack of smartness was a thing of the past. The general took the adivce in good part.

Mellenthin also felt that Hammerstein, who displayed undeniable originality, did not particularly fancy getting involved in work himself. Out of sheer laziness and indolence he did not even bother to read the reports prepared for him about maneuvers until von Mellenthin insisted that he do so. People who were themselves industrious thought Hammerstein dull. "Shrewd but lazy," ran one remark about him, "specially suitable for the General Staff. Shrewd and hardworking staff officers could become dangerous."

Politically, von Mellenthin's time as an aide-de-camp was highly dramatic, for it covered a crucial period in German history. Early in February 1933, Mellenthin had to make the arrangements for the first meeting between the senior Reichswehr commanders and the new Reichs Chancellor, Adolf Hitler. The meeting took place at Hammerstein's house. The invitations, my brother recalls, had been sent out at the request of General von Blomberg, who as yet had no residence in Berlin since he had only been appointed minister of defense a few days previously, on 30 January. The Reichswehr commanders had arranged themselves in a semicircle to receive Hitler, who was preceded by Hammerstein and accompanied by the state secretary, Hans Lammers and his Sturmabteilung aide-de-camp, Wilhelm Brückner. Hammerstein led the Führer into the room and announced, with a wave of his hand, "Gentlemen—the Reichs Chancellor."

Hitler bowed awkwardly a few times and was obviously ill at ease. Yet when he had an audience, he could not resist speechifying demagogically and at length, which in those days inspired a good number of his listeners.

Captain von Mellenthin himself felt an inner antipathy toward Hitler, which may have been influenced by Hammerstein's own very negative attitude to the new chancellor. My brother's personal impression of this the first of Hitler's encounters with the Reichswehr generals, was that he was taking great pains to win over the army. Yet at the discussion he seemed unable to establish any meaningful contact. He seemed unsure of himself, and his words came hesitantly.

From the start Hammerstein had been very strongly against Hitler, but his dismissal, which followed a year after Hitler took over, was not due solely to his growing and open rejection of the regime. He simply let things slide and betrayed a conscious lack of interest in his job. Lacking the energy and drive for innovation, he had allowed the War Ministry, now under von Blomberg, to gain predominance over the Army Command. The necessary preparations for increasing the size of the army that Hitler had in mind made it apparent that the commander in chief of the army would have to be replaced on professional and objective grounds.

Some of von Mellenthin's activities as aide-de-camp to Hammerstein's successor, Baron von Fritsch, have already been mentioned in the opening chapter of this book. He was delighted, however, when as of 1 October, 1934, only about two months after the passing of Field Marshal von Hindenburg had presented Hitler with the opportunity to consolidate his position, he could once more get out into the open air as commander of a horse-artillery battery in Potsdam. After that he had the good fortune to be appointed to command the Horse Artillery Battery of the 1st Cavalry Division for the next two and a half years, during which time he was briefly posted to the British Army and attached to the 19th Field Brigade at Bordon, near Aldershot. During 1938 he also spent ten days at a cavalry school in England at Weedon, not far from Northampton.

Already an enthusiastic horse-racing man, in his spare time during his Potsdam days he devoted himself to racing and managing a large officers' stable, and for two years he had the most successful stable in the army.

On 1 July 1937, he was appointed head of the Attaché Branch of the General Staff of the Army in Berlin, by transfer to Section 3 of the Army Staff. He held that post for two years in peacetime and several years more in war, during which time the branch was greatly enlarged. In the old Imperial Army of the days before 1918, there had been no particular department for military attachés, who belonged to Section 2 of the General Staff, but after World War I, Germany, who concluded the Treaty of Rapallo with the Soviet Union in 1922 and thus ended the diplomatic isolation of both countries entered into a special agreement with the Russians. Within its framework during the 1920's close cooperation was encouraged in the development of armor. This included a tank training school at Kazan and flying training, especially at the airdrome at Lipetsk. Only in 1933 did Colonel Ernst Koestring— who was to retain the post until the outbreak of war between the two countries—officially become German military attaché in Moscow, and from then on the army interested itself in sending officers to other countries and to foreign armies. Building up the German Wehrmacht made it necessary to adapt the experience of foreign forces for its own use.

In the meantime a number of foreign military attachés had been accredited to Berlin, and, even before the advent of Hitler, President von Hindenburg had ordered the dispatch of German attachés to other countries. In 1935, when the German General Staff again came openly into being, the affairs of all military attachés, including foreigners in Berlin with the Foreign Armies Section, were handled by the newly established Attaché Branch. In 1938 the Quartermaster-General's Section (formerly Foreign Armies) was established, with Foreign Armies East and West Departments and an independent Attaché Branch, which in 1940, became the Attaché Section.

As the head of the Attaché Branch von Mellenthin had the job of dealing with the reports and affairs of German military attachés, as well as working harmoniously with foreign attachés and promoting cordial relations with foreign armies, which included arranging for the exchange of officers.

These activities took him to many foreign countries, such as France, England, Italy, the Balkans, and others, and on such journeys he was given various political-military tasks by the chief of the General Staff. Through his contacts with horse lovers in other countries it was found that, as a well-known German horseman, he was able to foster good relations, as was the case with the French Army. The French riding team had often been invited to take part in gymkhanas in Germany, and the famed Cadre Noir of Saumur appeared in Berlin in January 1939, barely four months after the Munich crisis had brought Europe to the brink of war. A German team rode at Nice in 1938.

In friendly discussions between German and French officers, the general verdict of the French, it appeared to von Mellenthin, was that "we do not want war with Germany. We will go to war only if England forces us into it." In 1939, when Hitler occupied Czechoslovakia—which had become autonomous after the Munich Agreement of the previous year—the British prime minister, Neville Chamberlain, was completely disillusioned. But it was only after the French ambassador in Berlin had informed the German government that France refused to recognize the *fait accompli* that Britain announced a unilateral guarantee to Poland, to whom France was already committed by alliance.

The German foreign minister, Joachim von Ribbentrop, did not believe that Britain would ever join forces with the Poles if Hitler entered Poland, but at the same time von Mellenthin received an official report from Lieutenant Colonel von Bechtoldsheim, the German military attaché in London, that there was no doubt whatever that this time Britain was in earnest. Naturally the report was sent to Hitler at once, but he doubted its accuracy and believed von Ribbentrop, even though the Attaché Branch was excellently informed on the situation and feelings in Great Britain by continuous telegraphed press reports, all of which were passed on to Hitler. On 3 September 1939, two days after the German Army had crossed the Polish border to converge on Warsaw, Germany found herself at war with Great Britain and France.

During the war Colonel von Mellenthin remained chief of the

enlarged Attaché Section of the Army General Staff for three and a half years. The section had to be greatly expanded as cooperation with the liaison staffs of Germany's allies was added to its previous responsibilities. In addition, since contact had to be established and maintained with neutral countries, the courier service in the military attaché field was also enlarged, and information had to be issued to both German and foreign authorities.

Over and above coping with these various and sometimes delicate tasks, the chief of the Attaché Section also had to handle military-political questions personally. For example, before 9 April 1940, when the occupation of Denmark and the landing in Norway began, to forestall the British, who had tightened their blockade of the Norwegian coast to cut off Germany's iron-ore supplies from Scandinavia, von Mellenthin was told by Hitler's military aide-de-camp that he was to arrange a tour at once by all foreign attachés of the West Wall, or Siegfried Line—the German defensive positions against the French. The trip was to last three days, and by the time von Mellenthin and his party returned from this journey, the Northern Campaign had begun. Even as chief of the section, von Mellenthin had not been informed of this major diversionary measure, which took Germany's adversaries by surprise, though the British War Cabinet had been aware of German forces concentrating at Rostock, with their eyes on Scandinavia, since 3 April, and powerful British naval forces were at sea. The little destroyer *Glowworm*, on its way to lay the minefield off Norway, ran into the German warships heading for Narvik. She reported her encounter before heroically ramming the 10,000-ton German cruiser *Hipper* and going down, by which time it was too late for the British to take any effective action.

The campaign in France was nearly over—a new offensive against the French south of the Somme had been opened soon after the evacuation from Dunkirk ended. By 9 June 1940 the German forces were at Rouen and on the Seine, and the previously neutral Italians wished to enter the war on the side of those who at the time looked like the obvious winners. General Roatta, the Italian chief of staff, phoned von Mellenthin to tell him that he wished to inform the German Army Command that the Italians intended attacking the French Alpine strongholds through Savoy. Von Mellenthin in turn received orders from the Army Command to stall the Italian move, which Germany thought unnecessary. The chief of the Attaché Section therefore held back the German reply to the Italian proposition, and when they did actually launch their attack on the night of 10/11 June, with about 32 divisions facing only 5 French divisions, it was a dismal failure. The Italians immediately rang up von Mellenthin and begged him to do all he could to persuade the German Army Command to support them by attacking the French in the rear.

After the capitulation of France, von Mellenthin visited a prisoner-of-war camp for generals near Dresden, to assure himself that they were being correctly treated and also, of course, to find out something about what the French were thinking. The consensus among the French officers—perhaps not unnaturally, so soon after total defeat—was that France had gone unwillingly to war without any political objective, but forced into it by Great Britain. Considering that it was almost a tradition with the French to build up an alliance with the East—Russia, Poland and others—to contain Germany, such sentiments had to be treated with some reserve. The French Army had been administered rather than commanded, and the Maginot spirit—defense at any cost—had led them to defeat.

The French Army had been poorly equipped, and their armor—contrary to Guderian's adage, "Not a drizzle, but a downpour," had been widely dispersed over the whole front. Their generals were unanimously of the opinion that the British had left them in the lurch.

Von Mellenthin invited the Frenchmen to dinner in Dresden, and after a while, on his own responsibility, he arranged for General Renondeau, whom he knew well and who was in poor health, to be sent home. The last French military attaché in Berlin, General Didele, refused a similar offer, preferring to remain with the French troops who had been taken prisoner of war. He was given the task of representing the French prisoners doing agricultural work in East Prussia, with a certain amount of freedom to travel wherever he wished.

In the spring of 1942, von Mellenthin went to the Iberian Peninsula on military-political affairs. Even Gibraltar, as Britain herself was painfully aware, was dominated by Spanish guns, but my brother's journey to Franco's Spain and to Portugal was to gain a clearer view of the situation in North Africa. The publication of the Atlantic Charter by Churchill and Roosevelt on 14 August 1941 had given the German Army High Command plenty to think about, and, as we now know, the British were keeping two divisions in constant readiness to occupy the Atlantic islands or French North Africa if Germany made a move against Vichy France or through Spain. Reports had reached Germany about the road building in the southern part of the Northwest Africa area, and it was also known that the British were putting strong pressure on the Spaniards and on various Moroccan tribes. Morocco had already been discussed as a possible landing place for American troops by Churchill and Roosevelt, and it could certainly tempt them, with Ritchie's Eighth Army still facing Rommel in Libya.

The question to which von Mellenthin wanted answers could not be cleared up from Madrid, and so he was given permission to send a military attaché to Tangiers. During the trip it also became clear to him that Germany could not hope for any active support from Spain. A meeting between Hitler and Franco would bring no dividends. Spain was too dependent on Great Britain and America for her supplies. The ties between Portugal and the two Western Powers seemed even stronger, as von Mellenthin convinced himself on a visit to Lisbon, where the door stood open to the British and Americans.

Full of apprehension even though his activities had yielded not-insignificant results, von Mellenthin flew back to report to the chief of the General Staff in May 1942, at about the time when Rommel was on the point of launching his far-reaching attack against the Gazala Line.

When the British and American forces landed in Morocco and at Oran and Algiers on 8 November 1942—less than a week after Rommel was thrown back from El Alamein—Germany's military and political leaders could not have been taken unawares. Von Mellenthin's exhaustive report on the threatening situation had been made at the end of May, but in fact the Germans could not have done much to stop the Anglo-American operation, since by far the greater part of the German Army was tied down on the Eastern Front.

To illustrate the versatility of his activities, at about the same time as his Iberian visit, von Mellenthin arranged to transfer a former assistant of the military attaché in Tokyo to Bangkok as military attaché there, to get accurate and early information about the Japanese operations in Southeast Asia. This particular individual had close connections with the most important Japanese service departments.

During September 1942—in the promising days when Panzerarmee Afrika still stood before Alamein and the great thrust on the Russian Front was carrying the German armies to the Volga and southward to the Caucasus—an unusual political task was given to von Mellenthin. Hitler intended to give the Rumanian head of state, Marshal Ion Antonescu, command of the two Rumanian armies in the Stalingrad sector, as well as that of the German Sixth Army, as his own army group. The offer was ceremoniously made to Antonescu in Bucharest in August 1942 by the chief of the German military mission, General Hauffe, and it was willingly accepted by Antonescu, who was prepared to go anywhere his soldiers were fighting.

Rumanian political leaders, especially their ambassador, Gheorghe, who had been present at the discussion, felt that any such proposal was too dangerous. Setbacks might occur, and it would be unthinkable for the Rumanian head of state to be considered a defeated military commander. Gheorghe, who was friendly with von Mellenthin, flew to the Army High Command at Vinnitza to express his anxiety to the chief of the Attaché Section. The marshal was more important in Bucharest than in Stalingrad, in Gheorghe's opinion, and von Mellenthin, who wholeheartedly agreed, promised to do everything in his power to have Hitler's suggestion rescinded. He did manage to have the date of Marshal Antonescu's proposed takeover of command delayed, which pleased the marshal, who was not well and would certainly have been in even worse shape if he had to face responsibility for the disaster that ensued at Stalingrad and involved the Rumanians as well as Paulus' German army. Von Mellenthin has written:

> My political duties as Chief of the Attaché Section and as a vital link with the armies of our allies often created great difficulties. My immediate superiors placed great trust in me and gave me a free hand as long as their own operational interests were not disturbed by political matters. But my field also extended to authorities in the Army High Command, where important and interesting reports from German military attachés in neutral countries were often considered.
>
> I created my own link with Hitler's personal staff, who backed me up and saw to it that reports I considered important, and also my own sum-

marized notes, actually reached Hitler. As a result I was constantly in hot water with the Army Command Staff, since Hitler was far more interested and therefore often better informed than his foreign minister, Ribbentrop, or Field Marshal Keitel, who was chief of the Combined Staff of the Armed Forces. This made things difficult, but my conscience dictated that the real supreme commander should be given the unvarnished truth about conditions, the economy, and the equipment of neutral countries, and especially about whatever news came from the United States.

Toward our allies we ought to have adopted a more candid attitude. Often when they wished to know something about our own situation or about our forces, I was unable to produce the information to which they were entitled. After all, our allies had more than 50 divisions fighting and suffering on our Eastern Front, and, since I was the man responsible for liaison and good faith with them, my conscience forced me to be as open and forthcoming as possible. As a result I overstepped my authority on their account, but there was never any unpleasantness or trouble with the German High Command in this regard. Here I was lucky, but honor and decency should be the rule between nations fighting side by side.

To show the reverse of the picture, Mussolini, feeling himself poorly situated, attacked Greece through Albania without telling us anything in advance—an episode that developed into a major disaster. The Italian military attaché, General Marras, came to my house in Berlin only the evening before the attack to inform me about what was going on, so that it could be duly passed on to the Combined Staff of the Armed Forces and the Army High Command. When the Italian adventure led to disaster, it was the Germans who had to pull Mussolini's chestnuts out of the fire in Balkan operations, which were a drain on us for the rest of the war.

After three and a half years of purely military-political service— he had commanded an artillery sector on the Channel coast for two months during the autumn and winter of 1940—my brother was determined to get to the front. After the chief of the army staff, Halder, had already twice refused his request, during the winter of 1942 he put the question to the new chief of army staff, General Zeitzler, pointing out that he was a professional soldier and had not reckoned with fiddling about with military-political matters for the duration of the war. Zeitzler agreed to release him, and in the spring of 1943 my brother was sent on a course for divisional commanders. His place was taken by Colonel Schuchardt, who for some while had been head of the British group of Foreign Armies West in peacetime and more recently on the operations staff of an army group. Many another who spent the whole war cheek by jowl with Hitler could have done likewise. What a blessing it would have been for the frontline troops if the relief of men like Generals Keitel and Jodl, who spent the whole war at Hitler's headquarters, had been put into effect, as was so often suggested.

Some indication of the high regard in which von Mellenthin was held as chief of the Attaché Section can be gleaned from opinions expressed by his seniors, one of whom wrote of him as an "energetic, enthusiastic personality and dedicated soldier, combining a striking talent for command, as proved at the front, with political-military knowledge." Von Mellenthin's work as chief of the section, this summing up stated, undoubtedly contributed to influencing the general military-political situation, and he thoroughly deserved to be granted some precedence on the seniority list.

In 1941 a top-ranking army staff officer expressed complete agreement with this report on von Mellenthin, and volunteered the opinion that he had displayed outstanding organizing ability in his constantly expanding department and that his influence on foreign military attachés had been exemplary. In conclusion, this very senior officer had no hesitation in backing the proposal for von Mellenthin's promotion, "which he would long ago have earned in any ordinary unit."

On 1 May 1943, Colonel von Mellenthin was given the command at the front that he had wanted for so long. He was appointed commander of the 67th Grenadier Regiment—the Von Seekt Regiment—which thus had a gunner in command for the first time in its history. The regiment belonged to the 23d Division, and it may well be imagined how everyone from the divisional commander downward regarded the "outsider" as an absolute novice at commanding troops, after he had been hammering away at military politics for years. But after only two months the divisional commander was sent home, and von Mellenthin temporarily took over command of the division until 10 September 1943, when Major General Gurran appeared, and von Mellenthin reverted to command of his own 67th Regiment and then of the 93d Infantry Division.

The Chief of Staff of the 43d Corps, under whose command the 23d Division fell at the time, has recorded that

in the autumn of 1943, shortly after I became chief of staff of the corps, which was in the middle of the Nevel penetration by the Russians, the 23d Infantry Division arrived to reinforce us. I remember that we had to send the new troops into action as soon as they arrived, and even to detach some of them to other threatened divisions. It made the position of the divisional staff of the 23d Division particularly difficult.

The divisional commander at the time was General Gurran, who had risen from the ranks. He was a splendid commander of men, but not quite up to this sort of situation, so I was reluctantly forced to propose to the corps commander that there should be a change in divisional commanders. Colonel von Mellenthin was just the man, and I can recollect how very satisfied we were with the decision. We did all we could to get the Personnel Section to appoint him commander of the 23d Division, and it always remained a mystery to us why we never succeeded.

Why the appointment was never approved is now clear to me, and the reasons have been confirmed by my brother. Horst von Mellenthin had always held very privileged appointments. Before the war he commanded a horse artillery regiment at Potsdam, and then he became chief of the Attaché Section in Berlin. He was well known everywhere for his pronounced conservative, "Prussian" attitude, and in the prevalent Hitlerite view all this was too much for the Personnel Department, who could hardly appoint him commander of a richly traditional Potsdam division.

Not long afterward, on 25 November 1943, he was given command of the 205th Infantry Division, a fine Württemberg-Baden formation, which brought him simultaneous promotion to major general and of which he remained divisional commander until the end of 1944. His staff officer (operations), Hermann Linn, writes of his divisional commander:

His name is linked with the tough defensive fighting and withdrawal of the 205th Division in the sectors of Army Group North and in Courland. The loyalty he engendered dates from this time. He was certainly not one of your crude, thrustful types, but rather an affable commander. He had a deep sense of responsibility toward the men and material entrusted to him, and it was typical of him to weigh every decision carefully. His attitude was clear in everything he did or said and accounted for the trust and veneration he enjoyed. He leveled criticism with restraint but effectively, wherever he thought it justified, but he was protective toward everyone under his own command in respect of criticism from outside, and he looked after the interests of his own division in his dealings with superiors. He did it all without loud self-assertion or dramatics, but with quiet, objective argument. When all else failed, he had no hesitation in uttering an undramatic but most effective "No."

Under the heading "It is Better to Lead Yourself Than to Surrender Your Own Troops," my brother had this to say in one of his battle reports:

In the middle of January 1944 the Soviets attacked at various points between Kholm and Nevel [this was the so-called Second Baltic Front, where the Soviet 22d Army and 3d Shock Army were operating on the left flank of the Russian forces breaking the siege of Leningrad]. They managed to break through in some areas, but my division, holding the left-hand sector of our corps front, was not so hard hit and repulsed the enemy's attack. The division on our left, belonging to the neighboring corps, had to cope with a deep penetration, and Army ordered them to put in counterattacks, with reinforcements. From my division a whole regiment of three battalions and my fusilier battalion were to be detached for the purpose, and my whole divisional artillery was to support the attack.

I asked the corps commander for permission to take personal command of this substantial portion of my division instead of throwing them into heavy fighting "on loan," but he advised me in a friendly way not to look for trouble unnecessarily. At the next opportunity that offered, however, I put the same request to the general commanding the neighboring corps, since it was *my* men they were dealing with. He thought it over and said that I would be advised—but nothing came of it. Instead I learned that my unit commanders had been called to an order group at a point somewhat west of the Russian salient. I drove there uninvited, so as to be present when orders were issued to my unit commanders.

A frontal counterattack was ordered against the penetration, an operation for which the Soviets would most certainly have been prepared. Such a move would inevitably have resulted in heavy losses on our side, and I was just about to state my opinion on the subject when the divisional commander was suddenly called to the phone and given orders from army that I was to take command of the counterattack in his place.

I wonder what would have happened if I had not been on the spot on my own initiative, at that moment. It was late on a winter's afternoon, and I had little time left in which to issue orders. The screening off of the actual enemy breakthrough was the responsibility of the divisional commander concerned, and my own troops were allotted new assembly areas with substantially shorter approach marches. My final order group before the attack went in was held next morning, 18 January 1944, and I called the operation "Reichsgründung." We did not need to concern ourselves much longer with preparations. The artillery played its part, and then the infantry, reinforced by engineers and assault guns, attacked the Soviets by surprise in their flanks from north and south, along the old battle line.

Part of the old front line was retaken and held against Russian counter-attacks. To all outward appearances the whole operation had been improvised, as was my own command post, which was in part of a ditch. But the flank attacks had actually been precisely thought out, which was evident from our limited losses, which were bearable throughout.

Immediately after the attack, my troops returned to their own, now somewhat shortened, sector.

During the defensive fighting which followed, an unusual change in command took place under circumstances that General von Mellenthin has himself explained:

Shortly after a successful counterattack in the sector of my left-hand neighbor on 18–19 January 1944, my corps commander ordered me, by telephone, to report to Corps Headquarters at once, bringing all my personal belongings with me, since I was to take over another sector. For the time being my division was to be taken over by my staff officer (operations), a colonel. At corps Battle Headquarters the gravity of the situation on the right wing of the Corps was explained to me. The division in action there was unable to hold up the Russians, and in various places the troops were in precipitate retreat. Great confusion reigned.

The division in question had once been under my command at Lake Ladoga, and I was told that they knew me and had confidence in me. In view of this, I was to take command at once, and the previous divisional commander was to be relieved.

I insisted that he be given orders regarding his relief at once through Corps, so that he would not hear of his dismissal for the first time from me. As soon as this had been done I drove to my new division, where I arrived during the night of 21 January 1944, and got the divisional commander to put me in the picture as regards the situation. At divisional headquarters I came across many old friends among the officers, who were glad to see me again, which made things much easier for me. That night I held a meeting of commanding officers and discussed the coming attack, in which the commander of the artillery was particularly important. He seemed surprised to find a gunner as his new divisional commander and quickly agreed with the artillery deployment, which I sketched in detail. We would confuse the enemy about our own intentions by artillery fire from various localities at different times, a stratagem which proved successful.

The history of one of the grenadier regiments of the division records how, at this critical juncture, General von Mellenthin was detached from his own division to take command of theirs. In the days and weeks that followed, very heavy fighting took place.

Von Mellenthin recalls, and he was sent reinforcements including assault guns and a few tanks:

Higher command was fully aware of the importance of repulsing Soviet attacks and supported us to the best of their ability. I spent all my time with the troops and their forward tactical headquarters, and there were frightful crises and even Russian penetrations along our front. One had always to have small reserves ready to seal off any breach immediately. One had to keep something in hand—in other words, you had to decide in advance which positions would next face the most serious threat.

The winter weather alternated from heavy snowfalls to hard frost. Sadly needed sleep had to be carefully arranged, but after three weeks of severe fighting enemy pressure slackened. The sector north of Nevel (from which the Baltic States were directly threatened) was of considerable importance for our entire front, but it had been held. The division and I were commended by our army command and by Model's army group.

On 18 October 1944 the commander of the 205th Division, Lieutenant General von Mellenthin, was awarded the Knight's Cross of the Iron Cross. His hard-fighting division had been twice mentioned in the army communique during the past few weeks, during which time the Russians had been making an all-out thrust for East Prussia and had reached the Baltic coast at Memel, trapping Schörner's forces in the Courland Peninsula of Latvia. Official reports mentioned, among other things, that the "Pilz Division," as the 205th was called, had from 10 to 14 October fought against five Russian guards divisions and a rifle division, and had wiped out 41 enemy tanks. The communique added: "The Commander of these oft-tested troops, Lieutenant General von Mellenthin, embodies all those qualities of military leadership that maintain the morale of his men and encourage them to give of their best, not only in successful offensive but also in heavy defensive fighting."

From 19 October 1944 until 13 November 1944, von Mellenthin was temporarily in command of the 38th Panzer Corps. Of his activities as a corps commander in the Courland battles he has reported as follows under the heading "A Crisis of Conscience":

Before the fifth battle of Courland a corps headquarters was withdrawn and my own corps sector extended to cover four divisions. A hard battle lay ahead of us, and I figured there would be two main axes of attack, with the assaults being delivered at different times. The Soviets actually attacked the left-hand corps sector first, and made quite a deep salient into our front. By bringing up a regiment by train and with the help of a Panzer division, we managed to clear this up, but now a heavy attack on our right wing could be expected.

If I placed the few reserves I still had behind this sector, it would mean that the main battle line would run very unfavorably to us. The whole sector was really too long for us to occupy it effectively for defense, and so I wanted to withdraw my main line back into a more favorable area.

Even as a corps commander, as a result of Hitler's strict orders, one never had a free hand to better the front line without special permission, and so I informed Army Headquarters, who were well disposed toward me, of my intention to pull back. They duly forwarded the request to the top, and after 24 hours it was turned down by the High Command. Even this insignificant withdrawal of the front met with disapproval, and so I stood, not for the first time, divided between the dictates of conscience and obedience.

Obedience—quite apart from severe losses—would have led to an almost irreparable and deep penetration of our front, and so I decided to follow my common sense. I discussed the situation with the divisional and regimental commanders concerned at their tactical headquarters, explaining the situation and mentioning the veto on any pulling back of the line. I also indicated that I would accept full responsibility for acting against the veto.

In our old forward defended localities, only strong fighting outposts with plenty of ammunition were to be left. Everything else was to be withdrawn to prepared positions farther back. The fighting outposts could thin out in face of strong enemy pressure, but, on the other hand, towards the rear but in front of our gun positions a shortened defense line would be manned, especially by infantry with heavy support weapons. Everything was immediately prepared.

When the Russians did attack, those men in the forward defended localities, where the outposts lay, managed to delay the Soviets longer than we anticipated, and the Russians suffered heavy losses in tanks. When our outposts began thinning out to the north in face of ever-increasing enemy pressure, the Russians supposed that the way now lay open for a massive breakthrough, and they launched another attack in force. Completely to their surprise, they ran head on into our well-prepared new defense line about 41 kilometers to the rear. They went straight into our concentrated antitank and artillery fire, in a moment of surprise that was greatly to our advantage. They overestimated our strength, and the impetus of their attack petered out, so that they gained no further ground.

We had had to sacrifice 4 kilometers, in contrast to our neighbors, who lost 15 kilometers in a breakthrough. For quite a long time my corps front was left in peace. The army commander in chief remarked, "I see you've got things back on an even keel."

In the middle of March 1945, General Schörner, now commander in chief of Army Group Center, had von Mellenthin transferred to Upper Silesia to command 11th Corps. It is strange that Schörner, who was the glaring opposite of von Mellenthin in manner and background, apparently had a soft spot for this man of noble birth.

On 16 March 1945, von Mellenthin, promoted to general of artillery, and with the Oak Leaves to his Knight's Cross, reported on 11th Corps operations in Upper Silesia:

From the middle of March I commanded the reinforced 11th Corps, which consisted of four infantry divisions, a rifle division, and three Panzer or Panzer grenadier divisions in Upper Silesia, in the Ratibor-Leobschütz sector, near the Oder River. I had to throw back or hold off superior enemy forces to maintain the continuity of an unbroken front, and at the time two divisions in and near Ratibor were in such serious difficulties that on my own responsibility I gave orders for them to pull back. The army group commander in chief, Schörner, who was known to be particularly strict—and was soon afterward promoted to field marshal—met me at a command post. I gave him my appreciation of the situation and added quite calmly that I intended giving up Ratibor the next morning. It was an important point on the Oder River, one of the last natural barriers before Berlin, and at first Schörner would not believe me. He asked if I was becoming soft, besides which, he said, I should first have consulted him.

I replied that under such circumstances one had to be sensible. Tomorrow I might still have two divisions in the front line, but by the day after tomorrow they would certainly be partly wiped out, with the survivors in the bag.

Schörner asked me if this was my final word, to which I replied in the affirmative and added that I had already given orders for the withdrawal and would not alter them. This old soldier, known for his toughness, seemed to be convinced. Whether he liked it or not I leave to the imagination.

He immediately called up his own chief of staff from my command post and told him that von Mellenthin was now also getting soft but had managed to talk him over. With that he ordered his chief to include in the next day's Army Group "Sitrep" that Ratibor had fallen after hard fighting.

During the final weeks of the war Mellenthin fought as commander of 7th Corps in Silesia, where he did all he could to keep open the refugee escape routes over the high Riesen Mountains and withdrew his troops in small detachments across the mountains. The corps had meanwhile received orders to halt on the crest of the Riesen Mountains at midnight on 8/9 May 1945 and to surrender to the Russians, but von Mellenthin succeeded in getting complete formations in good order into Czechoslovakia, where they were taken prisoner by the Americans.

Since German prisoner-of-war camps had already been handed over to the Russians by the Americans and every officer and ten men had been permitted to retain their weapons, von Mellenthin threatened an American general with an armed breakout by his men if his camp was handed over to the Red Army. The general assured von Mellenthin that he would give him ample warning if such hand-over was planned, but the Americans then had release papers hurriedly flown in for the German prisoners, and 95 per cent of them were quickly released and sent home. A few, including von Mellenthin, were sent to an American camp at Pilsen.

After his release by the Americans, von Mellenthin was invited by General Reinhard Gehlen (who had been head of Foreign Armies East until dismissed on 9 April 1945 and had surrendered to the Americans at Fischhausen on Lake Schliersee) to join the "Gehlen Organization," which was transferred to the West German government in April 1956 and became the Bundesnachrichtendienst, or Federal Intelligence Service, with Gehlen a lieutenant general of the reserve in the Bundeswehr. In his book *The Gehlen Memoirs*, the author mentions that he established within his organization a "special connections" section under General Horst von Mellenthin, to maintain touch with government and industry and that Mellenthin was his deputy by 1951. He continued as such for five years. Among other things von Mellenthin's "special connections" kept in touch with the best and most reliable former General Staff officers to have them available for the future Bundeswehr, to which the Federal Intelligence Service later transferred no fewer than 56 of its coworkers apart from himself.

In 1956, von Mellenthin was at the German Embassy in Washington, where he remained for three and a half years in a capacity in which his diplomatic ability was particularly valuable. His various duties brought him into contact with the Pentagon, and he was personally well known to Allen Dulles, director of the

Central Intelligence Agency. He died while this book was being prepared for publication.

The old Prussians, of whom von Mellenthin was a typical example, are no more. Hardly anyone mentions Prussia these days. But even her enemies cannot deny that Prussian virtues, as von Mellenthin personified in war and peace under the motto "Ich Dien" ("I serve") remain indispensable for future military leadership. He did justice to his military-political duties, as well as to the responsibilities facing him as a military commander. By reason of his personality, his strength of character, and his intellectual integrity he stood the test at all times. He was respected, not only by higher command but especially by the men in the ranks.

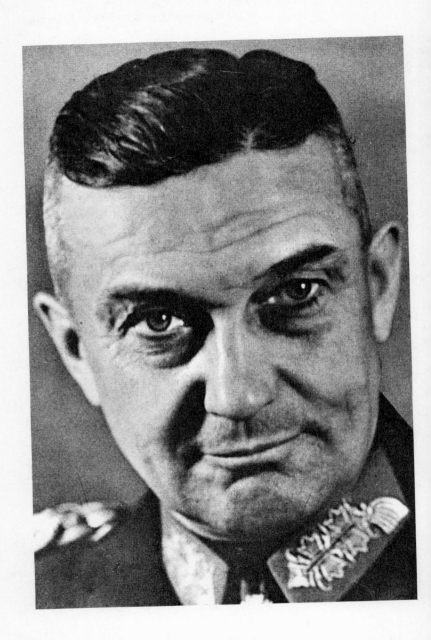

Chapter 8

FIELD MARSHAL WALTER MODEL

Master of Improvization

Field marshal Walter Model was born on 24 January 1891 in Genthin, a little town on the Magdeburg–Berlin road, about 10 kilometers east of the Elbe River. He was a small, one might almost say elegant man, remarkably versatile, and strikingly energetic. Always well dressed, he sported a monocle, which seemed to have become part of him. Not only physically but also mentally extremely active, he was bubbling over with ideas. Even in an apparently hopeless situation, something would always occur to him. When he wished, he could be most charming.

Model sprang from that upper middle class which was the mainstay of the state in the days of Kaiser Wilhelm, and his father was a Royal Prussian director of music. Young Model's military career began when he became an ensign, or cadet officer, in the 52d Infantry Regiment. During World War I he served on the Western Front and was posted for a while to the General Staff. He then fought at Verdun, where he was wounded more than once and distinguished himself to such an extent that he was awarded the Iron Cross, First Class, for bravery.

After the war he served in the 2d Infantry Regiment in the 100,000-man Reichswehr, stationed at Allenstein in East Prussia, and became its commanding officer. Not only was Model considered a hard taskmaster by his juniors but at the same time he was thought of as fractious by his equals in rank. Even among his superiors, including Hitler, he was never backward about expressing his own opinion, and the manner in which he did so earned even the Führer's grudging respect. Regardless of where or under what circumstances Model put in an appearance, he invariably had the effect of a cat among the pigeons, and one could never be sure when he might have a sudden or unexpected outburst of temper.

Since he had no great penchant for technical matters, it came as rather a surprise when in 1930 he was appointed head of the Gruppe für Kriegstechnik, a technical-warfare section of the ministry. Though only a lieutenant colonel with an infantry background, he was already in favor of motorization, and in 1931 he visited the Red Army to study technical matters in connection with armament. In spite of some mistaken decisions, there is no doubt that even at the ministry, where in 1935 he became head of the newly formed Abteilung für technische Fragen, dealing with the development and design of modern technical weapons, his drive contributed to considerable progress, which would probably have demanded notably more time under purely technical supervision. The impression of perpetual forcefulness that Model gave was no mere superficial pose. His restless spirit was always bursting with energy, and on top of that he was utterly convinced of his own ability.

During his service at the ministry Model had the opportunity of making close contact with Nazi party circles, and he made the most of it. Because his energetic and impulsive nature was highly thought of by Hitler—and even more so by Goebbels—he had no difficulty with lesser party bosses, and was accepted by the party.

He was almost ten years younger than most high-ranking German army officers, and his favorable attitude toward the Nazi party found expression in measures that were not entirely comprehensible in military circles. When he became an army commander, and then army group commander, he appointed as his aide-de-camp an officer of the Waffen-SS. The individual involved held the rank of major and was unquestionably a courageous and tactful officer, but in the army this move of Model's was interpreted as kowtowing to the party, and his fellow officers lost some of their confidence in him.

By the end of 1941 any German hopes of a quick victory in Russia had been dashed, and the Red Army's winter counteroffensive was in full swing. Having dispersed his forces by turning toward the south (Kiev), Hitler had sacrificed the possibility of taking Moscow. All four of his senior commanders—Rundstedt, of the Southern Army Group; Bock, of the Central Army Group; Leeb, of the Northern Army Group; and even Brauchitsch, the army commander in chief—departed for one reason or another, and Hitler made himself commander in chief of the army in Brauchitsch's place. Guderian, the armored expert commanding the 2d Panzer Group, was dismissed before the year was out. At a stage when the Ninth Army was almost isolated in a salient stretching north from Vyazma to Rzhev and was being heavily attacked in the depths of a bitter Russian winter, Model was appointed to its command. On arrival at his Tactical Headquarters north of Vyazma, he was faced with a truly desperate situation. The Russians had broken through both to the west and to the east of Vyazma and the front had collapsed, with the Russian 29th and 39th armies thrusting southward.

As one of his staff explained details of the confused situation before the new army commander, General Walther Krüger of 1st Panzer Division, and Colonel Wenck, the divisional chief of operations, someone put the question: "And what, sir, have you brought us to restore the situation?" With a great show of surprise Model glared at his staff through his monocle and then curtly replied, "Myself." A burst of laughter relieved the tension.

The Ninth Army, in imminent danger of encirclement, was in so critical a situation that, on 20 January 1942, Model flew to see Hitler and beg for a Panzer corps to be sent up immediately in support. Hitler agreed but wanted to throw the tanks into battle in the area of Gzhatsk, northeast of Vyazma, while Model intended to use them nearly 100 miles farther north around Rzhev. An acrimonious argument developed between the Führer and Model, leading to an unheard-of occurrence at Hitler's headquarters.

Staring coldly at Hitler through his monocle, Model demanded, "Who commands the Ninth Army, my Führer, you or I?"

Without waiting for any reply, he went straight on to assert that he knew what the situation was at the front and that in the Führer's headquarters they had nothing to go by but maps. Quite surprisingly, Hitler gave way, but he made it clear that Model alone must shoulder responsibility for the outcome of the operation.

When the Panzer Corps did go into action in the sector selected

Approx. Front, April 1942 ----
Maximum German gains ......
Front, March 1943 ———
0   300 MILES

Lake Ladoga
Leningrad
Lake Ilmen
Rzhev ● MOSCOW
Velikie Luki
Vyazma
Smolensk
Briansk
Orel
Kursk   Voronezh
R. Don
Kiev   Kharkov   Stalingrad
R. Donetz   R. Volga
POLAND (1939)
R. Dnieper   Stalino
R. Bug   Rostov
CASPIAN SEA
ROUMANIA   Maikop
Nalchik   Grozny
Sebastopol   Novorossisk   Tuapse   Tiflis   Baku
Batum
BLACK SEA

THE FRONT IN RUSSIA, APRIL 1942-MARCH 1943

From *The War, 1939-19*

by Model, it soon bore out his arguments. The Russians attacked just at that point, and he succeeded in reestablishing the German Front.

In his book *Verloren Siege,* Field Marshal von Manstein says this about Model:

His most outstanding characteristic was his extraordinary drive, which was not without a certain ruthlessness. To this he added great self-assurance in asserting himself and a determination in expressing his opinions. By his own reckoning he was an optimist who would not acknowledge difficulties. He pressed his own views quite frankly even on Hitler. In any event, Model was a brave soldier and, often bluntly demanded the same of those under his command. He was always to be found in the most critical sector of any front he commanded.

In the summer of 1943, after the failure of the German offensive near Kursk in July 1943, the full weight of the Red Army's counter-offensive struck the German Army Group Center, whose commander, Busch, was unable to cope with the perilous situation. Model, now aged fifty-four, replaced him, and it was thanks entirely to his tactical skill and genius at improvization that the Russian attack was brought to a halt. The methods he adopted certainly never pleased his subordinate commanders, for he ruthlessly broke up formations to close gaps as they appeared, and the scattered detachments often returned to their parent units only after long periods of action under strange command and after suffering considerable casualties.

Field Marshal von Rundstedt dubbed the Führer's habitual interference in the chain of command as "Hitler's Corporal's War." But on many occasions Model similarly fought a corporal's war, without limiting himself to "instructions," as was customary in the higher command of the German Army. He even issued direct orders to the smallest of units and would sometimes lead them personally into action.

Model was among the first to denounce the attempt on Hitler's life in July 1944, and on August 17, Hitler bestowed on him Germany's highest decoration for bravery or distinguished service, the Diamond Clasp to the Knight's Cross. On this rare occasion Hitler told Model: "Were it not for you, your heroic efforts, and your wise leadership of brave troops, the Russians might have been in East Prussia today or even before the gates of Berlin. The German people are grateful to you."

That same day Model, the only field marshal to be decorated with this highest of all German awards, was ordered to the Western Front, where he was to relieve Field Marshal von Kluge as commander in chief of Army Group B and to be confronted with an ambitious plan for a major offensive. The plan appealed neither to him nor to his commander in chief, West, the veteran Field Marshal von Rundstedt, when they first had sight of it in October. Two Panzer armies, the Sixth under Sepp Dietrich and the Fifth under Manteuffel, were to drive for Antwerp and Brussels so as to cut off Montgomery's British forces from their supply bases and force a second Dunkirk. Rundstedt retired into the background and left Model and Manteuffel to cope with Hitler.

Model seemed unable to warm to his new task. He was definitely a specialist in the kind of warfare experienced on the Eastern Front; he was a first-class stopgap in a tight spot and a master of improvization, but not a strategist. As von Manstein wrote: "Model never gained his laurels for success in any bold set-piece operation. He had become more and more the man whom Hitler sent to restore the situation on a threatened or tottering front, and in such situations he achieved extraordinary success."

During the whole planning of the Ardennes offensive, which was done under the general direction of Rundstedt, Model—like Rundstedt himself and Manteuffel—was convinced of the impracticability of the "Grand Solution," which on Hitler's orders named Antwerp as the objective. All efforts failed to convert Hitler to acceptance of an attainable "lesser solution," which envisaged a thrust through Aix-la-Chapelle to the Rur River, to cut off the Americans. Hitler stuck to his grand plan and even dictated details, such as the artillery task and its timing and zero hour for the attack.

A corporal's war indeed!

Before the opening of the offensive Model frequently visited his subordinate command staffs and with his usual energy concerned himself with steps already taken or appropriate to the situation. Reports about timing difficulties of designated units or material he brushed aside. He simply expedited matters and gave orders.

D Day for the offensive was 16 December 1944. A few days

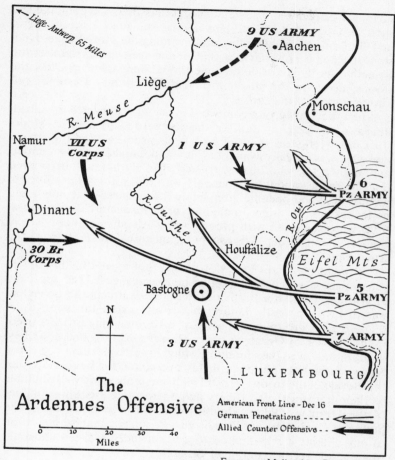

The
Ardennes Offensive

American Front Line - Dec 16 ▬▬▬
German Penetrations ‑ ‑ ‑ ‑ ⬅
Allied Counter Offensive ‑ ‑ ⬅

From von Mellenthin, *Panzer Battles.*

before the attack was due to begin, it became clear that nearly
all the supplies of fuel and ammunition and the reinforcements
promised by the Supreme Command had failed to arrive and could

no longer be counted on. Even to corps and divisional commanders such as General Krüger, commanding the 58th Panzer Corps, and General von Waldenburg, commanding the 116th Panzer Division, it was by now obvious that under such circumstances the objective set by Hitler could never be attained. Nevertheless, the troops, down to the smallest unit, did their best to cope with circumstances as they arose.

When the army group commander visited a Panzer corps headquarters, the chief of staff of the corps tried to present Model with precise figures of what had been promised for the attack and what was actually available. The field marshal lost his temper, and, like Hitler, who by now trusted virtually nobody, he poured out reproaches about commanders who did nothing but raise objections and had become completely defeatist, so that one could no longer rely on them. Immediate protests against these accusations were squashed with precipitate words and injunctions a la Frederick the Great: "If you need anything, take it from the Americans!"

The field marshal's behavior clearly betrayed that his much-vaunted nerve was failing and that he already sensed the approach of disaster. The bitter Battle of the Bulge, as it came to be called, was to prove a costly failure that sorely taxed the strength of Model's army group, but in spite of it commanding officers tried, in the interest of Germany's over-all war effort, to make the best of the situation as they found it, which in retrospect may be cause for astonishment. This is probably accounted for by the fact that the morale of the troops was still high and is also partly attributable to their faith in their officers and to the fine fighting qualities of the German soldier. On the other hand, confidence in the Supreme Command hardly existed any longer, and where it did to any extent, it was limited to certain individuals—Rundstedt, Manteuffel, and a handful of others.

The Rhine River, the last great natural barrier between the Allied forces and the German heartland, was reached by the 3d US Corps on 4 March 1945, General von Zangen, commanding the German Fifteenth Army along a sector about 25 miles west of the little town Remagen, warned Model of the possibility of an Allied breakthrough toward the Ludendorff railway bridge there. The army group commander dismissed the idea in the belief that no one but a fool would attempt crossing such a formidable barrier as the Rhine at so unfavorable a point. In fact, the Allies had barely considered the possibility, but on 7 March New American Pershing tanks and infantry reached the bridge, and under urgent orders from General Courtney H. Hodges of the First US Army, they went over it. Efforts at demolition had failed, and for the first time since the days of Napoleon the great river had been forcibly crossed by an enemy of Germany.

As has already been mentioned, to restore a situation under bad conditions Model often separated units and formations that belonged together. During the preparations for mopping up the American bridgehead at Remagen, Colonel Dingler, commanding the 9th Panzer Division, had some experience of how Model went about it.

For the attack the army had sent forward as reinforcements to the division an infantry regiment just arrived from Norway, superbly trained and equipped. The troops were young men who had not yet seen action.

When Model appeared on the scene shortly before the attack was due to start, he demanded details of preparations that had been made for the operation and strongly disagreed with plans that the regiment as a whole should be placed under command of the 9th Panzer Division. He was beside himself with indignation and gave orders for the regiment's three battalions to be split up, one going to each of the two Panzer divisions, the 9th and the 11th, assigned to the spearhead of the attack on Remagen, and the third to a new infantry division in the process of formation. The cohesion of a most battleworthy regiment was thus destroyed, and its striking power was frittered away. Insufficient forces were committed to the attack on Remagen, and it failed.

This setback occurred two weeks before General Montgomery's planned full-scale crossing of the Rhine farther north, which General Dwight D. Eisenhower—before the Battle of the Bulge threw his timetable off—had intended as the prelude to a drive on Berlin. Model, oblivious to warnings from Field Marshal Albert Kesselring, held to his assumption that the main thrust would come from Montgomery in this sector, and accordingly he moved his own headquarters to the far-eastern edge of the great Ruhr industrial area, where he set himself up in Olpe, a little town about 79 kilometers along the main road from Cologne to Göttingen and Cassel.

On 25 March, Hodge's First US Army attacked from its bridgehead at Remagen. Eisenhower had changed his plans. The thrust on Berlin had become secondary, and cutting off all German forces in the Ruhr now took priority. In thinking that the Schwerpunkt of the Allied offensive would be in the north, Model had fatally misjudged the situation. On 1 April 1945, the Ninth and First US armies joined hands near Paderborn. More than 250,000 men of Model's Army Group B and some 100,000 paratroopers were trapped in the Ruhr pocket. Any man with a wealth of military experience such as Model possessed could hardly have failed to realize that the fate of Germany and her army was sealed, and now the field marshal found himself in a cruel dilemma. Duty and honor as a top-ranking member of the officer corps demanded that he continue a battle whose ultimate outcome could only be defeat.

During the ensuing Battle of the Ruhr Pocket in the middle of April 1945, as the fate of Army Group B became clear, Colonel Dingler was on his way to a new divisional tactical headquarters when he met the field marshal, who was under the impression that Dingler was disengaging instead of advancing. Mistaking the situation, Model immediately began heaping reproaches on Dingler's head and pointed out the direction in which his division should be going. When it was reported to him that American tanks were already in position only a few yards ahead, under cover of a wall, he became thoughtful for a moment. He had hardly expected the Americans here so soon. Then he asked where Dingler actually intended setting up his new headquarters.

The tiny hamlet which Dingler had in mind rejoiced in the name Schieten, and as he blurted it out the colonel mispronounced it just enough to give it in German a meaning as vulgarly excremental as it would be in English. Model gave one of his rare smiles and decided on the spot to join up with Dingler.

Knowing the situation to be totally beyond redemption and that if he fell into Russian hands he would certainly be executed, Model was caught in circumstances that hourly grew less bearable. During these final days in the Ruhr Pocket, I was chief of staff to the Fifth Panzer Army, and I had many almost intimate conversations with the field marshal. He was visibly seeking a solution to his own inner conflict and clearly perceived that we had lost the war.

Yet, against Hitler's orders, he wanted to permit as few demolitions as possible. He discussed the question of capitulation with me, but we both rejected any such idea.

On 15 April 1945, Model issued an order that formations were to break out eastward in small groups and fight their way toward the mountainous country along the Weser River. I had no intention of being "put in the bag" if I could help it, and I headed eastward with a small group of officers. Lying up during the day and moving only at night, we covered more than 250 miles, but any hopes of joining our eastern armies were dashed. On 3 May, four days before the end of the war in Europe, we were captured by American troops at Höxter, on the Weser River, well east of Paderborn.

During the last few days of fighting in the Ruhr, Model himself tried several times to be killed in action in the front line, but by 17 April the Americans had already occupied the pocket for two days and he was still alive. Most of his army group—about 300,000 men all told—marched into captivity, but Model, three officers of his staff, and a few privates broke through an American column near Ratingen, only a few miles east of the Rhine, and took cover in the forest near Duisburg. There, on the morning of 21 April 1945, he told his companions that he wished to end his life, and he selected an oak tree under which to be buried. In vain they tried to dissuade him, but he bade each of them farewell with a handshake.

"I would never have thought that I would ever be so disappointed," he said. "My only aim was to serve Germany."

With that, he walked deeper into the thicket, followed by his intelligence officer. A single pistol shot was heard in the forest near Duisburg. Field Marshal Model was dead.

I served as a staff officer under Model, and I think that, in purely military terms, he was an outstanding soldier. In addition, he was a good and capable staff officer but inclined to rely too much on his own judgment and knowledge without as a rule being responsive to advice. He was a much better tactician than he was a strategist, and defensive positions were more to his taste than wide-ranging offensive operations. He possessed an astounding talent for improvization, and there can be no disputing the originality of his conduct of affairs.

He was extremely frugal in his habits. Hard on himself, he was just as demanding with his troops. Everyone who knew him laid great emphasis on his personal courage.

He was utterly convinced of his own superior knowledge, and in spite of his leanings toward the Nazi party, he never became what one might call a political soldier." There is no record that he ever exerted any influence whatsoever on Germany's internal or external political development. As a result, not one of the 20 July conspirators against Hitler approached Model to take part or even to give them his tacit support. It seems certain that if he had heard of any attempt on Hitler's life he would immediately have reported it. It remains an open question whether Model supported Hitler out of personal allegiance or to further his own ambitions.

Model was an extremely difficult man. In the course of long association with him, one gained the impression that he trusted no one but himself. He wanted to have every single thing under his own control. Lacking confidence in others, he found it difficult to delegate tasks and responsibilities.

In spite of such flaws in his makeup, Model must be considered an extremely strong personality and outstanding character. Following the collapse of Wehrmacht, which to Model was synonymous with the crumbling of all his life's desires, aims, and ideals, one can scarcely imagine any other end for him than the suicide he chose. It was his way of remaining true to himself.

Chapter 9

GENERAL
WALTER KRÜGER

A "Stayer"

Walter Krüger was born on 23 March 1892 at Zeitz, in Saxony. Of medium height and athletic build, he moved slowly and deliberately. He took a long time to make up his mind, but once he had reached a decision, he acted quickly. By nature he was invariably affable and friendly, and his most outstanding characteristic was an unshakable calm. Though certainly interested in politics, Krüger was not sufficiently absorbed in the subject to become involved. He was first and foremost a soldier, with extraordinary personal courage and was always in the thick of any fighting. His staff officers were given very much a free hand, and his gentlemanly manner made it easy and a pleasure to work with him.

He came from the Saxon cavalry, and before World War I was well known in the horse-racing world as a rider. Becoming a soldier in 1910, he was commanding a cavalry regiment by 1937. At the outbreak of World War II he was in command of an infantry regiment, but was soon appointed to command the 1st Lorried Infantry Brigade in Kirchner's 1st Panzer Division, of which he was to become GOC himself. The division formed part of General Höppner's Panzergruppe 4, which advanced rapidly toward Leningrad in the summer of 1941 and later took part in the critical fighting of January and February 1942 in the battle for Rzhev under Model, with Colonel Wenck as Krüger's staff officer (operations.)

General Krüger saw action in the Polish Campaign, as well as on the French, Greek and Russian fronts. Very much the frontline commander, he gained considerable experience in the most diverse theaters of war.

The most striking feature of his personality was his imperturbability. One example that comes to mind occurred in the French Campaign in 1940, in which the 1st Panzer Division began the thrust through Luxembourg and southern Belgium, in the center of General Guderian's 19th Corps. For the second phase a Panzer group was set up under Guderian, and at about midday on 14 June 1940, Guderian visited the 1st Panzer Division battle headquarters at Saint-Dizier and gave orders for the immediate pursuit of the retreating enemy to the day's objective at Langres.

The advance guard would be provided by the 1st Lorried Infantry Regiment, and it was taken for granted that, as regimental commander, Lieutenant Colonel Balck would be in the lead. The competition to accompany him was fierce, since Guderian liked to be at the head of his Panzer group with Balck, and General Kirchner was not the GOC of the 1st Panzer Division for nothing. As if anyone would want to be farther back than the Panzer group commander, Guderian! Colonel Krüger, who, as brigade commander, came next on the list to be in the lead, endured the whole "general inflation" with complete composure. His hour would also come one day, as the armed forces communique of 14 December 1943, was to show when it lauded the action of the 1st Panzer Division under his command in the fighting at Shitomir in the following words:

In the area of the attack northeast of Shitomir our troops mopped up dispersed enemy formations along the west bank of the Teterev. Between the 6th and 13th December 1943, the enemy lost 4,400 prisoners, about 11,000 dead, 927 guns, and 254 tanks. In this fighting the Thuringian 1st Panzer Division under Lieutenant General Krüger particularly distinguished itself.

General Krüger was simultaneously awarded the Oak Leaf clasp to his Knight's Cross.

From the many battles and actions in which Krüger took part, I have selected only one, which has previously been dealt with in only perfunctory fashion in writings about the war, owing to the fact that after the collapse of the German Front in Normandy during August and September 1944, practically all war diaries of higher formations were lost in the retreating flood of German units that had been dispersed. This episode illustrates the importance of calmness to any military commander at such a chaotic time, for it affects the success or failure of his direction of operations.

From mid-March 1944, the 58th Panzer Corps was in the south of France and had under command the 11th Panzer Division in the Bordeaux area, the 2d SS Panzer Division—"Das Reich"—at Toulouse, and the 9th Panzer Division near the mouth of the Rhone, north of Marseilles. At the beginning of August, Krüger's corps with the 9th Panzer Division and the SS Das Reich found itself involved near Caen and again at Avranches. After the collapse of the German Front in Normandy the British 12th Corps and the 15th US Corps closed in from north and south and trapped a mass of German divisions, including the 2d SS Panzer Division, which had gained unfortunate notoriety for a massacre at Odoursur-Glane on 10 June, while hurrying north harried by partisans. In the bottleneck of the Falaise pocket, the 9th Panzer Division was also caught, but Krüger's corps staff got out at the last moment and were able to take all their wireless equipment with them, which was later to prove of inestimable value.

In the pocket Hausser's Seventh and Dietrich's Fifth Panzer armies and the Panzergruppe Eberbach were threatened with annihilation by 16 August. The next day they were pulling out as Field Marshal Model hurried to take over command of operations from Kluge, with whom Hitler had become disenchanted, as he did with commanders who could not provide answers to insoluble problems. Model considered the Seine the nearest line where any sort of continuous front might be reestablished, and by 21 August all escape routes from the Falaise pocket had been closed. About 10,000 German soldiers had been killed, and 50,000 fell into the hands of the Allies.

Meanwhile, the US Seventh Army had landed in the south of France on the Riviera coast. As remnants of the German First Army tried to pull out from the south through Autun and Dijon between General George Patton's drive from Normandy and the Americans and French advances from the Mediterranean, the 11th Panzer Division bumped into the Seventh US Army near Bourg, causing only a slight delay as the German Nineteenth Army retreated headlong from the south toward the Belfort Gap. Unutterable confusion reigned among higher headquarters, which had no idea of the whereabouts of most of their units or even which had managed to evade annihilation or capture.

In the vicinity of Rouen, Krüger's staff, who no longer had any divisions to command, crossed the Seine. A continuous German front no longer existed, and nothing had been prepared for the defense of the north bank of the Seine; the formations that were to have gone into action there were mere remnants flooding back from Normandy and barely deserved the name divisions.

Once over the Seine the corps staff received orders from Model's army group that all Panzer formations retreating between Paris and the sea were to assemble in the area round Beauvais and reorganize rapidly for further action. That it was in any way possible, in the confusion that reigned, to halt a number of German units of various sorts from retreating further, and then to concentrate them was a notable achievement for Krüger, who set about the task with the utmost energy.

However, Waffen-SS units very soon pulled out from corps command by referring to Army High Command orders, under which they were to be sent home at once to refit. Krüger's corps now looked round for other formations, especially those that had been left without instructions from higher authority. A training school for officers at Beauvais—which lay almost on the boundary between the Americans of the Twelfth Army Group under General Omar N. Bradley and the British Twenty-first Army Group under General Montgomery—was absorbed into the corps as a combatant battalion. A strong motorcycle unit was brought under command, and the corps staff actually had some battleworthy units at its disposal again. On 24 August 1944—only three days after the Allies' pincers closed at Falaise and the day before they liberated Paris—Krüger's staff reappeared as the command headquarters of a corps.

Model's Army Group B was falling back in three main columns. The Fifteenth Army's nine fresh but raw reserve divisions from the Pas de Calais lay ahead of Montgomery, the remnants of the Fifth Panzer Army were northwest and north of Paris, trying to hold up the Anglo-American forces for the shattered Seventh Army to reorganize farther north behind the Somme. What was left of the First Army pulled back east of Paris, while from the south of France the Nineteenth Army was withdrawn rapidly before the Allied forces that had landed there on 15 August.

On 26 August, Krüger's corps received orders to move eastward from the Oise and place itself under the command of the First

Army. No reliable information about the enemy was available, and no one knew for certain any details about the situation. Only on 27 August did several reports regarding the enemy reach Krüger's corps, which had meanwhile taken up positions on the northern outskirts of Paris, which was in the hands of the French 2d division and the 4th US division. Then came indications of a concentrated enemy attack in the direction of Soissons. This attack was actually being launched by the 7th US Corps on the right of the 5th US Corps, and General Krüger at once gave orders to fall back several kilometers so as not to be cut off, but the next day the enemy broke through the thinly held corps front. The few days between August 20 and 28 had been sufficient to coordinate communications links between the various units that had been thrown together, and so Krüger's corps headquarters already had a pretty firm grip of the controls.

It was perfectly clear to his headquarters that, should the Allies attack with any degree of forcefulness, they would break through and score successes all along the line with no great difficulty. To make matters worse, the corps received orders on 29 August to recross the Oise and join the Fifth Panzer Army because the First Army would be forced to withdraw to the northeast—which seemed to Krüger's corps a hardly convincing reason for them to pull back over the Oise. But the general remained totally unperturbed by all this ordering from pillar to post.

West of the Oise his corps was to cover the eastern flank of the Fifth Panzer Army, and this army order was the last instruction received by Krüger's corps from any higher authority. From then on the corps staff was left completely without orders. All attempt to reestablish contact by radio with various army staffs failed, and Krüger was out of touch.

His corps had now to fend for itself and try to act within the framework of the situation as they saw it. It was necessary to try to maintain contact with as many units as possible to keep them together and delay the Allies' advance. If the whole business was not to deteriorate into a rout, that could only be achieved by withdrawal, sector by sector, but it was obvious to Krüger that the sectors thus envisaged could only hold out for a day at most, and possibly for only a few hours.

All immobile units—meaning those on foot—were pulled back in forced marches of 50 to 60 kilometers a day. The motorized formations held their positions as long as possible, but it was clear to corps headquarters that all this could only be done for a few days in view of the Allies' superiority.

At Villers-Catterets the staff came across a Luftwaffe station from which they hoped to gather more accurate information regarding enemy movements, and, although American tanks were already pushing into the area, General Krüger calmly sat down to enjoy his pea soup, which he had obtained from a field kitchen. In fact, he had to be asked to hurry up a little.

The corps staff managed to escape the advancing enemy by using byroads, and on the western bank of the Oise they disengaged near Compiègne. It now seemed that the enemy's main thrust would be made toward Rheims, and parts of the 9th Panzer Division (previously under corps command) were forced to deviate to the east. Between the Oise and Rheims there now seemed to be no battleworthy German formations. As far as the corps could determine, its own eastern flank was completely open and uncovered. Unknown to Krüger's corps, the 2d SS Panzer Corps, which had been in action west of the Oise, had crossed to the east bank. All they did know was that the 1st Panzer Corps was still in action west of the river, and Krüger tried to get in touch with them. The more confused the issue, the calmer he became. Fortunately, too, an acute shortage of fuel caused General Hodges to delay the American corps link with the British for three days.

When at last he managed to establish contact with the commander of the 1st SS Corps, Krüger was not shaken to be told that he could not count on support from the SS, since they had been pulled out and were being sent back to Germany, where the Siegfried Line held out vague hopes of a stand. Krüger left the SS general not with the customary, "Heil Hitler!" but simply with, "Well, then, adieu."

Subsequently the staff of the 58th Panzer Corps was informed that enemy tanks had also broken through on the western wing of the 1st SS Panzer Corps. Krüger's corps thus had enemy forces on both flanks, ready to follow up their advantage with determination at the earliest possible moment. Immediate steps were taken by corps headquarters to gather all the units previously under the command of the 1st SS Panzer Corps but not withdrawn with it, as well as any other units still in the area.

Now the question of fuel for the motorized units became urgent.

Fortunately on one of the Oise canals a patrol discovered a barge with enough fuel on board to meet the immediate needs of the vehicles. Another problem was how to carry out the withdrawal. Considerable enemy air activity made it essential to move only under cover of darkness. But with their limitations, night marches were nowhere near enough, and so there was no option but to move by day also, in small units over little known roads. Even so, losses mounted as infantry on foot straggled and were taken prisoner.

Without accurate information about the enemy's intentions, it was difficult to make any decisions about our own withdrawal. Here the Americans helped. They kept transmitting, mainly in clear, so that the corps headquarters could soon deduce in what direction the next heavy attacks were likely to be launched. Even the British were kind enough to transmit easily decipherable messages, from which the corps learned that they were trapped between British and American armies—at that time by the Second British and the First US armies. From the British, Krüger's headquarters also regularly learned the enemy's objectives for the day. It was interesting to discover that Montgomery went about things extremely methodically, risking nothing, a practice that under normal battle conditions might be generally adopted. But in pursuit one should drive forward with a certain ruthlessness, as the Third US Army on the Allies' right did under General Patton. The Americans became the greatest threat to the 58th Panzer Corps, who could never be quite sure just where and when they might appear.

From other information that had meanwhile come in, General Krüger got the impression that Patton was heading more to the east. In fact, Hodges' First US Army was now advancing between Montgomery and Patton. Consequently, Krüger's Corps came to the conclusion that it should keep more to the north so as to remain on the left flank of the American thrust in hopes of escaping through a loophole between the two advancing armies. The British seemed to be moving in a northerly direction, presumably on Brussels, as corps concluded pretty accurately.

General Krüger now decided to abandon the idea of withdrawal by sectors, and to thin out as quickly as possible in smaller units.

Near Amiens on 31 August, General Eberbach, who had taken over command of the Seventh Army, succeeding Hausser, was captured with his tactical headquarters by the Allies, who also got possession of an operation order revealing the German High Command's plan to pull back to and fortify a line on the Somme. Two days later, on 2 September, a radio message was received by General Krüger's headquarters from 2d SS Panzer Corps, revealing that that corps was still fighting in the area around Laon, in the path of the US First Army. Several other fighting-fit units were also there, including the 116th Panzer Division and part of the 9th Panzer Division, which was withdrawing to the northeast.

Krüger's 58th Panzer Corps now had to coordinate its moves with those of the 2d SS Panzer Corps. Though information about the enemy was vague, the situation now appeared not quite as hopeless as before. In fact, three British armored divisions, the Guards, the 11th, and the 7th Armored, were advancing rapidly, with the Guards directed on Brussels, the 11th Armored on Antwerp, and the 7th Armored on Ghent, while the Americans on their right headed in the direction of Valenciennes, Charleroi, and Namur.

Of paramount importance on our side was the establishment of a single controlling headquarters from which both the 58th and the 2d SS Panzer Corps could be directed. Here fortune smiled on them. The corps staff of the 74th Corps was available under General Straube, who was later to oppose the Twelfth US Army along the Rhine south of Wesel, in command of the 86th Corps on the right of the 58th Panzer Corps, then under General Abraham. Straube's headquarters had no more troops under command, but they were still completely ready for action as regards their vital signals organization.

At a meeting of the three corps commanders General Straube as the senior was elected commander of the "Straube Group," now consisting of the 58th Panzer Corps and the remnants of the 2d SS Panzer Corps, with the formations under their command. At a conference orders were jointly drafted for all formations under command, clearly stating their respective destinations. These "tickets to the end of the line" as Guderian called them, were made out to the Brussels-Mons-Charleroi Canal, where the Straube Group was again to deploy for defense. Everything depended on their reaching this objective as quickly as possible. General Bradley, commanding the Twelfth US Army Group, had meanwhile been doubting the British ability to keep up on his left flank and had turned the full weight of Hodges' First US Army's drive onto Mons and Tournai. That accomplished, Hodges was going to swing to the east to close the gap between his First Army and Patton's Third, which was held up in its drive for the Rhine by lack of fuel.

Under command of the 58th Panzer Corps were now the remnants of seven divisions, including a cycle formation and smaller units that had joined the corps in dribs and drabs. None of them was really battleworthy. They had no tanks, and the bulk of their artillery and antitank weapons had been lost. The meager information available about the enemy confirmed that their estimate of the situation more or less coincided with the facts. The axis of the main American thrust seemed to be toward the northeast, while the British were moving northward. Krüger's corps found itself in, and remained in, the narrow gap between the two enemy armies, and this became more apparent with further withdrawal, as enemy air activity over the corps sector grew less, with the result that they could move at greater speed even by day.

It was amusing to note that, as far as British aircraft were concerned, the morning and afternoon tea breaks were strictly observed. For about half an hour in the morning and again in the afternoon the sky was more or less clear. But for the retreating troops a further difficulty now entered into the picture. A civil uprising against the Germans had been proclaimed over the radio and began on 4 September, the day after British Cromwell tanks, driving 50 miles an hour, entered Brussels. In almost every village German troops were now fired on as they passed, and they often had to wage quite a battle to force their way through, with not inconsiderable casualties.

In spite of everything, by 5 September appreciable parts of the corps had managed to reach Belgian soil in the area south of Mons, where they still faced the First US Army. There, on 3 September, an American corps had run into the remnants of three German corps, and before the fighting was over, 25,000 Germans had been taken prisoner and many more had been killed. Owing to unexpected attacks by Allied armor, a large part of the German forces that had got that far was encircled. Only small units that had been immediately following Krüger's corps headquarters remained under command. Corps headquarters itself, having intercepted an enemy radio message, managed to escape eastward toward Charleroi in time and so avoided capture. Well over to the east, meanwhile, Patton's Third US Army had refueled and was driving over the Meuse to cross the Moselle.

On the way from Charleroi to Liège, Krüger's corps received unexpected reinforcements in the form of German troops retreating north of the canal toward the east. Other splinter groups from the south also joined them, including a few tanks. General Krüger once again had a more or less battleworthy force at his disposal.

They were able to reach Liège, where, for the first time in many days, they found a higher command in charge—the staff of the Seventh Army under General Erich Brandenberger. While the American drive was slowed by lack of fuel, Hitler decided to halt the enemy on the Siegfried Line, long neglected but now to be hastily set in order, with veteran Field Marshal Gerd von Rundstedt reinstated as commander in chief, West, to halt the Americans at the Meuse and release Model to concentrate on the affairs of his Army Group B.

If Krüger's corps, on arriving at Liège, imagined that they were at last to be pulled out for rest and refitting, they were sadly disillusioned. They were ordered to leave for Lorraine at once and go into action against the Americans advancing on the Nancy-Metz Line. There Krüger and his staff would soon again bump into the Third US Army under Patton. This unexpected development General Krüger met with his usual imperturbable calm. It was at this stage that General Balck took over command of Army Group G, whose front ran more or less from Luxembourg through Metz and Lunéville to the Swiss border.

As Balck's chief of staff, I drove to the vicinity of Lunéville during the second half of September, 1944. There, on 18 September, the Fifth Panzer Army launched a counterattack against General Patton's 12th US Corps, which was pressing on across the Moselle near Nancy. We used the 47th Panzer Corps (the 15th Panzer Grenadier Division and the 111th and the 112th Panzer brigades) and the 58th Panzer Corps (the 11th Panzer Division, the 21st Panzer Division, and the 113th Panzer Brigade). It was a great pleasure for me to visit the battle headquarters of 58th Panzer Corps and to renew acquaintance with my old friends of many actions in Russia, including General Krüger and his chief of staff, Colonel Dingler. By looking at them, no one would have

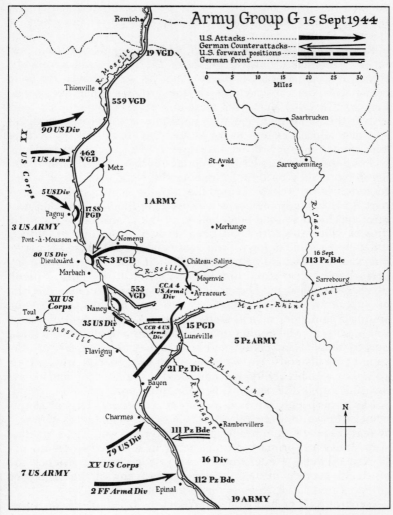

From von Mellenthin: *Panzer Battles.*

guessed that both men had just come through weeks of heavy fighting on the withdrawal. They still showed all the offensive spirit of Panzer commanders.

In mid-December 1944, General Krüger and his staff took part in the Ardennes offensive, but after the withdrawal across the Rhine at Cologne, on 24 March 1945, he was relieved on Field Marshal Model's instructions on the grounds "that he was no longer sufficiently alert"—an incredible reason, since for six years of war this same man had time and time again proved both his alertness and his eagerness for action. On 10 April 1945, Krüger became commander of the 4th (Reserve) Corps in Dresden.

The employment of Krüger's 58th Panzer Corps, from the fighting in Normandy until the retreat to the vicinity of Liège, which took only a few weeks, seemed like months to everyone who took part. In Normandy the corps had been engaged in full-scale warfare, and its losses had been heavy. In the confusion of the withdrawal, when the corps had been thrown on its own resources, it had taken some doing for the commander not to lose his nerve, but Krüger remained calm and collected. His characteristic imperturbability had stood him in good stead in the most difficult of circumstances, and because of it he managed to make the best of apparently hopeless situations. He was no spectacularly inspiring commander such as Guderian, Balck, or Manteuffel, but he was a "stayer," who could sum up formations at a glance and knew how to handle them calmly and in a businesslike manner with the support of his staff. He was one of those generals who, in accordance with his ability, was employed in the right job and always measured up to the demands it made upon him.

I have purposely devoted a chapter to General Krüger simply because he was not one of the conspicuous commanders of World War II. I knew him in peacetime and after the war. Field Marshal von Manstein's primary requirements in a military commander fit Krüger well: "Understanding, knowledge and experience are all decisive prerequisites, but the lack of any of them may be compensated for if necessary by good staff officers."

General Krüger had Colonel Wenck as his staff officer (operations) in the 1st Panzer Division. As commander of the 58th Panzer Corps, Colonel Dingler was his chief of staff. Both these officers outstandingly complemented Krüger as a commander and contributed greatly to his success. What they did not need to provide was the fortitude with which Krüger was so richly endowed. This and his inborn imperturbability earned him the trust of all his troops.

Chapter 10

FIELD MARSHAL FERDINAND SCHÖRNER

A Courageous Commander and Practical Fighting Man

Ferdinand Schörner was born in Munich on 12 June 1892. He was the son of a police officer and originally wanted to take up teaching, for which he studied at the Universities of Munich, Lausanne, and Grenoble after performing his year's military service in the Royal Bavarian Prince's Own Infantry in Munich. In August 1914 he went on active service with that regiment as a lance sergeant (Vicefeldwebel), and by November 1914 he had already been commissioned a second lieutenant in the reserve. He soon attracted the attention of his superiors by displaying great dash and courage. During 1916, when Rumania entered the war against Germany with sparkling initial success before being driven back, it was Schörner's company that blocked crossing places over the southern Carpathians and thus forced a great part of the Rumanian Army, which was flooding back into its own country, to withdraw in haste over trackless mountains.

During the twelfth Battle of the Isonzo on the Italian Front, in 1917, Schörner was awarded the Pour la Mérite, Germany's highest decoration for valor. On his own initiative he had suddenly assaulted and captured Monte Kolovrat, a key point vital to the outcome of the battle. In point of time the bestowal of this distinctive eight-pointed decoration coincided with that of the Pour le Mérite on Field Marshal Rommel.

On the Western Front, at Verdun and at Rheims, Schörner was badly wounded, but his untiring personal efforts and bravery resulted in his appointment as a regular officer and earned him promotion to lieutenant. After the end of the war he saw action in the "Freikorps Epp," one of the volunteer units that fought against the Communists in the Ruhr area and against the Poles in Upper Silesia, that part of Germany along the Oder from the region of Breslau downstream to Rothenburg. He was then absorbed into the 100,000-man army, serving in the 19th Infantry Regiment in Munich.

In 1922, Schörner passed the entrance examination for staff training, and in 1926 he was promoted to captain and became a company commander in a rifle battalion. Because of his sound knowledge of languages, he was then seconded for a while to the Italian Army as an interpreter, but this posting ended when he assumed duty as an instructor in tactics at the military College in Dresden. Hitler had been chancellor for more than a year when Schörner, who had meanwhile been promoted to major, was transferred to the General Staff in Berlin, where his work was mainly concerned with the countries of southern and southeastern Europe.

Fundamentally he was no desk officer, and, having been promoted to lieutenant colonel, he was greatly pleased when on 1 March 1937 he was appointed commanding officer of the 98th Mountain Rifle Regiment. His very robust and loud-mouthed manner went down well with the other ranks, especially since they also felt that they were under an outstanding expert on military matters.

On 27 August 1939, a few days before the beginning of the Polish Campaign, Schörner was promoted to colonel, and in the subsequent fighting he again distinguished himself on several occasions—as, for example, when he attacked Lemberg with elements of the 98th and 99th Mountain Rifle regiments and defended the heights east of the town against very heavy Polish attacks. During the campaign in France he was in command of the 6th Mountain Division and was promoted to Major general. In the Greek Campaign of 1941, Schörner's mountain riflemen broke through the strongly defended Metaxas Line covering Salonika, and, working closely with 2d Panzer Division in the 18th Corps, the 6th Mountain Division drove the New Zealanders through Olympus Pass, occupied Gonnos on 17 April, and pushed the New Zealanders and Australians southward as the main British withdrawal moved through Larissa, while the Yugoslavs sued for peace and the Greek government headed for a crisis. There was a sharp action by the 6th Mountain and 5th Panzer divisions against the New Zealanders at Molos before the British withdrew from Thermopylae. Schörner's troops continued the pursuit to Athens until the British forces finally evacuated the mainland. Schörner earned the Knight's Cross of the Iron Cross, and one of his mountain regiments was attached to the force earmarked for the grimly contested capture of Crete, with the rest of the division at call.

From the warmth of Mediterranean Greece, Schörner and his 6th Mountain Division went to the other extremity, the bitter cold of the Arctic on the Murmansk Front, where despite all efforts Dietl's troops had failed to reach the Murmansk railway, and his Mountain Corps had had to dig in along the Litsa River, which runs into the Arctic. There, with elements of the division still arriving, natural disaster in the form of a gigantic landslide that heralded the onset of a bitter winter completely destroyed the wooden bridge that formed the only link with the forward troops. In the rear, the Arctic Ocean Road on the south formed the vital lifeline along which came all supplies and reinforcements. Immediately Schörner threw all his available men, staff included, into work right through the night to reestablish communication and to carry forward food, fodder, and ammunition, while sappers battled to build a new bridge. It was completed on 8 October 1941, but within twenty-four hours an overwhelming Arctic gale again brought movements to a standstill. Not one of the Greek mules brought north with Schörner's division survived the rigors of the cold, but the Litsa Front held, and at the end of October the 6th Mountain Division moved into the bridgehead and along the Titovka.

There Schörner became commander of the 19th Mountain Corps, which was a constant threat to Russia's northern lifeline, along which British and American arms and supplies were reaching the Red armies after being carried at immense cost in the Arctic convoys.

At the end of April 1942, the Soviet Fourteenth Army under Lieutenant General Frolov, commanding the Karelian Front of Finland launched a major offensive with far superior forces, with the object of annihilating the German Mountain Corps before Murmansk. The Soviet 10th Guards and 14th Rifle Divisions fell upon the Litsa bridgehead in a frontal attack, which broke against the tough 141st and 143rd Rifle regiments for three solid days of bitter fighting. Then on 1 May six Russian ski brigades outflanked the German line on the south to envelop the rear of the 6th Mountain Division, and a reinforced Soviet naval brigade covered by gunfire from torpedo-boats landed in Motovskiy Bay to cut the German supply route.

In the face of a major crisis Schörner displayed a noteworthy steadfastness and tenacity of purpose. He personally led forward rear elements, B Echelon, and supply personnel and men from headquarters staffs to reinforce the tenuous defense of his supply line. He was in the thick of the fighting himself and personally led counterattacks, determined to gain time. In fact, he held out so tenaciously that there was time for units of the 2d Mountain Division, now well back west of Kirkenes, to move up and restore the situation. Just before midnight on 3 May two of their rifle regiments went into action, and a week later the Russian marines withdrew. Farther south Schörner launched a counterattack, which smashed the Soviet attack before nature came dramatically to his aid. The Russian 155th Rifle Division, earmarked to finish off the Germans, had not yet received its winter clothing when the worst of the weather hit, freezing the men to death by the hundreds. The Arctic Front ground to a standstill.

On 1 June 1942, Schörner was promoted to general of mountain troops. He held the Murmansk Front until October 1943 not allowing the Russians to gain ground. Hitler was greatly impressed by the steadiness and toughness of the general, who was a man such as he wanted—ruthless, boorish, and harsh toward his subordinate commanders and all "base wallahs." He insisted on the strictest discipline and was unshakable in any crisis. Schörner was just the man to suit someone of Hitler's disposition, while like Generals von Manstein and von Witzleben, with their refined manners, never appealed to him. He was worlds apart from them.

From now on Hitler sent in Schörner whenever the German line began tottering. Like Field Marshal Model, Schörner became part of Hitler's "fire brigade," and in October 1943, he took over as commander in chief of the Nikopol Army Detachment, (an "Armeegruppe," not a "Heeresgruppe") on the southern sector of the Eastern Front. The Stalingrad disaster of January 1943, was already history; Kleist's forces had had to fall back from the Caucasus; the German divisions averaged little more than half establishment strength, and in the center of the endless Russian Front the Germans had been forced out of Orel early in August. Though slowed down, the Russian advance had continued. By the

RUSSIAN ATTACKS ON FINLAND

ARCTIC OCEAN

Kirkenes

Motov-skiy Bay

Petsamo

Litsa R

Nautsi

Murmansk

Kandalaksha

SWEDEN

Kemijärvi

Salla

FINLAND

WHITE SEA

Kemi

Lulea

GULF OF BOTHNIA

Oulu

Suomussalmi

Murmansk Riy

Kuhmo

RUSSIA

Lieksa

Vaasa

Ilomantsi

Tolvajärvi

Suojärvi

Kollaa

Kitela

Pori

Tampere

Pitkaranta

LAKE LADOGA

Lahti

Viipuri

Turku

Helsinki

GULF OF FINLAND

LENINGRAD

N.D.O.

Map by Colonel Neil D. Orpen.

time Schörner took over in the Nikopol sector, the Red Army had already crossed the Dnieper and threatened to cut off the German forces in the Crimea.

Schörner succeeded in repulsing all Soviet attacks. When the Russians managed to break through the German Front in the neighboring sector in January 1944, his own front became precarious. He never let himself be unduly influenced by the imminent danger of encirclement but attacked with all available forces and succeeded in cutting a 3-kilometer-wide corridor through the Russians and keeping it open long enough to extricate all his divisions from a very threatening situation.

There he had to hold a bridgehead on the east bank of the Dnieper and repulsed all Soviet attacks, but when the enemy succeeded in breaking through an adjoining sector, Schörner's front was also seriously endangered. Again he gave evidence of his iron nerve and willpower. He knew that if he obeyed Hitler's orders, which forbade any withdrawal, then his 22d Corps in the bridgehead would be lost. On his own initiative he ordered a withdrawal and, although he lost all the artillery and heavy weapons, he saved every one of his men. Hardly any other general could have pulled off anything like that against Hitler. Schörner's position vis à vis Hitler had become so strong that he did exactly what he thought the situation demanded.

At the beginning of March 1944, Hitler appointed Schörner chief of the National Socialist Command Staff at Army High Command. The general's reputation as a truly devoted Nazi did not stop him from relinquishing the post after a few weeks, for he had very quickly come into conflict with Reichsleader Martin Bormann, who had become deputy leader under Hitler after Hess's flight to Scotland and wanted to appoint old party associates as National Socialist leadership officers, to ensure that the training of the army would be prescribed by the party. This certainly did not suit the military expert, Schörner.

On 31 March 1944, Schörner became a colonel general and took over Army Group South, whose sector included the whole area of the Crimea, the Carpathians, and Rumania. It was at a time when Hitler's insistence on "no retreat," while continuing German losses made it ever more impossible to hold so long a front, was rapidly diminishing any chance of stemming the Red Army's westward flood. While Marshal Zhukov, in command west of Kiev, was sweeping down through Galicia, Marshal R. Ya. Malinovsky's forces were closing the other side of the pincers from Nikopol and Krivoi Rog.

Great masses of men were on the move, and Nikolayev, at the mouth of the Bug River, had fallen on 28 March after bitter resistance. By the end of the month the Russian spearheads had reached the Pruth near Jassy, in Bessarabia, and far upstream they had taken Cernauti and, still farther west, Kolomyya, within easy reach of the Carpathians and the border of Hungary.

Here, when wide-ranging strategic thinking was demanded, Schörner, with several armies to command, showed himself to be more a tactician than a strategist. His task was certainly not to bother about cleaning up B Echelon or lines of communication or personnel or to spread fear and terror among them; but, following ingrained habit, that is what he did once again.

Konev had failed to take Jassy, but his left wing was wheeling southward down the Dniester River, threatening to get behind Schörner's Sixth Army in the area around Odessa, on which Malinovsky's Russian forces were advancing westward from Nikolayev. On the advice of his staff Schörner asked Hitler for permission to give up Odessa. The Führer refused on political grounds, with his eye on Rumania. But Schörner was not prepared to throw away the lives of his men senselessly. He flew to Hitler's headquarters and again stated the position. Again Hitler refused and ordered Odessa held to the last man.

Against this clear edict from the Führer, Schörner returned to the front and ordered the evacuation of Odessa and the Sixth Army pulled back behind the Dniester. Hitler simply had to put up with it.

On 20 July 1944, Schörner was entrusted with the command of Army Group North, fighting in Courland, where he was no longer in a position to stop the Russians from breaking through the German Front. Finland's surrender had removed the threat to the Russian right wing and left her free to concentrate the forces of two of her "fronts" against Schörner. More than 125 Soviet divisions from the Gulf of Finland down to the vicinity of Minsk were involved in a colossal drive on Riga to split and wipe out Army Group North and to occupy Estonia, with the support of the Red Navy. Schörner was faced with the choice between contesting every inch of ground to the last man and last round in accordance

181

with Hitler's habitual instructions or withdrawing to establish a new line farther back. In spite of Hitler he decided on the latter course. Against the massive Soviet numerical superiority, the Germans had managed to gather 49 infantry and 7 Panzer or mechanized divisions and a handful of motor brigades. On 14 September 1944 the offensive opened.

Constantly visiting the front, Schörner was well aware of the gravity of the situation, which became perilous when the 1st Baltic Front forces drove more than 30 miles in three days on his right, to within 16 miles of Riga and threatened to cut off all his troops in the Baltic States. He pulled his army group back, which meant surrendering the Baltic provinces but saved his own formations from complete annihilation, in spite of bitter fighting. The Russian attacks were held by the newly deployed army group as it withdrew, and Hitler simply had to accept Schörner's measures, for which he was awarded the Diamonds to his Knight's Cross of the Iron Cross. Failing to reach Riga, on 5 October the Russians launched an offensive toward Memel farther south. They reached the coast near there five days later but failed to take the city or to force the surrender of 33 German divisions of Army Group North cut off in Courland.

Before the end of 1944, Foreign Armies East Intelligence reports indicated that no fewer than 225 Russian infantry divisions and 22 armored corps were poised for attack on the Eastern Front, but Hitler, disbelieving, refused to evacuate the army group cut off in Courland or to stop his Ardennes conteroffensive in the West in order to provide troops to bolster the divisions opposing the Red Army. On 12 January 1945, after many weeks spent in building up supplies, and with industrial Upper Silesia as their primary objective, the Russians launched their offensive. Konev, commanding the "First Ukranian Front" in southern Poland, attacked from the Baranov bridgehead over the Vistula. Within three days the Russians, with an over-all numerical superiority of about five to one, were pouring through a gap at Pinczow and over the Nida River, heading for the Oder.

Within a matter of hours massive Russian attacks were launched all along the hundreds of miles of the Eastern Front. Hitler held the unfortunate General Harpe, commander in chief of Army Group Center, responsible for the failure, and he was dismissed. Schörner took over command of Army Group Center at this critical moment, but even he could not perform miracles. Attacked by vastly superior forces, the German armies had no alternative but to retreat.

At his new battle headquarters in Upper Silesia, Schörner received an order from Hitler, that Upper Silesia was to be held regardless of cost. With its steel and coal production it should not be allowed to fall into the hand of the enemy if the German war machine as a whole was to continue running. In fact, Konev's forces crossed the Silesian border on 20 January and were on German soil. Schörner took a very realistic view of the situation. He would hold Upper Silesia just long enough for thousands of German refugees to save themselves from the Russians by crossing the Oder.

Having made his decision, Schörner phoned Hitler to tell him that he was going to evacuate Upper Silesia. In face of the army group commander's determination, Hitler was resigned. He answered wearily that so far Schörner had always managed well and so he agreed. Any other commander in the same situation would certainly have been relieved on the spot. But Schörner was an exception. On 5 April 1945, with the Allies in the West thrusting eastward from the Rhine and the Russinas across the Oder, ready to drive on Berlin, Hitler promoted Schörner to field marshal.

So much for Schörner's methods of command and his relations with Hitler. From July 1944 onward, Lieutenant General von Natzmer was his chief of staff, and he is thus well qualified to give an opinion of Schörner as a military commander:

The legendary Field Marshal Schörner, whose thick-set figure immediately attracted attention, spread fear and alarm by his blustering and stern appearance, no matter where he turned up. With his staff, a single gruffly delivered instruction to his chief was valid for several days, and was frequently all that he thought necessary for commanding an army group, the largest of all German fighting formations. Details in the sphere of command did not interest him. His chief of staff had to cope with any alteration in the situation or of fundamental factors affecting it, and he would accept what was done as long as it accorded with his own ideas. that, as Schörner put it, was what the man was paid for.

The necessary authority for command in such a situation was expressly delegated to the chief of staff, who was promised complete protection as far as Hitler's headquarters was concerned and this was always maintained. On the other hand, the chief of staff was allowed no say whatever in the posting of personnel or the maintenance of discipline within the army group. Taken all in all, it was the ideal situation for any general staff officer, though the load of responsibility often bore heavily on his shoulders, and the mass of work could become almost overwhelming. Such a division of authority was completely unusual and without precedent.

Some foundation for this lay in the fact that Schörner enjoyed Hitler's confidence. He wore the golden party badge and never shrank from ringing up Hitler personally at any time to express his own opinion, his own views, and his own wishes, often in a profusely unbridled outburst of temperament. By contrast, Hitler seemed barely capable of standing up to him. In fact, we have William Shirer's word that in his last will and testament, drawn up shortly before he committed suicide, Hitler named Schörner, whose army group was still holding out in the Bohemian Mountains, the new commander in chief of the army.

In trying to form any estimate of Schörner, one must constantly bear in mind that he went about things in a way that would have been quite impossible for any of his fellow officers of equal rank. He had no need to fear the displeasure of his supreme commander or even sudden dismissal. It is profitable, yet a trifle absurd, to consider in broad outline the manner in which things were run on Schörner's staff, though a special chapter would be needed to give a comprehensive picture of the whole curious method of military command, which was nevertheless completely successful in the end.

Schörner generally left his tactical headquarters shortly after 7:00 A.M. His own quarters were always carefully sited from the point of view of comfort and set well apart from the rest of the staff because of his raucous irritability. Without even telling anyone where he was heading, he would set off either for B Echelon or for the front line. But his destination never remained secret for long. Very soon indignant telephone calls were coming in for the staff from generals in whose sectors Schörner had seized vehicles found without route forms or from sectors where he had demoted captains to second lieutenants for having their collars unbuttoned or stripped NCO's of their stripes. For absolutely trivial reasons he even took away the Ritterkreuz from men entitled to the decoration. Once he appropriated a medical officer's birthday cake and gave it to some troops in the front line. Such telephone calls kept the chief of staff's exchange very busy, and to get some relief the chief had to organize a special "complaints department."

When Schörner returned in the evening and asked the chief of staff if there was anything new, the chief then reported that he had released some vehicles, promoted two second lieutenants to captains, awarded stripes to a few lance corporals, presented one Ritterkreuz, and so on. The response was a roar of laughter from the field marshal, and open satisfaction with the steps taken. Schörner had achieved his aim of manifesting and consolidating his authority and spreading fear and alarm, so that no one within the B Echelon area of the army group could permit even the slightest negligence to be passed over. Some dangerous consequences were thus avoided.

Had anyone pictured a field marshal—a rank seldom granted in earlier times—as the representative of an over-all strategy, holding the cards of command over large military formations in any situation, then he would have learned better from Schörner. He was born under a different star and was a practical commander of men and a tactician, not a strategist. He had firm control over all his troops, including those in the lines of communications. It pleased him when old, humdrum ways, which are almost inevitable in a long war, were automatically abolished in his vicinity. Over and above all that, Schörner had a pronounced flair for meeting the demands facing a military commander and a remarkable ability for recognizing the courses open to the enemy against which countermeasures needed to be taken.

With enemies such as the Russians, who left nothing to be desired as regards brutality and ruthlessness in their methods of fighting, it was perhaps not altogether out pf place to have a brutal commander on the German side, where no one normally dared stray from the path of correct, soldierly conduct. But such a man had to have correspondingly capable general staff officers.

So many false and offensive remarks have been made about Schörner's last days as commander in chief of an army group at the very end of the war and during his time in captivity that I would not like to add any comments. He was released from Russian prisoner-of-war captivity on 28 January 1955, at a time when consideration was being given to the introduction of general conscription in West Germany. Circles opposed to conscription attacked the Wehrmacht in general and Schörner in particular, basing their allegations principally on material published by the official journal of the Nationalkomitees Freies Deutschland (the National Committee of Free Germany) in the East. They would employ any means to stop the rearmament of West Germany.

After his release as a prisoner-of-war, Schörner was charged before a German civil court, which upheld only a few of the charges brought against him. Nevertheless, he was deprived of his right to a pension. It is significant that former members of the 6th Mountain Division which he had commanded got together and through monthly contributions collected a sum of money that just about equaled the pension that would have been his due.

I would summarize the cardinal points of Schörner's personality and character as follows: He was a most uncomplicated character, very straightforward and with few inhibitions. He was energetic, brave, and, as a soldier, a practical commander of good tactical but lesser strategical ability. Command of an army group was really too much for Schörner, and the responsibility it placed on him weighed heavily on his shoulders. His manner of speaking can only be described as coarse, and he was feared by his men but respected in spite of it. He looked after them, and they trusted him.

Chapter 11

GENERAL
HERMANN BALCK

Steadfast and Inflexibly Determined—A Highly Gifted Commander of Armored Forces

By way of introduction to this chapter, I would like to explain why it is the most comprehensive. I was with General Balck from December 1942 until the end of 1944 almost without a break—from the Chir near Stalingrad, when Balck was commanding the 11th Panzer Division and I was chief of staff to the 48th Panzer Corps, under whose command his division operated. We were then together as corps commander and chief of staff of the 48th Panzer Corps, commander in chief and chief of staff of the Fourth Panzer Army, and commander in chief and chief of staff or Army Group G in the West to the end of 1944.

The Balcks come from a very long line and belong to one of the oldest Finnish families, who migrated from Sweden in the year 1120. In 1308 a certain Gregor Balck was the Fourth Bishop of Abo in Finland. There was a General Balck who belonged to a still-existing Swedish branch of the family; he was a fine horseman, a good swimmer and swordsman, an officer in the Swedish Army, and a founder of the Olympic Games.

Hermann Balck's family moved to Germany before the Thirty Years' War and belongs to the Hanoverian branch. His forebears were senior civil servants in Rothenburg and Isenhagen. A great-grandfather emigrated to England and served as one of Queen Victoria's officers, after taking part in the Peninsular Wars as a member of Wellington's staff. Balck's father was a lieutenant general when he was awarded the highest German decoration for valor, the Pour le Mèrite, in recognition of his personal bravery and outstanding leadership.

Hermann Balck was born on 7 December 1893 in Danziglangfuhr. He owed a great deal to his father as regards his military ability and general education. When he was only ten, his father would discuss military matters with him, and took his son with him on excursions on horseback. His father's military career took young Hermann to the most diverse parts of Germany, west of the Rhine, to Berlin and Silesia, to Posnań, and to Thorn. At Eastertime in 1913 Hermann was accepted for service in the Goslar Rifles as a candidate for a commission. He could not have wished to be in a better unit.

Respect for the ordinary man, freedom of speech, strictness and justice in the service, and joy in accomplishment were taught as axioms to the riflemen. In February 1914, Balck was posted to the Hanoverian Military College, where he underwent the toughest schooling of his military life.

On 4 August 1914 the rifle battalion entrained for Liège, and the train pulled out of Goslar station to the accompaniment of cheers. The journey across Germany was like a triumphal procession, in marked contrast to our march off to war at the end of August 1939. Everything on the latter occasion went off without hurrahs. Everyone was ready to face whatever might happen with quiet determination, but there were no enthusiastic crowds to applaud their soldiers on their way.

In the attack on the Belgian fortress of Liège in 1914, Balck commanded a platoon of No. 2 Company. After a few days, though still only an ensign, he became battalion adjutant. During the course of World War I he was wounded seven times, and a measure of his bravery lies in the fact that as early as November 1914 he was awarded the Iron Cross, First Class, the first recipient of the award in his battalion. When he was transferred to the 22d Reserve Rifle Battalion in Russia after recovery from a wound, he had to report to the GOC of the sector, General von Schaeffer, who invited him to dinner. When the general toasted him, as is customary in Germany, Balck naturally rose to his feet. But the general also stood up, with the words, "For a knight of the Iron Cross, First Class, I must certainly also rise."

Balck's battalion fought in various sectors of the Eastern Front during 1915 and 1916, and meanwhile he became commander of the machine-gun company. Here, while under the command of the 5th Cavalry Division, he spent weeks leading a fighting patrol, which carried out successful raids behind the Russian lines in the Rokitno swamps. In the autumn of 1916 his rifle battalion was sent into action in Rumania and Italy, where it belonged to the German Alpine Corps, which succeeded in breaking through the Italian front on the Isonzo and pushing on to the Piave.

Balck wrote of one attack by his battalion on this front:

> The Italian position fell, and on the next ridge there was the same performance, with the enemy again waving white handkerchiefs. Deserters appeared, but a single Italian machine gunner fought on desperately. I leapt at one of my own machine guns, as the rifleman in charge did not seem to be too expert with it. I had fired half a belt from the gun when something hit me in the chest, my hands, and my back. I was lying right in the middle of an Italian burst of fire. So as not to be suspected of telling a rifleman's fairy tale, I quote from the history of the 10th Rifle Battalion: ". . . two flesh wounds on the right hand, one on the left, another on the chest, and one on the left shoulder blade. But all only slight."

The oldest of soldiers could not recall anyone else having had such good fortune, and for the next few days Balck continued to command his company with both arms in a sling.

At the beginning of 1918, after Christmas leave, Balck rejoined his battalion in Lorraine. The German Army in the West was preparing itself for an offensive with the object of smashing the British and French before the Americans came on the scene. Balck describes the preparations of his own battalion for this great effort:

> On 23 April 1918 we went forward from Lille by sections, to relieve the infantry. The enemy were sitting on the Kemmelberg, from which they could rake our positions with machine-gun fire. We simply had to dislodge these troublesome French machine guns. Behind me German trench mortars had taken up position, and I ordered them to put down fire on the enemy machine guns, but the platoon commander refused. He could only open fire at the beginning of the actual attack. Apart from which, he contended, he would draw fire from the French artillery onto himself.
>
> I drew my pistol abruptly: "I'll count to three—then there'll be a shot, either from your mortars or my pistol. One, two . . . !" With a crack one of our mortar bombs landed slap among the French machine guns. All further preparations for the attack went ahead undisturbed.

During this offensive Balck was once again wounded, but his injuries were not excessively serious. When his battalion was pulled out of the front line, he disappeared from the field hospital and made his way back to his company by dog cart.

In mid-October 1918, the Alpine Corps, as well as the riflemen, entrained for the Balkans, where they were to form the backbone for a disciplined and orderly withdrawal. In the meantime however, on 9 November 1918, revolution had broken out in Germany. The Alpine Corps, withdrawing through Hungary and Austria, maintained good discipline, and on 23 November 1918 they crossed the German-Bavarian border at Salzburg. The troops became aware of the altered circumstances only on seeing the red cockades and a sergeant's red collar band with the words "Soldiers' Councilor" embroidered on it. The Goslar Rifles called out, "We don't need any soldiers' council!" at which the Reds disappeared.

On the evening of 25 November the Goslar Rifles' train pulled into Goslar station, and one of the Soldiers' Councilors came on the scene to receive them. The battalion commander, Captain Kirchheim, ignored him and ordered his battalion to detrain, march off, and enter the ancient garrison town with him in their customary soldierly way. The streets were packed with people who greeted their returning riflemen with great enthusiasm. But, somehow, something was different.

The mayor greeted the battalion in front of the Town Hall with a colorless speech. What could he say? Then the battalion moved into badly prepared quarters—no tables, no chairs, no light, everything completely cheerless.

To be sure, there was a Social Democratic government in the Reich, but at the time the workers' and soldiers' councils were largely in control over considerable areas. The rifle battalion had no option but to elect a soldiers' council also, and Balck's company unanimously elected him chairman of its council. A few days later at a full sitting of the workers' and soldiers' councils, he was also elected to their head committee. Still wearing uniform and badges of rank on his shoulder tabs as before, he took part in the government of the city and district of Goslar.

Then once again the old 4th Company had to bid farewell to its company commander when demobilization was ordered. The whole battalion marched to the station with drums beating, and a peasant farmer from Oldenburg got out of the carriage and said to his old company commander, "I thank you, Sir, in the name of all my comrades for everything you have done for our company." The tears ran down the old soldier's cheeks.

Without the old cadre of men, the devil was now on the loose in barracks. On 12 December 1918 the company refused to go on duty. One of the leading agitators fired into nearby houses from the roof of the barracks and then let fly at Balck. He never got any further. The remnants of the old-timers, about twenty men who had served in the field with Balck, hurled themselves on the culprit and gave him a thorough thrashing.

Shortly afterward volunteers were called for by the government to protect Berlin and the eastern frontier, which was threatened by the Poles. Balck's company volunteered for duty on the Eastern Front, but most of the German formations employed there were a haphazardly thrown together rabble whose discipline was less than imperfect. When Heinz Guderian, then a staff officer, visited Balck and his company on a tour of inspection, he told Balck that the situation was everywhere the same. On the whole of the Eastern Front there were only three dependable battalions, the 6th Rifles, the 10th (or Goslar) Rifles, and the 6th Grenadier Regiment.

On 2 August 1919, Balck again returned to Goslar with his riflemen, and the battalion was re-formed as the Hanoverian Reichswehr Rifle Battalion.

In March 1920 there was unrest throughout Germany. The "Kapp Putsch," led by Wolfgang Kapp (a politician of the extreme right and director of agriculture) and General von Lüttwitz, collapsed, but in the Ruhr area the Communists were in control, and the government had to act against them. Balck's rifle battalion was entrusted with the task of covering the approach march of considerable Reichswehr formations against the Ruhr. The battalion attacked and captured the Dülman returned-soldiers' camp, which had been strongly fortified by the Communists. This was accomplished by close cooperation between Balck and the commander of the 3d Company, Captain Guderian, so as to take the camp by surprise.

In January 1922 Balck requested and was granted a transfer to the 18th Cavalry Regiment at Stuttgart. The mobile role and operational tasks of the cavalry had for a long time stimulated Balck's intense interest in that branch of the service, and very soon he took over command of the regiment's machine-gun platoon. He devoted special attention to the supervision and care of his men, who, in a twelve-year period of service, naturally faced a mass of problems. Apart from training in military leadership, during this period he particularly concerned himself with training his men for a future job in civil life.

In the course of these years Balck twice took part in general-staff tours and obtained the appropriate qualifications, but staff work did not particularly appeal to him. He loved regimental life, in constant contact with men and horses.

Once he expressed his outlook on the subject by saying that on the staff one easily became "secondhand," as he called it. A man became smothered in routine office work. I cannot share my highly respected commander in chief's opinion in this regard, though we agreed in most other matters. Did staff officers such as Manstein, Wenck, and Busse—to mention but a few—become "secondhand" men?

In mid-1933, Balck was transferred to the 3d Infantry Division as staff officer, personnel, and in the autumn of 1935 he was appointed to command a newly established cycle battalion in Tilsit, East Prussia, forming part of the 1st Cavalry Brigade. During this period of his service he was given two postings, one of which took him to the Finnish Army, which he considered very good. The other was to the Hungarian Honved, with whom he declined to become a "poodle trainer," as he called it.

After becoming a lieutenant colonel on 1 February 1938, Balck had to give up his cycle battalion, and was transferred to Berlin to the High Command of the Army, in a post in the newly formed Inspectorate of Mobile Troops. His field of work covered care and control not only of the cavalry but also of the lorried infantry regiments and reconnaissance units attached to the cavalry.

While the Inspectorate of Cavalry wished to resuscitate the old cavalry divisions in the form of so-called light divisions, Balck was opposed to the idea, and the Polish Campaign proved his point as regards a lack of efficiency and penetrative power in such formations. They were regrouped after the Polish Campaign as Panzer divisions.

To his sorrow, at the outbreak of war Balck had to remain with the Inspectorate of Mobile Troops in Berlin, and once the Polish Campaign was over, he was sent to various Panzer divisions to speed up their refitting and general improvement. Finally, on 23 October 1939, came his appointment as commander of the 1st Lorried Infantry Regiment at Weimar. He was exceptionally pleased, for this was the very regiment he had helped equip with the most modern weapons and vehicles.

The regiment, which belonged to Major General Kirchner's 1st Panzer Division in Guderian's Panzer Corps, was transferred to the middle Moselle in February 1940. The division's task in the forthcoming French Campaign was to break through the French fortifications at Sedan.

On 10 May the Wehrmacht attacked. Having located a ford across the Samois, during the night of the 13th Balck's regiment reached the Meuse at Floing, to force a crossing over the river. Their position on that day had not been too good, and the French artillery was on the alert. Our own approach routes were choked with traffic, and our artillery had not yet moved up. Furthermore, the sappers had not yet come forward with their bridging train. Balck reported to divisional headquarters that the attack across the Meuse was hardly feasible without first wiping out the French artillery, and he reckoned maximum air support to be necessary. This came at about midday. The Luftwaffe attacked in waves, using about 1,000 aircraft, and the French guns were put completely out of action. They never recovered from this blow.

The complete cessation of enemy fire had a remarkable effect on the morale of the men of the Lorried Infantry Regiment, and though every man had been seeking cover only a few minutes earlier, that was now completely forgotten. Assault boats were carried down to the river bank, and there they were launched within full view of French bunkers only 50 to 60 meters away. The selected assault companies of the 1st Lorried Infantry Regiment crossed the Meuse under cover of a German air attack so overwhelming that they never even noticed that the enemy had not been annihilated.

Once in possession of bridgeheads over the Meuse, the operation of the Lorried Infantry Brigade in the center of Guderian's Panzer Corps went like clockwork. By sunset Balck's regiment had captured the dominating La Marfée heights on the south bank of the Meuse.

During the evening the 1st Panzer Division decided to enlarge the bridgehead at once and to push on to the region of Chémery, which lay more than 9 kilometers south of the Sedan bend of the Meuse. It was a daring decision, for neighboring formations were hanging back, and a full-scale crossing of the Meuse was making only slow progress.

Balck decided, regardless of the exhaustion of his men, to thrust farther into the depths of the French defensive area. After a night march of more than 9 kilometers the 1st Lorried Infantry Regiment occupied Chémery. The morning of May 14 brought the crisis Balck had feared. A French armored brigade, actually two ill-coordinated groups, one of which was not ready, supported by dive-bombing, launched an attack. Only the French 7th Tank Battalion and the 213th Infantry Regiment actually went into battle, but near Chémery they caught 1st Panzer Brigade vehicles refueling. Balck's own regiment, thrown in to reinforce the 1st Panzer Brigade, held its ground. Fifty French tanks were knocked out. Then German Panzers smashed their way into the flank of the 213th Infantry Regiment from Chémery.

The battle for Sedan in May 1940 is of considerable significance in the development of armored warfare. Until that time it was customary to draw a sharp distinction between the employment of infantry and armored formations—there were still lorried infantry regiments (Schützen-Regimenter) on both sides, instead of Panzer-Grenadiers, or motorized brigades, as they became in British armored divisions. In Balck's view the distinction between infantry and armor in such situations was not justified. If the 1st Lorried Infantry Brigade had had tanks under its command and immediately available during the crossing of the Meuse, the attack would have developed with considerably fewer complications. Accordingly, at Balck's suggestion, after Sedan tanks and infantry were combined in mixed battle groups.

Balck's regimental adjutant, Lieutenant Braune-Krickau, reported of the battle at Sedan:

It was 15 May. The regiment had been through the heavy fighting in the Ardennes, the artillery fire from the Maginot Line in front of Sedan, and finally the breakthrough of these supposedly impenetrable lines. As we set out on the morning of 15 May, no one suspected that one of the toughest days of the whole campaign lay before us. Soon the spearhead of the attack struck resistance at the hamlet of La Horgne, 30 kilometers southwest of Sedan. We thought we'd quickly cope with the situation, as on the previous day, but for the first time during the war the companies were pinned down by enemy fire. The village appeared to be a well-prepared fortress.

The regimental commander, Lieutenant Colonel Balck, accustomed to satisfying himself personally about any situation, hurried forward. Suddenly he appeared right at the entrance to the village and in the middle of the front line. Inspired by the presence of their commanding officer, the companies renewed the attack and, in tough fighting, forced their way into the first houses of the village. But again they had to go to earth. There were casualties, and the wounded came back with chilling reports—a crisis had arisen, but everyone kept his head, for the regimental commander was there with the men.

When calm and morale had been restored by the CO's example, he immediately gave orders for continuing the engagement. One battalion was ordered to make a thrust in rear of the enemy, and the main weight of the attack now shifted to that point. Lieutenant Colonel Balck also took up his position with them. It was obvious to him that the other ranks would soon start thinking "Aha, now things are going to get hot, the CO's soon going to be here. . . ." But again fighting came to a halt. A crisis had again arisen, and again it was the CO who worked miracles in the front line by his own example.

After hours of bitter fighting the worn-out battalion found itself facing the enemy-occupied village of Bouvellemont. . . . Most of the officers had been killed or wounded, and the companies had suffered heavy losses. Ammunition was running short. Since early morning the men had had nothing to eat and had been unable to have a drink during the fighting in the scorching heat of a hot day. They were at the end of their tether. On their own they began to dig in. "Just one night's good sleep," they seemed to be thinking," and then we'll get cracking early tomorrow morning."

But the CO had other ideas. He had already recognized that the village in front of them represented the very last part of the enemy position. If it were taken, then tomorrow the whole wide district of Champagne would be before us, and a breakthrough to the sea could begin. But if the village remained in enemy hands, then he would have time to consolidate, to bring up reserves and offer bloody resistance again next day. Final victory was beckoning, the ultimate reward for such heated battle. Should this be denied the regiment?

The regimental commander called up the surviving officers and ordered an attack. Misgivings were openly expressed. "Then I'll take the place myself!" asserted Balck, gripping his knotty stick and setting out straight across the field towards the objective.

The men in the ranks watched wide-eyed. "D'you see the 'old man'? Are you going to let him go on alone?" They shouted out to one another. Then, still dead-tired, half-sleeping men sprang electrified from their slit trenches, and all of a sudden they had caught up with the regimental commander. They charged past him and burst into the enemy's very last position with cheers.

The next morning forward reconnaissance reported the countryside free of the enemy over a large area, and by that evening the regiment was already another 130 kilometers to the west, on the River Oise at Saint Quentin. Everyone in the ranks knew from experience what the inflexible determination and example of a single man could accomplish.

In the history of the 1st Lorried Infantry Regiment, 15 May will always be linked with the name of Lieutenant Colonel Balck. When the radio two days later broadcast the news that the Führer had awarded Lieutenant Colonel Balck the Knight's Cross of the Iron Cross, every man in the regiment was rightly proud of it. Every one of them regarded it as his own Knight's Cross, for it was his own regimental commander who wore it.

The last organized resistance by the French was now broken. On 16 May, General Guderian called on Balck's regiment and visited every company. The personal, human, and soldierly manner of both commanders, Guderian and Balck, worked wonders. In the briefest possible time the troops were once more fully organized and pressing on to the next objective.

When Colonel Nedtwig, commanding the 1st Panzer Brigade, collapsed from exhaustion, Balck took his place in command of the armored regiment. During the next few days the 1st Panzer Regiment took over a bridgehead at Peronne, on the Somme, from which they were to push on to Amiens as soon as another formation from the 10th Panzer Division took over from them. The commander of Balck's relieving regiment expected a regular handing-over ceremony, but since there was not a sign of the enemy for miles, Balck simply refused. He wanted to push on at once, and when Colonel Landgraf protested anew, Balck brusquely concluded the discussion with the remark, "I'm advancing on Amiens. If you lose the bridgehead you must just retake it. I've done it. And what's more, my field kitchens will stay with you for a while!"

By the middle of that morning, after advancing nearly 58 kilometers, the 1st Panzers were on the outskirts of Amiens. Guderian's corps had bumped into the British for the first time, but that night of 20 May tanks of the 2d Panzer Division reached the sea at Noyelles.

On 22 May, after taking Amiens, Balck's regiment was diverted northward toward Calais and Dunkirk. After his battle group had taken a bridge over the canal at Bourbourgville and established a bridgehead there, further advance was stopped on Hitler's orders.

As regards the behavior and fighting ability of the British at Dunkirk, Balck's verdict is of interest:

As soldiers the British are brave men and our equals. After capture they made an excellent impression. Whistling and singing, their prisoner-of-war columns marched off in step, and when our men offered them cigarettes, they refused. A proud nation. It's a pity that Germany and Britain could not come to terms.

During the second phase of the French Campaign, which ended with the destruction of the French Army, Balck and his regiment were in action at all the main focal points of the fighting. Guderian now commanded a Panzer group of two corps facing south across the Aisne on the German left, west of the Maginot Line. The French fought hard, and Balck personally captured the colors of one of the French regiments before resistance collapsed. With the end of the fighting the Lorried Infantry Regiment was left in peace for half a year, which was used for refitting and training.

On 15 December 1940, Lieutenant Colonel Balck was appointed commander of the 3d Panzer Regiment at Moedling, near Vienna, and on 5 March 1941 the regiment was sent off to Greece to help the Italians in their mistaken Albanian and Greek Campaign.

The Metaxas Line, which had been strongly fortified by the Greeks, was to be penetrated by mountain and infantry divisions, while the 2d Panzer Division, to which Balck's 3d Panzer Regiment belonged, was to outflank this position on what were, to say the least, very poor roads. Then they were to drive on Salonika. By 7 April the Metaxas Line had already been broken at several points, and two days later the 2d Panzer Division occupied Salonika.

Balck wrote in his diary: "Is the world crazy? The city is packed with people shouting, 'Heil Hitler! Heil Hitler!' Flower after flower is thrown onto our vehicles. There is not a single hand which is not raised to greet the Germans. Applause. Hurrah! Hurrah!"

The British forces sent to Greece, two infantry divisions and an armored brigade, were much too weak to stave off the defeat of Greece. Rommel's rapid advance on Cyrenaica in March 1941 had wrecked any plans General Archibald Wavell might have had for sending more troops to help the Greeks.

With the Greek forces hard-pressed, the battle group formed on 15 April under command of Balck, who had recently been promoted to colonel, as to launch an enveloping attack on the New Zealanders, who early next morning had to fall back on the Pinios River gorge, the Vale of Tempe.

I have described the course of this hard fight in *Panzer Battles*. A report by the British on enemy methods that fell into German hands commented on the progress of Balck's armored battle group:

The German 3d Panzer Regiment acknowledged no difficulties of "going," and successfully coped with the terrain, which had been considered absolutely impassable for armor. Quite apart from that, one must ascribe Balck's success to the audacity of his decision to dismount his lorried infantry and to employ them without their transport in a sweeping outflanking movement which should really have been entrusted to mountain troops trained for the purpose.

In his battle report Balck mentions that his tanks and tractors were the only vehicles that succeeded in coping with the generally difficult terrain. He drew the conclusion that all wheeled motor vehicles should be eliminated from an armored division and that even supply vehicles should be tracked or half-tracked. Balck realized that in practice it would be impossible to send wounded back or fuel forward to the troops until Larissa had been occupied. It could not be done even if jerry cans of fuel were brought up by boat on the Pinios River and then off-loaded onto oxen and donkeys.

The campaign in Greece now hastened to its end. On 23 April 1941, the capitulation was signed by the Greeks. The British and Greek governments had agreed that the British should hold a bridgehead behind the Thermopylae line to cover evacuation, which proceeded from 24 April to 1 May, by which time 50,732 men, most of the New Zealanders, Australians, and part of the British 1st Armored Brigade, had got away after suffering about 12,000 casualties and losing 8,000 motor vehicles.

After the 3d Panzer Regiment had been moved back to Germany following the Greek Campaign, Balck was appointed to command the 2d Panzer Brigade. However, on 7 July 1941 he was given a new task as a sort of "economy commissioner" ("Sparkomissar") at the office of the director of army equipment in Berlin. His job was to make up for the high losses in tanks and motor vehicles on the Eastern Front. After four months of such activity, at the beginning of November 1941, he succeeded in bringing about a saving of about 100,000 vehicles and their personnel. Then he was appointed general of mobile troops at the Army High Command. The commander in chief of the army, Field Marshal von Brauchitsch, sent Balck off to the Eastern Front at once, especially to the vicinity of Moscow, to form a personal impression of the situation.

First of all, Balck flew to see General Guderian, his former corps commander in France and Germany's greatest authority on tanks. On the same trip he saw for the first time the Russian T34 tank, which was more or less impervious to German antitank weapons. Every commander to whom Balck spoke in the course of his tour considered the state of our forces to be very serious.

It was at this point that Hitler dismissed the commander in chief of the army and took over command of the army himself. On 30 December 1941, at the time the German formations were beginning to disengage before Moscow, Balck had to make his report to Hitler on his recent tour of the front. It took about two hours, during which Hitler said hardly a word. Balck advised Hitler not to withdraw on any account, regardless of the difficult situation. With snow two meters deep and the temperature at 40 to 50 degrees below zero celsuis, it would be impossible to operate, to prepare new positions, or to provide adequate roads for a withdrawal. In addition, Balck gave Hitler his views on tactical experiences of the Russian campaign, on the Russians' new rocket launchers, their assault guns and tanks, their mass employment of infantry—who were barely trained—and on many other matters.

He expressed to Hitler his concern about their own troops' excessive demand for tanks, at which Hitler interrupted him and quoted a figure of tanks supposedly delivered to the forces. Balck cut in with the words, "You are mistaken," and went on, "My own figures are correct."

In spite of Hitler's protests Balck got the impression that in his own way the Führer admitted the facts and would take heed of what he had said. As a result of Balck's report Hitler summoned the minister of armaments and munitions, Albert Speer, to discuss the question of increased tank production. Thus Balck's activities as general of mobile troops bore fruit.

General Halder, chief of the army staff, eventually acquiesced to Balck's repeated requests to be transferred back to the front.

On 16 May 1942 he was appointed GOC of the 11th Panzer Division, which was deployed east of Smolensk to fight Partisans. The division was being thus employed because it consisted of remnants who had survived after suffering heavy losses. The division enjoyed a particularly good reputation in the army and was rapidly refitted and again brought up to full strength under Balck.

The great spring offensive of 1942 at Kursk was approaching, and the 11th Panzer Division's task was to cover the left flank of Army Group South and then thrust on Voronezh, breaking through the Russian positions along the Tim River. At 2:15 A.M. on 28 June 1942—with German hopes high after Rommel's glittering successes in Africa—the offensive began.

General Balck went forward to his regiments at once. When he appeared in the most advanced position, his men—in most unwarlike manner—saluted as in peacetime. Balck clearly had everything well under his thumb once again. In a mere two months of fighting, which Balck directed by attacking as always, his division knocked out 501 Russian tanks and was twice mentioned in the Wehrmacht communique. The commander in chief of the Second Panzer Army spoke very highly of the division.

At the conclusion of this bitter fighting the division was pulled out and transferred to the area of Bryansk for rest and refitting. Balck displayed particular concern for the welfare of his men, even to the extent of bringing in performers from an army theater. One of them sang the men the song "O welche Lust, Soldat zu sein" ("What Fun to Be a Soldier"), at which the audience turned the show into a whistling concert until the vocalist countered with "Das kann doch einen Seeman nicht erschüttern" ("But It Can't Shock A Sailor"), at which Balck broke into a roar of laughter.

On about 20 November the Russians broke through the front northwest of Stalingrad, in the sector held by the Third Rumanian Army. Stalingrad was cut off. On 1 December the 11th Panzer Division was placed on standby. They were to be put in along the Chir River to help establish a new line there. The 48th Panzer Corps, of which I was the chief of staff, was in command of the sector. Balck wrote in his diary: "A completely happy partnership between Mellenthin and me began in those days and lasted for the rest of the war."

On 7 December the Soviet 1st Tank Corps forced a crossing of the Don from the east and thus drove in behind the Chir Front.

We—the 48th Panzer Corps—ordered Balck to attack the Russian armored corps on the move with his 11th Panzer Division. The 336th Infantry Division, which was particularly threatened by the Russians, wanted the 11th Panzer Division to launch a frontal attack on a collective farm (Kolchose) occupied by the Soviets, but Balck never considered such a course. He decided on an out-flanking thrust to take the Russians in the rear with an armored battle group. Frontally he sent in only a Panzer grenadier regiment—as the earlier lorried infantry had become—to hold down the enemy on their existing line. Then, in an outflanking thrust, the selected battle group drove into a long column of Russian motorized infantry approaching from the north. Panic broke out among the enemy troops, who were totally surprised by Balck's unexpected appearance and were completely wiped out. The 11th Panzer Division managed to cut off the Soviet armored corps entirely and knocked out 53 tanks.

The position of 336th Infantry Division was thus cleared up, but during succeeding days appeals for help came from various quarters the Russians had succeeded in penetrating. Balck's 11th Panzer Division now had to play "fire brigade" and were indefatigably on the move, sealing off one penetration after another.

On 18 December, I rang up Balck and told him about yet another deep Russian penetration 20 kilometers farther west. His reply was: "OK, that's fine—first we'll just clean up the break-in here and then get down to the other."

I replied, "Sir, this time it's a bit more than ticklish. The 11th Panzer Division must move at once. Every second counts."

Balck came back: "OK—we'll do it."

With his attack already in progress, he halted it, refueled, issued a meal, and immediately prepared for the 20-kilometer move. On reaching the assembly area, he deployed his 11th Panzer Grenadier Regiment to cover his right flank so that his 15th Panzer Regiment and 110th Panzer Grenadier Regiment could drive into the left flank of the enemy, who had broken through. After the heavy losses of 1941 the Panzer Division establishment had considerably increased the Panzer Grenadier element of the formation to compensate for lack of tanks.

At 5 o'clock on the morning after my call to Balck the Russians again attacked. Their armored and other formations rumbled past Balck's battle headquarters toward the south. Colonel Graf Schim-

203

melmann, commanding the 2d Panzer Regiment, as if on parade, ordered his tanks to wheel in behind the advancing Russians who until that moment had no idea that the tanks behind them were German.

Within a few minutes Schimmelmann's Panzers, 25 in all, had knocked out 42 Russian tanks without a single loss to themselves. Then the Panzer regiment turned about into a depression to get ready to tackle the second wave of the Russian attack.

When the Soviet armor appeared over the crest of a ridge, that engagement was also settled in favor of the Germans within a few minutes. The 25 German Panzers knocked out another 65 Russian tanks without loss, and, thanks to the activities of 11th Panzer Division as a "fire brigade," the situation on the Chir River was to some extent cleared up. The corps of Romanenko's 5th Russian Tank Army had been smashed up one after the other by Balck's division, and on 20 December 1942 the 11th Panzer Division was again mentioned in the Wehrmacht communique.

But they were allowed no rest. They had to get to the area of Tatsinskaya in a hurry on 23 December 1942. The front held by the Italians farther north had been broken by the Russians and for all practical purposes no longer existed. On Hitler's orders the Morosovskaya locale and airfield had to be held at all costs. Only weak "alarm units" that had been thrown together were available there.

Balck's battle-weary division could count on nothing but boldness in their task. Any idea of a defensive solution would have meant their annihilation. On the morning of 24 December, with only 20 Panzers, one battalion, and his divisional artillery, he thrust into the Russian flank and was again successful. What is more, he was now at the rear of the enemy. Over the air he ordered the rest of his division, which had remained farther back, to concentrate on the village of Tatsinskaya, where Russian units far outnumbering his own forces were encircled. The pocket burst only on 28 December, after many crises had been weathered. Only 12 enemy tanks managed to break out. The Soviet 24th Tank Corps was wiped out.

The fighting that followed centered on the occupation of Rostov-on-Don, where the German 1st Panzer Army was to—in fact, *had* to—get through from the Caucasus to avoid being cut off by the Russians. In these engagements the 11th Panzer Division again invariably distinguished itself whenever it was sent into action. Twenty-one years later Balck had the pleasure of receiving from his former army commander, General Hermann Hoth, a letter saying that "had it not been for the 11th Panzer Division we [the 4th and 1st Panzer armies] would never have escaped that trap."

After heavy fighting, greatly hampered by deep snow, Balck had to attack the Russian 5th Shock Army under Lieutenant General M. M. Popov, which had been established on 9 December and then deployed between the Fifty-first Army and the Fifth Tank Army, which had got in behind Stalingrad from the south and north. Balck, using tactics that he greatly favored, wanted to tackle this army from the rear and put some snowplows at the head of his division. After about two hours of difficult going he was actually behind the Russians with part of his division, on the runway that was the enemy's supply line. The Russians were taken completely by surprise.

From that point Balck thrust southward, deeper into the rear of the main Russian forces, but since he wanted to get forward himself as quickly as possible, he wished to have the commander of his Panzer Regiment actually with him in his Kübelwagen (the wartime military version of the Volkswagen). He sent out orders accordingly, but the Panzer commander's orderly officer returned with the reply: "The Count [Graf Schimmelmann] reckons that there is still some lively fighting going on in the village ahead of us. He thinks it would be better if General Balck transferred from the Kübelwagen into his tank."

This was, in fact, a more suitable arrangement, but Balck's answer to the proposal was, "Oh, no! From a tank you can't see anything!"

The general again ordered Graf Schimmelmann to report to him, but the Panzer commander's orderly officer told Balck, "The Count states that if the general has not the courtesy to travel in his tank, he won't go with him."

Balck had a good laugh and climbed into Schimmelmann's tank. The thrust into the rear of the enemy by 11th Panzer Division spelled the end of Popov's army.

Balck, who was promoted to lieutenant general on 1 January 1943, was awarded the Swords to his Knight's Cross for this achievement. Then the 11th Panzer Division was ordered to the Kharkov area, where Balck received the news that he had been transferred to the commanding officers' reserve. He was already on the way home when he was hauled out of the train to take over the elite Gross Deutschland Division for a while. He commanded it until May 1943, and after a leave, had to deputize for the corps commander of 14 Panzer Corps for four weeks. The corps was near Naples, Italy (in September 1943), and Balck took over from Lieutenant General Hans-Valentin Hube on 2 September, less than a fortnight before the Allies faced their greatest crisis in the Salerno bridgehead. The British and Americans had managed to weather the storm, but on 18 September Balck's corps, facing the British troops, with 76th Panzer Corps on his left facing the Americans, was ordered by von Vietinghoff to prevent any Allied attempt to advance north or northwest. In the face of overwhelming Allied air superiority and fierce attacks on 26 September the Tenth Army issued a directive for a fighting retreat into the Bernhardt Line. With part of the Italian population involved in bloody rioting, at the end of the month Balck realized that he could keep no troops south of Naples after the end of the month. Von Vietinghoff agreed, and the British entered Naples on 1 October as part of the Fifth US Army under General Mark Clark. Balck, wanting to visit his frontline troops in a hurry, took off in a Storch, which turned a somersault and left him seriously injured, with almost every rib broken.

Having recovered from this mishap, on 12 November 1943 he was appointed to command 40th Panzer Corps, which was holding a bridgehead at Nikopol on the lower Dnieper. He was back in Russia again, almost three months after the launching of the Red Army's major offensive to retake the eastern Ukraine and cross the Dnieper, which by the time Balck arrived they had already done at several points north of Nikopol and on both sides of Kiev. Kiev was the key point in the German defenses along the right bank of the great river. The Red Army's striking force on the 1st Ukrainian Front had launched their main offensive to take Kiev on 3 November, and with overwhelming local superiority they had entered the city on 6 November.

Immediately on his arrival Balck reported to the commander chief, Army Group South, Field Marshal von Manstein, who told him: "You are to take over 48th Panzer Corps at once. It is fighting at Kiev, and that's where the decision will be. That's

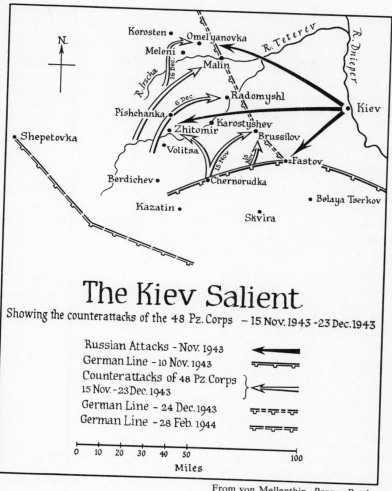

The Kiev Salient

Showing the counterattacks of the 48 Pz. Corps — 15 Nov. 1943 -23 Dec. 1943

Russian Attacks - Nov. 1943

German Line - 10 Nov. 1943

Counterattacks of 48 Pz. Corps
15 Nov. - 23 Dec. 1943

German Line - 24 Dec. 1943

German Line - 28 Feb. 1944

0   10   20   30   40   50   100

Miles

From von Mellenthin, *Panzer Battles.*

where I need the best commander of armor. Hitler agrees that you should take command of 48th Panzer Corps."

In Balck's diary there is an entry:

The chief of staff of 48th Panzer Corps was Colonel von Mellenthin, whom I had known from the Chir River days. An extraordinarily happy partnership began with this outstanding staff officer. On the Chir we had already got to understand one another quickly and with few words. Now a brief discussion every morning—often simply a short indication of something on the map—was enough to put the two of us in tune for the whole day.

During years of working together not the slightest ill-feeling ever arose between us, and we also agreed that one should get things done with as little staff work as possible. We never loaded units with unnecessary bits of paper. Whatever could be disposed of verbally—and that meant most things, including operation orders—was done verbally.

We often changed places on visits to the front line, as a staff officer can also only work properly when he maintains the closest contact with the men on the spot and knows the terrain himself.

The task given to Balck for his 48th Panzer Corps was to take the locality of Shitomir and then attack Kiev. He concentrated his corps tightly together, and at the focal point of his operation he attacked with the 1st Panzer Division and the SS Leibstandarte Adolf Hitler, both first-rate fighting divisions. The attack drove into the flank of the Russian forces advancing westward, and three days later Shitomir fell, on 19 November 1943. Among others under the command of Balck's corps was the 25th Panzer Division under General von Schell.

This division had been formed in Norway, but both the commander and his troops were unaccustomed to battle, not yet fully trained, and, what was more, had had no experience in Russia. They were thrown in precipitately by higher authority, frittered away in the battle, and smashed up. All their equipment sacrificed, the men lost faith and their self-confidence.

Balck's judgment on this effort runs more or less as follows:

It is absurd to throw into battle in particularly critical circumstances a newly formed division whose members—including their commander— have no battle experience and have not completed their training. It would have been better to have brought two or three battle-tested divisions up to strength with the available officers, other ranks and all the equipment and vehicles.

Meanwhile, the enemy had welded together a strong battle group of two tank corps and a cavalry corps at Brussilov. So far all Russian attacks had been repulsed, but Balck correctly concluded that, before any further attack on Kiev could be made, this Russian battle group would have to be destroyed.

Three more Panzer divisions were brought up to Balck's corps for the Kiev task, and he then decided on a double enveloping attack. On 20 November the German Panzer divisions began their moves, and progress was good on both wings. But in the center the Leibstandarte's attack did not break through. One difference of opinion now followed another. The 19th and 1st Panzer divisions, which had been sent in on the left and right, never exploited their initial successes, and they were brought to a halt.

The controlling Fourth Panzer Army wanted to scrap the attack completely, but Balck would not consider it. At his own energetic intervention the 1st and 19th Panzer divisions thrust farther forward one pitch-dark night and closed the ring around the Russians shortly before midnight. The enemy had cleverly pulled out the unit command staffs and specialists in time, but nevertheless our booty was not bad: 153 tanks, more than 70 guns, and 250 antitank guns. In addition we counted some 3,000 enemy dead and took many prisoners. But the fighting had provided time for the Russians to establish a new front between us and Kiev.

Bad weather now aggravated the difficulties, and when a vile thaw set in, wheeled vehicles especially got bogged down. Balck himself, trying to get forward to the 1st Panzer Division, got stuck in the mud time and again. Because of the weather he had no alternative but to call off any determined attack on Kiev. Losses would be too severe.

On 27 November I wanted to reconnoiter the position myself once again, and at 5:00 in the morning I set off. At 10:00 that night I got in touch with Balck on the radio to tell him that I was completely stuck. It was impossible to shift the vehicle an inch, and I had to make my way to the nearest village on foot.

Throughout December the 48th Panzer Corps was involved in very heavy fighting, about which I have written in detail in *Panzer Battles*. Here I would like to relate just one incident concerning Balck personally.

On 22 December 1943 he was with the heavily engaged 1st Panzer Division and subsequently reported:

As I was about to drive off, someone called out to me, "Russian tanks 100 meters from the village. Our infantry moving out!" At the entrance to the village I had to turn around, for Russian tanks popped up just in front of me. I wanted to turn back. Everywhere infantry were pulling back, and the area was packed with horse-drawn vehicles and motor lorries, with Russian tanks firing into them all without a pause. But they were firing on the move while going flat out and hit nothing—especially as visibility from a T34 is miserable. All of a sudden I was in the midst of a Russian tank attack. To my front, to left and right, and behind me were Russian tanks. "Go with them!" I shouted to my driver.

It must certainly have been the only occasion on which a German corps commander in a Kübelwagen flying his GOC's pennant actually joined in a Russian tank attack. I couldn't shake off the feeling that I'd never get out of the mess.

A railway embankment ran on our right, and at some distance you could see a culvert. "Flat out for the subway!" I yelled. We slid past the Russian tanks and with a spurt our Kübelwagen was through the subway. On the other side was a second lieutenant with five tanks from 1st Panzer Regiment, sitting quite peacefully and suspecting nothing. I sent him off at once behind the Russians, and a little later on one T34 after another was in flames. The subaltern beamed, and I attributed the smile to his success in knocking out the tanks—but I was miles out.

"It's just great that we of 1st Panzer Regiment had to get the general out of a fix!" he grinned.

"So? Why?"

"Well sir, you've ticked us off so often—and now this!"

On 23 December, in view of the general situation, the Panzer Corps had no option but to go over to the defensive. The German 14th Panzer Corps had been wiped out by the Russians, and the 19th Panzer Division, under Balck, never reached its objective. The enemy had forced their way between it and the 1st Panzer Division, from whom we received a last signal: "Thirty enemy tanks ahead. Am being attacked by strong armored units. No fuel. Help."

Then the radio went silent. For hours we heard nothing about the division.

Meanwhile, elements of the Leibstandarte had reached us, after toiling wearily through the completely blocked Shitomir. Should we send them into action again immediately, throwing them in toward the 19th Panzer Division?

No decision ever weighed so heavily on Balck and myself.

Should we wait and then put in the Leibstandarte only when it was fully concentrated?

Balck was sitting gloomily in a house when I went to him about an hour and a half later with a radio message from 19th Panzer Division: "Am withdrawing westward in fairly good order."

On 27 December contact with the division was finally restored. Their divisional commander, Major General Källner, had led his division back brilliantly, shot up many enemy tanks, and brought out practically all his equipment. A new front could be established as a result, with our weak divisions covering a sector of up to 40 kilometers.

Finally we were able to go over to the offensive again along the whole of our corps front, concentrating strong Panzer units and turning the flank of the Russian assembly position parallel to our corps front line.

When things subsequently quieted down somewhat, Balck immediately concerned himself about adequate recreation for his own units. He invited hundreds of frontline soldiers to friendly evening gatherings, film shows were arranged, and bathing and laundry facilities were laid on for the troops, together with new uniforms and much else.

In general, the situation on the Eastern Front did not look too bad at the beginning of 1944. But there was a great, gaping breach between Army Group Center and Army Group South. The staff of 48th Panzer Corps was pulled out and given the job of closing this gap with newly brought up troops. But on the evening of 2 March 1944, after we had already got involved in our task, Balck received orders from the army under whose command we fell to pull out 48th Panzer Corps Staff and 7th Panzer Division immediately and move to the vicinity of Tarnopol. It was all very irritating.

When we reached the Tarnapol area, we ran into a really desperate situation. The Russians were attacking again, and with no contact to right or left the Leibstandarte and the 7th Panzer Division were alone in the area. In Tarnopol itself there were only some standby units and three armored trains. Both divisions were being bloodily attacked but held their ground, and in 30 hours they knocked out 100 Russian tanks. But of what significance was that in the surging flood that was rolling toward us? On Hit-

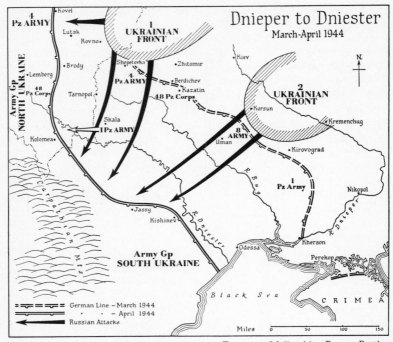

From von Mellenthin, *Panzer Battles*.

ler's orders Tarnopol could be evacuated only on his own special instructions.

To Balck it was obvious that the extremely bad situation could not be cleared up by any local defense of the city, and so he sent off the corps staff officer (operations), Major Erasmus, with the three armored trains, a sapper battalion, and some assault guns to meet the advancing Russians. They managed to hold up the onset of the 6th Soviet Guard Corps for two days, and during that time three newly deployed infantry divisions came on the scene. The gaps could at last be sealed.

On 21 March the Russians attacked yet again on a broad front, and bad tidings flooded in one after the other. We had no more reserves available, and the enemy were penetrating our line everywhere. In the circumstances General Balck, though usually accustomed to attack, could see no way out but a snap decision to withdraw behind the Sereth River. The move, difficult and critical though it turned out to be, was successful. Another crisis had been weathered.

Field Marshal Model, who had succeeded Field Marshal von Manstein in command of the army group, visited Balck at his battle headquarters on 1 May 1944. Balck's impression of the field marshal was that he stirred up considerable trouble through his very impulsive and disjointed way of tackling things. On the other hand, he recognized that Model achieved a great deal and that his defensive measures were sound both in general terms and in detail.

Balck reckoned that a man would not be prepared to put up with as much from Model in peaceful times, for he often meddled in matters that did not fall within his field of authority. At the time they met in Russia, the field marshal was naturally carrying immense responsibility, and so one had to excuse him a great deal, but it was most unpleasant that on each of his many visits to the front he raised such a colossal whirlwind, often issued contradictory orders, and in dealing with others seldom spoke in what one might consider the proper tone.

Balck let Model know that he wished to have a strictly private discussion with him and then told him straight out that things could not go on in such a way. The field marshal was putting everyone on edge before they went into action, and then, inevitably, they broke down in battle.

Model listened to all this quite calmly and acknowledged the justice of much of what Balck had said. As a result of the interview he no longer paid visits to 48th Panzer Corps.

On 14 July the long-awaited Russian offensive began against the front of Army Group North Ukraine. Artillery, tanks, and antitank weapons were thrown into the battle by the Red Army on a hitherto unheard-of scale. As could be gathered from the very earliest reports, our forward infantry divisions were hard-hit. Balck faced this new crisis imperturbably, and on the morning of 15 July, he launched an attack with two Panzer divisions that had been held in reserve. The enemy was brought to a standstill, but in the sector of his 8th Panzer Division developments took an extremely unfavorable turn when the division was attacked during its approach march by strong Russian air formations and suffered catastrophic losses. This put paid to any hopes of a successful counterattack by the two Panzer divisions, and the enemy penetrated deeply into the left wing of 48th Panzer Corps, which somehow managed to contain the enemy thrusts.

But things had gone even more disastrously for the neighboring corps on the left, where the enemy had broken in at several points. There seemed to be something lacking in the handling of 8th Panzer Division, and Balck took a step that is always difficult for any commander. He relieved the divisional commander of his post. He sent me there with orders to take over command of the division and attack from south to north into the Russian flank, so as to close a gap between us and our neighboring corps. The enemy, suspecting that such a thrust would be made, had established an impenetrable antitank barrier in the sector, and the attack never managed to get through. Withdrawal was the only way out for the army, and on 22 July it began.

On 27 July, Lemberg (Lwow), a city of considerable importance to the Germans, was taken by Konev's Russian forces. Our Fourth Panzer Army was forced back over the Vistula. The First Panzer Army—and the 48th Panzer Corps with it—was pushed back into the Carpathians. A disaster was approaching. The attempt on Hitler's life had been made on 20 July, heads were rolling as a result, and in the west American tanks were ready to pour out from Normandy, where they broke through at Avranches on 31 July. At this critical juncture Balck was appointed to command the Fourth Panzer Army. I followed as his chief of staff fourteen days later.

As was to be expected, the situation at the Fourth Panzer Army was more than tense. The Russians had broken through on a broad front on each side of the Upper Vistula. Virtually nothing by way of German forces stood between them and the province of Silesia. Then the enemy drove northward and threatened to roll up the whole Vistula line from south to north. Barring the way was the 40th Corps, facing south. In contact with them behind the Vistula but facing east was the 56th Panzer Corps, but even in their sector the enemy had already gained some bridgeheads on the western bank of the Vistula. The 3d Panzer Corps was in process of assembling, and our proven 48th Panzer Corps was moving up.

The position as Balck found it would have appeared completely hopeless to an amateur strategist, but when the enemy situation was calmly considered, things did not seem quite as desperate as at first appeared. It could be assumed that, after heavy fighting and extremely long marches, the Russians would also be pretty near the end of their tether. Supplies needed for further advance could be available only in inadequate quantities, while on our side supply lines were short and still in good order, so that reinforcements of men and material could be brought up very quickly.

Balck determined to stem the Russian tide moving north from Baranov—naturally by attacking. With Rumania having changed sides on 23 August and Bulgaria offering no resistance to the Russians, the German forces were left with their southern flank wide open, but in our extremely vulnerable sector, where Konev's Soviet forces had already established a bridgehead above the confluence of the Vistula and the San, the corps sent in to attack knocked out 120 Russian tanks on 8 September in heavy fighting. A few days later they accounted for another 56. Meanwhile, the 3d Panzer Corps and the 48th Panzer Corps had come in on right and left, closely concentrated and sent in by Balck against the left flank and rear of the enemy's Baranov battle group.

Ground gained by the two corps covered a considerable area, and their counterattack brought the Russian offensive in the great bend of the Vistula to a standstill, driving the Red Army bridgeheads back into a relatively limited space. Once again Guderian's precept, "Not a drizzle, but a downpour," had proved its validity. In his book *Erinnerungen eines Soldaten,* General Guderian wrote, "Thanks to Balck's indestructible energy and skill, in the end we were once again able to ward off extreme catastrophe."

For his achievement Balck was awarded the Diamond Clasp to his Knight's Cross by Hitler, and on 21 September 1944, with the British and American armies already sweeping across France and through Holland and Belgium to the Rhine, he was appointed commander in chief, Army Group G, and had to report to the Führer before assuming command. Hitler gave Balck the following report of the situation:

215

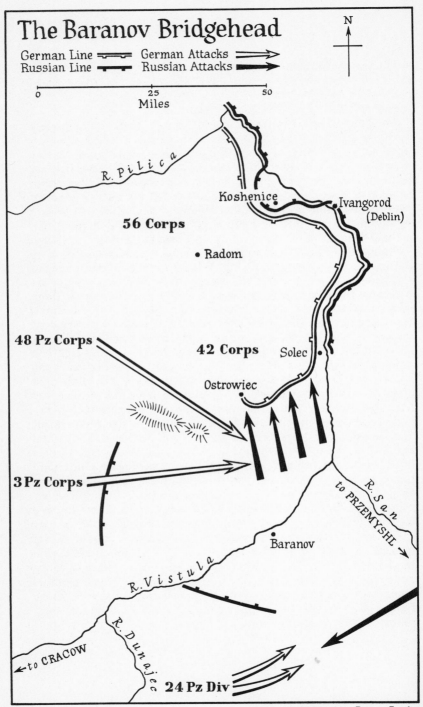

The Baranov Bridgehead

German Line   German Attacks
Russian Line   Russian Attacks

N

0   25   50
Miles

R. Pilica

56 Corps

Koshenice

Ivangorod
(Deblin)

• Radom

48 Pz Corps

42 Corps   Solec

Ostrowiec •

3 Pz Corps

R. San
to PRZEMYSHL

• Baranov

R. Vistula

to CRACOW

R. Dunajec

24 Pz Div

From von Mellenthin, *Panzer Battles*.

The Allies have come to a halt on the present line owing to supply difficulties. This must be exploited by a counterstroke. If we break through anywhere, they have nothing to put in against us. I hope to be able to attack in mid-November with strong forces, including ten Panzer divisions and powerful air forces.

A prerequisite for this is muddy ground and fog, so that the Allied air forces and tanks are at least hampered. To begin the offensive [the Ardennes offensive], the situation in the West will be changed as follows: On the right we will have returned to the Rhine. In the center we must be able to hold the West Wall. Your task, General Balck, will be to get by with the fewest possible troops. Under no circumstances can troops earmarked for the offensive be diverted to you. Should you manage to hold Alsace, it would be greatly appreciated, as it will put a pledge in my hand, for use if necessary.

This was certainly a perfectly clear and straightforward evaluation of the situation, and it impressed Balck, who concluded during the interview that Hitler was completely normal and fully in possession of his mental faculties. As he took leave of Hitler, Balck asked him if he could take me with him as chief of staff of the army group, and Hitler agreed. Balck contended that one should not separate two men who had worked well together for a long time.

On 21 September 1944, Balck took over command of Army Group G, which had previously been under General Blaskowitz. The army group battle headquarters was in Molsheim, just west of Strasbourg in Alsace, and the situation did not look at all bad. In fact, the German defense had stiffened all along the front, which now ran from near Antwerp, in a wide sweep east of the Albert Canal, then south in front of Maastricht and Aachen, and west of the Rhine in a generally southerly direction. However, between Lorraine and the Vosges and in keeping with General Eisenhower's concept of advancing on a broad front all the way from Holland to the Swiss frontier, the Americans were trying to push on from Metz, where Patton had been held up. There they were fighting bitterly but without success for the strong points of the ancient fortress of Metz, which was bravely defended by members of an officers' training course, who thus gained for higher command the time needed to refuel and refit the First Army, which held positions extending from a right flank in Luxembourg down to the area south of Metz.

The Fifth Panzer Army operating in the center of Army Group

G stretched down to the Vosges. Then the Americans thrust at the junction between the First Army and the Fifth Army, toward the Saar. Balck realized that the great danger lay there, and everything available, including the oft-proven 11th Panzer Division, was brought up and launched in a counterattack. When the weather was not good for flying, our attacks quickly smashed their way through, but as soon as the skies cleared and the enemy air forces could hammer us, every effort became paralyzed.

Balck discontinued his attacks, for we had formed a straight and favorable defensive line, and at the time we reckoned that we had achieved complete success. In reality, Eisenhower was holding back Generals Bradley and Patton because he had directed all his supplies to the north, to take the Ruhr area in a great offensive before winter set in.

In contact with Manteuffel's Fifth Panzer Army in the Vosges and in front of Belfort to the Swiss frontier was the German Nineteenth Army, which consisted entirely of units that were barely battleworthy and, in addition, very thin on the ground. Now American spearheads were approaching the Nineteenth Army positions, and Balck ordered that they should be recognized for what they were and halted by attack. Both the army commander, General Wiese and his chief of staff, General Botsch, looked at Balck in amazement and asked, "With what?"

After poring over the map, Balck ordered a thinning out of the army front along the less important sectors and had "hard-hitting packets" formed into shock groups that, in the event, managed to halt the Americans, who showed no great love of fighting in the woods.

Then Balck dug deep into the rear echelons of the army group. All communications units were gone through with a fine comb, and he established, among other things, that one division had about 300 men in action in the forward area, while there were some thousands available in their "rest area" west of the Rhine. Within a few days this division was occupying a 25-kilometer sector of the front with 3,000 men.

Most of the Panzer divisions had pulled their repair units behind the Rhine, which meant a great delay in bringing up repaired vehicles. Balck ordered all repair units immediately moved close up to the front line.

On his various trips Balck also discovered that many detachments had no army post-office address and got no mail from home. In unmistakable terms he let the responsible senior officials know what he thought of their unbelievable negligence and drastically reduced their ration scale. The matter was very quickly set right.

The army group headquarters reckoned on an early resumption of the American attacks, and orders went out that every division was to have an infantry regiment with an assault gun battery and an antitank company held in reserve. The object was to have battleworthy units immediately available to launch counterattacks from any quarter, and Balck personally supervised the formation of these reserves.

The fortress of Metz remained a problem for the army group, for it could be expected with certainty that Hitler would order that it had to be held under any circumstance. To avoid having particularly battleworthy units left in the fortress and cut off if it was encircled, the only troops that were moved in as a garrison were of limited fighting value.

On 8 November 1944, on the eve of a general Allied offensive along the whole of the Western Front, where they had missed an opportunity in September, the Americans resumed their attacks, as had been expected. The numerical comparison between the opposing sides is interesting—in Lorraine we had 30 tanks and assault guns against 700 American. Air squadrons on the German side were nil, on the American, about 1,200 aircraft. Yet we were not immediately overtaken by catastrophe. Why not? There were several reasons:

1. All German troops, officers and men, were fighting with a rare devotion to duty.
2. We were not bound by any edict of Hitler's to "hold at any cost" and could adopt mobile-warfare methods.
3. The obsolete fortress of Metz gained us five valuable days.
4. Because of the peculiarities of their command (other than General Patton's) the Americans failed to understand how to exploit success or to concentrate their powerful resources in time and space and then get the utmost from them.
5. The Allied idea of "unconditional surrender" only reinforced the German determination to fight.

We extricated ourselves from many a really desperate situation only because we knew for certain that no action would be taken by the other side. In this defensive fighting it was most important to Balck that his own units should not be smashed up, and his tactics therefore consisted of withdrawals linked with counterattacks, at times tenacious resistance with small counterthrusts. It was in this way that he kept the enemy constantly guessing about what had happened to us in the fighting and about our real intentions from day to day. Though in all essentials we actually fulfilled our allotted task of holding up the enemy until the beginning of the Ardennes offensive, we knew in our heart of hearts that every day we were standing on the brink of disaster.

Balck was clearly transferring the main effort of his own Army Group to Lorraine. If the front collapsed in Alsace, a local enemy offensive in that quarter would quickly reach the Rhine, and it was a miracle that the weak Nineteenth Army held in that sector for so long.

On 16 November 1944, French divisions penetrated our positions at Belfort and during the next few days reached Mulhouse. At the same time French and American forces launched attacks at Sarrebourg, in Alsace.

The army group proposed to the Army High Command that the Nineteenth Army be pulled back behind the Rhine, so that their better fighting units could be moved over to Lorraine as reinforcements in that area. Hitler turned down the proposal, and instead the Nineteenth Army was ordered to stabilize the position at Mulhouse.

After four days of vigorous argument I finally managed to convince the Supreme Command that, as far as the over-all situation of Army Group G was concerned, southern Alsace, including Belfort and Mulhouse, was completely unimportant. At last I could signal Balck that we could evacuate the Belfort Pocket.

Meanwhile, the French 2d Armored Division had taken Strasbourg. We pulled the Nineteenth Army back into a large bridgehead around Colmar to stabilize the position in Alsace. Our own counterattacks against the rear of enemy forces that had pushed through to Strasbourg—for which the Panzer Lehr Division had been sent to us—did not manage to smash their way through. We purposely kept our front line well forward of the West Wall so as to retain freedom of movement in depth. What is more, we had our doubts about the West Wall itself. Its works—like those at

Tobruk in 1942—had grown obsolete; its weapons had for the most part been removed and installed elsewhere.

At the end of November 1944, I was suddenly transferred to the commanders' reserve of the army. General Balck wrote in his diary:

Today my chief of staff, von Mellenthin, has been transferred. The reason is obvious. Mellenthin has committed himself very keenly and with all his powers of argument determinedly in favor of all our decisions. The evacuation of unusable remnants of forces from Alsace, the withdrawal from the Belfort Pocket were his work. And he battled hard for our latest decision. To me he was a chief of staff and a prop such as one seldom finds. For 2 years we have stood firmly together in the most difficult of crises and have mastered the situation every time. Here in the west also, I believe we have made possible the impossible.

Only three weeks later General Balck also had to relinquish command of his army group. In his book *Erinnerungen eines Soldaten,* General Guderian says that he believes Balck was a victim of Himmler's intrigues. As commander in chief, 6th Army, within the space of 24 hours Balck had to report to Hitler's headquarters for information and then to Budapest, where two Hungarian armies deployed in the area were also put under him.

Since I was not with Balck during those final months of the war, I would prefer not to say anything further about his direction of operations during that time, but it seems to be worth relating how Balck, in the very last days of the war, still clung to his belief that one should match "fairness against fairness."

East of Graz the Russians isolated the Sixth Army, and it was there that the last German breakout from a pocket was achieved by attack, shaking off the Russians. The survivors were determined not to fall into Russian hands, but a very capable officer had established that all German units were to become the captives of those against whom they had been fighting. It was a stipulation that would have to be met, and troops were being shoved in against the Americans from all sides, giving the appearance of a concentrated German pincer attack.

Contact was established with General McBright, who was in command on the other side, and a shrewd stroke was agreed upon. On arrival at the American's headquarters, General Balck was given a cool but correct reception. A guard presented arms, Balck gave the German salute, stepped to one side, and showed McBright a map with the German axes of advance clearly indicated on it. "We do not want to be taken by the Russians," Balck told the American, "but if necessary we will attack the Americans."

The conversation, strictly between the two of them, was conducted in English, and McBright revealed himself as a distinguished and true soldier, accepting the capitulation without any reference to higher command. The Sixth Army was saved.

Released from American captivity in 1947, Balck supported his family by working in a warehouse. Thanks to his vitality and energy, he quickly worked his way up and soon became the representative of well-known firms. It was a great pleasure for me, as marketing director of the South African private airline, Trek Airways, to enlist his support as their representative. Now Balck's former chief of staff and adviser became his boss, and our collaboration, as in the past, proved an outstanding success.

Chapter 12

WAFFEN-SS GENERAL
JOSEPH ("SEPP") DIETRICH

The Obedient Party Soldier and Father to His "Lanky Lads"

There may be a question why I should devote a chapter to one of the most prominent Waffen-SS commanders when considering a cross section of German generals. The answer lies in the fact that, in spite of all the differences between the German Army and the Waffen-SS, one cannot ignore the truth—that this man, a sergeant at the end of World War I, rose during World War II from brigade commander to commander in chief of the 6th SS Panzer Army. I was in contact with Dietrich at the capture of Kharkov in March 1943 and when he was an army commander during the Ardennes offensive at the end of 1944. His formations fought shoulder to shoulder with those of the army, and Dietrich showed himself to be a courageous commander of troops. What, then, was the difference between him and the other military commanders commented upon in this book?

Nearly all these generals fought as young officers for Imperial Germany during World War I, and all the other military commanders I have sketched went through the schooling of the 100,000-man army—the Reichswehr—after the war. General von Seeckt, the creator of that army declared as a fundamental principle that the army should stand aloof from all internal political events. And we aimed to live up to this principle.

We did not agree with all that national socialism brought about after 1933, and we certainly did not approve of the "playing at soldiers" by the Brownshirts, the party Sturmabteilungen. Naturally we approved the reintroduction of conscription, and we were pleased by the great successes scored by Hitler in the foreign political field before the war. But in spite of all that, we remained nonpolitical. That is where we differed from Sepp Dietrich and the Waffen-SS formations, originally fanatically indoctrinated political troops who carried out blindly and as a matter of faith every order of Adolf Hitler's, right or wrong. What, then, is the story of "Sepp" Dietrich, one of the most devoted of Hitler's followers?

Joseph ("Sepp") Dietrich was born in Hawangen, in Bavaria, on 28 May 1892. He was of medium height, stocky and powerfully built, handsome in a pugilistic way, and lively both in manner and in the way he moved. His ideas and his conversation were often disjointed, and as a result he gave the impression of uncertainty in expressing himself. But he was always ready for anything and had a sense of humor, which was rather on the robust side.

In 1911, at the age of nineteen, he joined the 4th Field Regiment, and with that artillery unit he went to the front in 1914. Later he was transferred, first to 8th Field Regiment and then to the 5th Assault Battalion. Tanks were used on the German side as well at the end of World War I—25 German tanks against 5,000 of the enemy's—and Sepp was among the few members of German tank crews. He earned the Iron Cross, both Second and First Class, the Tank Badge, the Bavarian Cross of Merit, and the Austrian Medal for Bravery. In 1918 he joined the Oberland Volunteers and fought in Upper Silesia against the Polish insurgents.

He became one of the most faithful of Hitler's followers and was destined to become famous in the strictly military branch of the SS, the elite corps of shock troops within the Sturmabteilungen, called the Schutzstaffel. Virtually a bodyguard for Hitler, to whom they swore a personal oath of loyalty, members of the SS numbered only about 200 by 1929. when Heinrich Himmler was given the title Reichsführer. It was still a small organization, descended from the shock troops created by Hitler in 1922–23 as a bodyguard "made up of men who would be enlisted without conditions, even to march against their own brothers." The first group was formed in Munich, and Himmler was member number 168.

With an increasing accent on racism and the most rigorous discipline, and, after June 1931 with the assistance of Reinhard Heydrich, a sadistic former naval officer who had been dismissed from the service, Himmler was to build the SS into the most sinister power in Germany. It controlled its own Security Service under Heydrich, the Gestapo, or secret police, and the notorious concentration camps. But the original bodyguard of the Führer remained apart from these perverted groups infecting the life of Germany. It had little in common with any of them except its black uniforms, a ruthless efficiency, and absolute loyalty to Hitler.

In the spring of 1933, Hitler and the war minister, von Blomberg, entrusted Sepp Dietrich with the task of forming a special Wachbattaillon Berlin of selected men. They were apart from the Allgemeine-SS, the general run of Himmler's thugs, and later became known as the SS Leibstandarte Adolf Hitler, with the strength of a reinforced infantry regiment. They fell directly under Hitler and were commanded by SS-Obergruppenführer Sepp Dietrich, whose men became excellent soldiers. All were at least 1.8 meters tall—almost 6 feet.

Dietrich enjoyed the trust of his men to a degree seldom equaled by other military commanders, but he remained fanatically faithful to Hitler, in whose political mission he firmly believed. And it was in this spirit of blind obedience to the Führer that his SS men were trained, with the inevitable accompaniment of that ruthlessness inseparable from unquestioning obedience to the will of an absolute dictator. On 30 June 1934 it was Dietrich and his men who shot the leader of the SA, Röhm, and a number of his associates in Munich on Hitler's orders, on grounds that are dealt with in detail in the chapter on General Baron von Fritsch.

During World War II, with its motto "Meine Ehre Heisst Treue" ("Loyalty Is My Honor") this Waffen-SS grew into a massive military shock force, fighting side by side with the regular army and eventually comprising no fewer than 39 divisions united in hatred of Russian communism and in loyalty to the Führer.

Dietrich, with his personal courage and loyalty already well proved, served throughout the war in the lower, middle, and highest ranks of the Waffen-SS, and his name remains inseparably linked with that of the Leibstandarte Adolf Hitler, whose achievements in action were exceptional. During the occupation of Austria before the war, he had moved his Leibstandarte 598 miles from Berlin to Vienna as part of the 16th Corps under General Heinz Guderian, and in the Polish Campaign he commanded a lorried infantry brigade. In France in 1940, though the SS Division "Totenkopf," which had never been in action before, was initially inclined to panic when attacked by British tanks, the Leibstandarte—now also a division—again under Guderian's 19th Corps, thrust forward onto the Aa canal at Watten. On 25 May an order was received from Hitler that further advance was to be halted, on the grounds that Dunkirk was to be left to the Luftwaffe.

Guderian has written about it in his book *Erinnerungen eines Soldaten*:

Early on the 25th of May I went to Watten to visit the Leibstandarte and to make sure that they were obeying the order to halt. When I arrived there, I found the "Leibstandarte" engaged in crossing the Aa. On the far bank was Mont Watten, a height of only some 235 feet, but that was enough in this flat marshland to dominate the whole surrounding countryside. On top of the hillock, among the ruins of an old castle, I found the divisional commander, Sepp Dietrich. When I asked him why he was disobeying orders, he replied that the enemy on Mont Watten could "look right down the throat" of anybody on the far bank of the canal. Sepp Dietrich had therefore decided on the 24th of May to take it on his own initiative.

Unquestioning obedience of orders clearly did not extend to disregard of tactical requirements, and Guderian approved his decision on the spot in view of its obvious advantages. The incident and many others of the war provided evidence of Dietrich's simple yet daring qualities as a military commander. The next day, when a British party holding out in a house behind the lines opened up on his staff car with a machine gun, Dietrich and his aide-de-camp had to take cover in a large storm-sewer drain, where he covered his face and hands with mud as protection against burning petrol. When the 3d Panzer Regiment got him out of this awkward predicament, he came in for some ribald leg pulling at Guderian's headquarters before the corps went in to attack toward Dunkirk, greatly hampered by orders from Supreme Headquarters to halt the advance. On 5 July 1940, Dietrich was awarded the Knight's Cross of the Iron Cross.

Following the Belgrade coup d'etat in March 1941, Hitler decided to smash Yugoslavia and attack Greece simultaneously. Moving rapidly from east to west across Bulgaria, the Twelfth Army sent the 40th Corps, including the Leibstandarte Adolf Hitler, into Yugoslavia on 6 April. General Sir Iven Giffard Mackay's small Amyntaion detachment, reinforced with what troops of the 6th Australian Division had arrived in time, made contact with Dietrich's brigade in front of Veve on 10 April. The Greek troops under British command had little transport and were not well trained to defend the passes, but there was a brisk action at

Ptolemais, east of Lake Kastoria. The British were pushed back, but the Leibstandarte and the 9th Panzer Division were too short of fuel and ammunition to follow up at once.

Greek morale was already tottering, and it was clear that the British had no option but to begin evacuating Greece. In a determined attack on British, Yugoslav, and Greek troops in the Klidi pass and at Lake Kastoria, the Leibstandarte under Dietrich's command forced the capitulation of the Greek Northern Army. Pushing on, they crossed the Gulf of Corinth in fishing boats, took Patras, and headed for Pyrgos on the west coast of the Peloponnesus. By 29 April the last remnants of the British forces in Greece were being evacuated from the beaches near Kalamata, farther south. Greece was in German hands, and preparations could be made for the capture of Crete.

During 1941, Dietrich and his brigade, excellently equipped with self-propelled assault guns, heavy weapons, infantry carriers, and everything else they could wish for, fought in the southern sector of the Russian Front, where a milestone along their road was the Uman Pocket, south of Kiev, where the Germans took 103,000 prisoners in August in a classic encircling move. They were at the storming of Nowo-Danzig and Cherson and the crossing of the Dnieper at Berislav and were already speeding toward the Tartar Ditch to break into the Crimea when they were called back from Perekop to help stem a Russian thrust through the Rumanians, who were supposed to cover Manstein's flank while his Eleventh Army smashed its way into the Crimea, in addition to trying to take Rostov-on-Don. With the second objective reallocated to Kleist's Panzer Group, Sepp Dietrich's Leibstandarte was placed under its command and took part in the drive through Mariupol and Taganrog to Rostov.

On 31 December 1941, Dietrich was awarded the Oak Leaves to the Knight's Cross for his dashing leadership, the 41st recipient of the award in the German Army. Five days earlier Hitler had dismissed General Guderian as commander in chief of the 2d Panzer Group facing Moscow, putting him on ice for reasons explained in the chapter on Guderian. He had to sit idle in Berlin while his men fought on doggedly, and few visitors cared to call on one who had thus fallen from grace. Dietrich, who was on a few days' leave after his investiture by Hitler, telephoned from the Chancellery to say that he was coming to see his old corps commander. He ex-

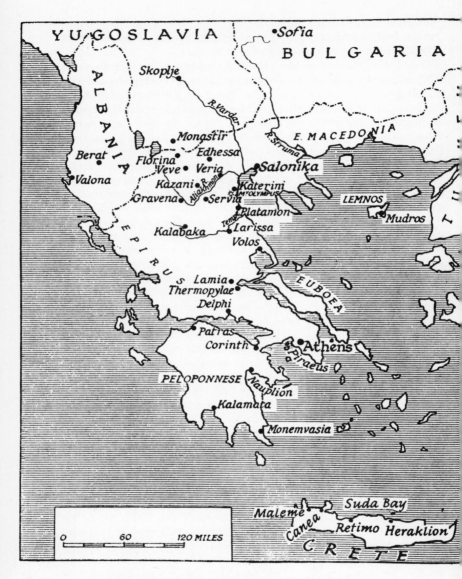

GREECE & CRETE 1941

From *The War, 1939–1*

plained that he had done so deliberately, to let the "big shots" know that they had done Guderian an injustice with which he did not wish to be associated. He had no qualms about letting Hitler know his feelings on the matter, which was remarkable evidence of his soldierly decency, regardless of his political loyalty to Hitler.

In June 1942 the SS Leibstandarte Adolf Hitler became a Panzer grenadier division. They fought with their accustomed bravery between the Don and the Donetz before being pulled out and moved to France for rest and reorganization as a Panzer division. The Waffen-SS was expanding considerably and was receiving much of the finest equipment Germany's war industry could provide. Strangely at variance with Himmler's racial doctrines, enrollment now embraced Latvians, Hungarians, Belgians, Frenchmen, Estonians, Hollanders, and others—hardly the "elite" of Dietrich's original Leibstandarte.

On 22 February 1943, after the withdrawal of German forces from the Stalingrad area, Manstein started his famous counterattack from the region north of Stalino against vastly superior Russian forces advancing through Kharkov toward Saporoshe. The 48th Panzer Corps, with whom I served as chief of staff, was directed on Kharkov in a northeasterly direction toward the area east of the city, with General Paul Hausser's SS Panzer Corps (consisting of Das Reich and Leibstandarte Adolf Hitler Panzer divisions) assembling round Krasnograd, and the 48th and 57th Panzer Corps at Krasnoarmeyskoye, so as to converge to throw back the Russians across the Donetz and then regroup, drive northeast toward Voronezh, and retake Kharkov and Bielgorod. Hausser himself, incidentally, was a qualified staff officer in World War I, and had been entrusted with the training of Waffen-SS leaders before the war.

In this surprise attack the Russian forces suffered very heavy losses at the hands of the 48th and SS Panzer Corps and were put to flight. By 15 March 1943, Kharkov had been captured by the SS Panzer Corps, with Dietrich and his division again distinguishing themselves. The next day he was awarded the Swords to the Oak Leaf clasp of his Knight's Cross for personal bravery during the action.

As chief of staff of the 48th Panzer Corps, I again found myself fighting shoulder to shoulder with SS Panzer formations, including

Dietrich's Leibstandarte Adolf Hitler, at the fateful battle of Kursk, the last German offensive in Russia employing virtually our full armored strength. The objective of this Operation "Zitadelle" ("Citadel") was to wipe out the big Russian salient that cut deep into the German Front around Kursk to a depth of about 120 kilometers. Powerful Russian forces were to be destroyed by thrusts from the south and north into the area east of Kursk, and the drive would have been successful had it been carried out at once, in April 1943.

Hitler went on delaying the offensive to be able to employ the "wonder weapon," our new Panther tanks, and it was 4 July 1943 before our divisions, including Dietrich's Leibstandarte, went in to the attack. Meanwhile the Russians had dug in so effectively and laid mines so thickly that the whole area round Kursk had become a Soviet fortress. As a result, our attack came to a standstill after about a fortnight, and Dietrich's Panzer division, in action in the Bielgorod sector, also suffered heavy losses. On 13 July we were informed that Operation Citadel was to be stopped at once, as the Allies had landed in Sicily. Several divisions, including Dietrich's severely mauled formation, were hastily pulled out to prepare for the invasion of Italy, which was expected at any moment. Dietrich lost his Leibstandarte and was given the task of forming the 1st SS Panzer Corps, with SS Panzer divisions Leibstandarte and Hitler Jugend and the Panzer Lehr Division under command.

With the fall of Mussolini in July 1943, Hitler had quickly determined to take complete control in Italy. Rommel was to take over Army Group B, and among reinforcements to be rushed to the scene was the 2d SS Panzer Corps from the Eastern Front. Rescued in dramatic fashion by the Waffen-SS daredevil Otto Skorzeny and a small airborn force, Il Duce set himself up in an out-of-the-way spot on the shores of Lake Garda, and was guarded by a special detachment from the Leibstandarte. Dietrich suffered the indignity of having to escort Mussolini's mistress back to her lover, and his men rounded up Allied prisoners of war from Italian camps with an efficiency that might have been admired had it not been for the callousness of their treatment of all ranks, whom they packed into cattle trucks and locked in for almost the whole of a snail's-pace journey to Germany without food, water, or sanitary arrangements and with punishment amounting to sadism of any attempts to escape. It was an episode not in the Wehrmacht manner, of which I knew nothing until I was told about it by South Africans after the war.

The Waffen-SS, which until 1942 accepted only volunteers, since conscripts went to the army proper, had by now begun to take in selected national servicemen. Discipline within its own ranks was harsh, and in some way its very fanaticism seems to have contributed to a measure of brutality that went beyond the needs of war. Indeed, against combatants the British Commandos with their tough tactics would take some besting, but by the time Dietrich—for all his loyalty to Hitler—found it no longer possible to pretend to himself that the situation was not steadily deteriorating for Germany, the Waffen-SS had expanded far beyond the personal influence he originally exercised over his original select Leibstandarte of tall, lanky lads. Before the war was over, there were to be no fewer than 39 Waffen-SS divisions, and the SS as a whole was a far more serious rival to the Wehrmacht than Röhm's Sturmabteilungen had been. But the two "armies" were staunchly united in their defense of Germany, which was a common bond between them, reinforced by a mutual hatred and dread of Bolshevism and the Red Army, whose behavior was not necessarily governed by the niceties observed by the British and Americans in their conduct of operations.

The 1st SS Panzer Corps under Dietrich's command was to attack, together with the 58th Panzer Corps, in the area of Caen, where the 12th SS (Hitler Jugend), 1st SS (Leibstandarte), 9th SS (Hohenstauffen), 2d SS (Das Reich), and Panzer Lehr divisions were concentrated—left to right—at the end of June 1944, facing the Second British Army. The 21st Panzer Division was on their right, and the 2d Panzer Division on their left. Petrol was short, the woods hampered armored movement, and, though, fighting was bitter, the German attacks never got far beyond their start lines owing to massive bombing of their assembly areas by the Allied air forces, in the face of which there could be no serious thought of attack with any real promise of success. Hitler, completely ignorant of actual conditions at the front, expressed his extreme displeasure to the army headquarters in control of operations and in addition accused the troops of cowardice. Dietrich's indignation knew no bounds.

At a briefing shortly afterward with Dietrich and two army

corps commanders, at which my friend Dingler was also present as one of the chiefs of staff, Dietrich said things one would never have expected of him, of all people. The gist of his assertion was that it was high time "Adolf" was induced to give up supreme command over the armed forces. If any one of the army commanders in chief could muster the courage to take over command of the whole army, he would back him with his Waffen-SS. This viewpoint and his disenchantment with the idea of Hitler's infallibility as a warlord undoubtedly had its roots in his own long experience of war under Hitler's supreme command.

Dietrich had become a realistic, experienced fighting commander. He was always among his men, whom he looked after in an outstanding manner. He understood their way of thinking and their troubles and in the course of time he realized the senselessness and other-worldliness of so many of Hitler's orders and actions. Dietrich was no political philosopher. The great complexities of world politics were certainly unfathomable to him. He may still have believed in his Führer as a stateman and as a strong leader of the German people, but in Hitler as a warlord he certainly no longer had any faith.

On 6 August 1944, Dietrich was awarded the Diamonds to the Knight's Cross, and at the same time he was promoted SS-Oberstgruppenführer and colonel general of the Waffen-SS.

During the Ardennes offensive, which began on 16 December 1944, the Sixth SS-Panzer Army under General Dietrich was to contribute the main effort to the attack. It was unusual, but perhaps significant, that during the planning and preparation for the offensive neither Dietrich's advice nor his opinions regarding the feasibility of the operation were sought. Rundstedt, commander in chief, West, as well as Field Marshal Model as commander in chief of the army group, and General von Manteuffel who was in command of the Fifth Panzer Army, next to Dietrich's, had their say. Their proposals, which related to the situation as it actually was, were noted but rejected by Hitler. At least they were asked. But not Dietrich.

Hitler thought little of these military commanders' opinions. He laid down every detail for conducting the offensive—when zero hour for the attack should be set, when the artillery preparation should begin, how long it should last, and so on. There was no talk about opinions or suggestions for improvement from

Dietrich. Possibly he was already resigned to the inevitable. His own Waffen-SS troops and the army formations under command of his army attacked with their usual élan and bravery but gained little ground. The plan of attack for his army had not taken sufficient account of the prevailing conditions—the exceptionally difficult terrain, with few roads and bridges—and the consequent problems of bringing up reinforcements and supplies to the point of main effort at the required time. A false start to any attack can be rectified during the course of subsequent operations only in the rarest of cases.

The personal initiative of General von Manteuffel, who simply ignored many of Hitler's orders, brought his Fifth Panzer Army notable success, but Hitler's instructions were carried out more or less to the letter by the Sixth SS-Panzer Army, with the result that they failed to achieve even initial success.

Hitler was caught, and remained so, by his recollections of World War I. In spite of his undeniable genius in certain fields, he was conducting what Field-Marshal von Rundstedt called a "corporal's war." In this respect Dietrich somewhat resembled him.

At the beginning of 1945, Dietrich's Sixth SS-Panzer Army was transferred to the Hungarian theater to halt the major Soviet offensive there in heavy, costly fighting after fewer than 700 out of almost 30,000 Hungarians and Germans had managed to break out of the Russian ring around Budapest on the night of 11 February. Having struggled through snow and ice from the Ardennes, Dietrich's divisions floundered through the mud to reach the Hron bridgehead and attacked successfully on 17 February. General Wöhler, commanding Army Group South, conferred with Balck, commanding Sixth Army, and Dietrich, again commanding Sixth SS Panzer Army after a brief detachment to his headquarters in Berlin.

An offensive was to be planned between Lake Balaton and the Danube. The weather was shocking, and on 6 March the Sixth SS Panzer Army's attack went in as a blizzard subsided. Only the 1st SS Panzer Corps was ready, and the Russians expected the attack. Within a few days Tolbukhin had committed virtually all his Russian reserves, and on 13 March he counterattacked on both sides of the Sárviz Canal. On 16 March the Russians launched a counteroffensive on the front between Lake Velencei and Bicske, the

Hungarian 3d Army collapsed, and the enemy drove through the Vértes Mountains well north of Dietrich's forces. Wöhler had to call off the German offensive and ordered the Sixth SS Panzer Army north.

By the 20th, when the Russians thrust toward the tip of Lake Balaton, Dietrich's army was gone, and, in spite of Hitler's orders to hang on, Balck's Sixth Army also slipped out just in time to avoid encirclement. There was no longer any real hope of stemming the tide.

Dietrich's troops fell back to the foothills of the Alps near Vienna. By mid-April the Sixth SS Panzer Army, the Sixth Army, and the Second Panzer Army had somehow managed to establish a front from west of Saint Pölten to the Drava River east of Varazdin. At the end of the month the Third US Army entered Austria from southern Germany, threatening the army group in the rear. On 8 May, General Lothar Rendulic, now commanding the army group, surrendered to the Americans at Saint Pölten.

Perhaps the following incident, which occurred during the last few months of the war, is characteristic of Dietrich's nature.

An eighteen-year-old soldier, much pampered by his mother, was sent to the Waffen-SS units in Hungary in the middle of very severe defensive fighting. He was posted to a tank crew, who naturally showed him no particular consideration and made life pretty tough for the youngster who had led so sheltered an existence at home. He could not bear it and headed for home and mother.

On the way he was arrested, charged before a court-martial and sentenced to death by shooting. Oberstgruppenführer Dietrich had to confirm the death sentence. After studying the records, Dietrich ordered the eighteen-year-old to appear before him and listened to the youngster as he described his mental anguish. Then he stood up and thoroughly boxed the ears of the condemned youth, with the remark that he was to go to his mother for one week's leave and then return to duty and become a decent soldier. At the end of the week the youngster returned to the front and turned out to be a thoroughly good soldier. Nothing more was heard about the sentence that Dietrich had annulled with a slap on the head.

It was alleged that during the Ardennes offensive Colonel Joachim Peiper's tough battle group of the Leibstandarte Adolf Hitler, short of fuel, turned into the Hitler Jugend zone, seized a petrol dump at Büllingen, forced fifty American soldiers to fill the tanks, and then shot them in cold blood. That afternoon the Waffen-SS group captured an American artillery observation battery of 125 men at the Malmédy crossroads, and a couple of hours later the prisoners were machine-gunned while they stood in a field waiting to be sent to a POW cage. Eighty-six lost their lives, but a few survived to bear witness to the event, which is recorded in Purnell's *History of the Second World War*. In *The Rise and Fall of the Third Reich*, Shirer puts the number of dead at 71.

The full truth about the Massacre of Malmédy will never be known, but a most detailed investigation has been made in the years since the War Crimes Commission trial in 1946. Charles Whiting, recording the results of his minute investigations (which include some damning reflections upon the methods adopted by the American prosecuting team before the trial and during the trial itself), has shown almost conclusively that Colonel Peiper was not personally involved and that Sepp Dietrich knew nothing about the murders or the atrocities committed by the Leibstandarte Adolf Hitler until well after the event. In his *Massacre at Malmédy* (first published in Great Britain by Leo Cooper Ltd. in 1971), Whiting tells the full story of this tragic episode, for which Peiper was originally condemned to death but was released after nearly thirteen years in prison.

Dietrich, who was undeniably a most courageous fighting soldier, could never have held high command without the backing of well-trained staff officers from the regular army. He had neither their background nor their training. Shirer, who can be suspected of journalistic hyperbole, recalled Dietrich as "one of the most brutal men of the Third Reich." However that may be, I cannot say that in my own dealings with him I found him so. Nevertheless, after the war he was sentenced by an American court to 25 years' imprisonment for complicity in the Malmédy massacre. After ten years he was released, but in May 1957 a Munich court sentenced him to a further eighteen months for his part in the executions of 30 June 1934.

Chapter 13

GENERAL HASSO VON MANTEUFFEL

The Zieten* of World War II

Hasso von Manteuffel was born on 14 January 1897 in Potsdam, near Berlin, and attended the Royal Prussian Cadet School. Like so many of the best-known and most-distinguished commanders of Panzer formations, he began his military career in the cavalry. During World War I he was promoted to second lieutenant in the 3d Hussars—the famous Zieten Hussars—on 22 February 1916.

Short and slightly built, he was lively, agile and always on the go, a typical cavalryman. Both on duty and off he was invariably friendly and courteous, though his manner never affected the clarity and precision with which he expressed himself, leaving no room whatever for any doubt about what he meant. Whatever the situation, he never failed to behave like a gentleman, in the best sense of the word.

Manteuffel was only a lieutenant when he became a squadron commander, one of the youngest in the Reichswehr of his day. In his efforts at improvement and innovation in the field of military training while still only a subaltern, he published a pamphlet entitled *The Squadron Commander*, in which he not only recorded his own experience of teaching horsemanship and caring for animals but also discussed infantry training for mounted troops. This was in 1932 or 1933, and when one bears in mind that not long before—in 1928—the highest military circles were striving for the retention of cavalrymen's lances, it is understandable that new-

*Hans Joachim von Zieten, a dashing Prussian cavalry commander who distinguished himself under Frederick the Great by his daring attacks.

fangled ideas about the use of cavalrymen as infantry were not everywhere well received. Even in Britain, with her South African war experiences to call on, among the establishment mounted infantry was not exactly something to be encouraged.

Manteuffel's paper, written by a young squadron commander only recently appointed, naturally did not enjoy the undivided approval of older squadron commanders with ten or more years of experience in command. In spite of this, Manteuffel remained popular not only among his fellows but also with his superiors and those under him. He had a sense of humor in his approach to life, and his wealth of new ideas and dash ensured extraordinarily rapid advancement and a brilliant military career. Within six years he rose from the rank of major to full general, and became commander in chief of a Panzer army.

General Guderian first noticed Manteuffel when the latter was conducting cadet officers' courses in the 2d Panzer Division, which was under the armored expert's own command. He again attracted Guderian's attention at the Armored Corps Training School in Wünsdorf, near Berlin.

Manteuffel somehow left the stamp of his own personality on his trainees, and he taught them independent action within the framework of an integrated team effort. His career led him to the inspectorate of armored troops, and from there he moved to the post of training officer in the Armored Corps Training School II at Potsdam-Krampnitz. There he was responsible for lecturing to and training cadet officers and serving officers up to the rank of company commander of lorried infantry in armored divisions— later to be known as Panzer grenadiers— and he also trained scouts and antitank gunners.

When his turn came for frontline service, he asked to be given a battalion, so that he could gain experience of battle in action, and of tactics and command under conditions of modern warfare, so different from those of World War I. He was given command of a battalion of 7th Lorried Infantry Regiment in 7th Panzer Division in June 1941.

When the commander of the 6th Lorried Infantry Regiment was killed in action, Manteuffel was entrusted with command of this unit as early as August 1941, after which employment of the regiment was for a long time inseparably linked with his name. They were the first through the breach in the Stalin Line as the spearhead of the Panzer Group under General Hoth. They led the thrust over the Dnieper, during which they took a bridge by storm and established a bridgehead that provided the firm base for a further successful drive. They broke through the Soviet defenses northwest of Moscow, and in a dashing coup on 27 November 1941 they captured a road bridge across the Moskva–Volga Canal, though it had been mined for demolition.

Manteuffel, who had meanwhile been given command of the Lorried Infantry Brigade of the 7th Panzer Division, had to relinquish command when posted elsewhere in July 1942. His divisional commander gave him a farewell in front of all his assembled officers and spoke of him as the "schoolmaster" of the division. He went on to explain that the accent should be equally on "school" and on "master."

In November, 1942, Manteuffel was given command of what came later to be known as the "Manteuffel Division." It was a mixed formation but a good one, about a division in strength on the right flank of the Axis Line in Tunisia, southwest of Bizerte, where it was to break through the British positions in the Sedjenane Valley, cut their lines of communication, and cover the flank of Weber's Corps farther south. This operation, "Ochsenkopf" began on 26 February 1943, and von Manteuffel's troops, facing the British 46th Infantry Division, carried on the fight until 1 April making considerable initial gains but eventually driven back. It was not until the end of April that the advance by American and French troops forced Manteuffel to withdraw through Mateur. In the midst of the fighting he fell ill and had to leave the battlefield. He was taken aboard the last hospital ship to leave Tunis for Europe.

In spite of clear Red Cross markings, the ship was bombed several times and developed a heavy list after a near miss. The ship's captain wanted to make for the Pantelleria Island, but very strong objections from Manteuffel persuaded him to alter course for Sicily in spite of the list, and the ship managed to make port and disembark its passengers safely. After recovering from his illness, about mid-August 1943, Manteuffel was appointed to command the 7th Panzer Division in Russia, and Hitler briefed him personally. An extract from my book *Panzer Battles* tells how well the division acquitted itself under his leadership. I was chief of staff to the 48th Panzer Corps when I wrote:

241

Our trump card was the 7th Panzer Division, which had now been brought up to full strength in men and material. Forty-eighth Panzer Corps intended to send 7th Panzer on a wide swing to the left of the 1st Panzer Division, and to move it far behind the Russian front. For this complicated plan to succeed it was of the utmost importance that the thrust should come as a complete surprise. . . . The role of this division required great skill, adaptability, and energy. However, it was commanded by General Hasso von Manteuffel, an officer who possessed these qualities in abundance, and also had the personal dash and courage required to inspire his men in this very difficult and dangerous task.

Events justified this opinion. After Shitomir had been taken by the division on 19 November 1943, Manteuffel earned for himself the title "the Lion of Shitomir," and from there the division attacked on the march, succeeded in taking the enemy by surprise, and managed to free a German armored division from encirclement.

Around Christmas 1943, Manteuffel was summoned to report to Hitler to receive an award for bravery, and the Führer personally gave him orders to take over the Panzer Grenadier Division "Gross Deutschland" and build it into the strongest armored division in the army. Manteuffel found the Gross Deutschland Division engaged in heavy defensive fighting in the region of Kirovgrad and Krivoi Rog, and in the months that followed he led it back deep into Rumania. It was due to his energy and wariness that the Gross Deutschland managed to reach the area east of Jassy in Rumania still intact. There Manteuffel repulsed attacks by two Soviet armies and six lorried infantry divisions directed on the Ploeşti oil fields. In the course of one of the tank battles that developed during this effort, several hundred enemy tanks were destroyed.

However, as the general situation deteriorated, it became necessary to move the Gross Deutschland to East Prussia, where the division assembled near Trakehnen, about 40 kilometers behind the front line. Since the German Front was crumbling there too, Hitler personally ordered the division to attack immediately, and on 9 August 1944 they were successful, and it became possible for the German defensive front to be more or less reestablished.

In referring to the action, the divisional history states: "Lieutenant General von Manteuffel sent his division into the attack without so much as one shell on the German side and without any artillery preparation whatsoever. Surprise was complete."

At the beginning of September 1944, Manteuffel was summoned to the Führer's headquarters and appointed commander in chief, Fifth Panzer Army and promoted to general of Panzer troops. The army was then on the Western Front, west of the Vosges Mountains, and that is where I—as chief of staff, Army Group G—met General von Manteuffel again.

After the Fifth Panzer Army had held the front on both sides of Lunéville in Lorraine until 15 October 1944 in a series of local but nevertheless hard-fought battles, Manteuffel and his staff were called back from the front on 18 October. The Ardennes offensive was casting its shadow before it, and the briefing for the operation, which had been worked out by Hitler to the smallest detail, took place in November at the headquarters of Field Marshal Model. The commander in chief, West, Field Marshal von Rundstedt, Field Marshal Model, and General von Manteuffel were present. Waffen-SS General Sepp Dietrich, who was to command one of the armies actually involved in the assault, was not present. Field Marshal von Rundstedt first called on Manteuffel to express an opinion about the plan of attack.

General Jodl, who was presenting the plan on Hitler's behalf, repeatedly interrupted Manteuffel's comments with a curt, "This plan of operations is irrevocable. Those are the Führer's orders." Jodl remained totally unreceptive to all objections put forward by Model and Manteuffel. Suggestions by von Rundstedt had no result, and finally Manteuffel proposed that he be allowed to present his ideas to Hitler personally. Rundstedt agreed, and Model decided to accompany Manteuffel on his visit to Hitler.

Manteuffel's interview with Hitler took place on 2 December 1944 in the Chancellery in Berlin and lasted for five hours. Manteuffel now discovered that many important prerequisites for a successful operation that he had mentioned to Jodl were in fact not available, though only ten days remained before the opening of the offensive. Model supported Manteuffel's arguments. Hitler listened to them without interrupting and allowed the members of his entourage who were responsible for the plan to have their say. The discussion proved fruitless, and so did a subsequent meeting between Manteuffel and Hitler in the latter's private study.

During a further private discussion between Manteuffel and Jodl, the latter assured him that all prerequisites would be provided, though he must well have known that neither the manpower nor the material was in fact available. The only thing to which Hitler agreed was a suggestion by Manteuffel that the attack should be launched without the artillery preparation originally proposed by Hitler, who wished to open with an artillery barrage — as the commander in chief, Sixth SS Panzer Army, duly did. Manteuffel was convinced that this would merely alert the enemy. He wanted to attack without any artillery preparation at all, an exercise that in the event proved outstandingly successful.

Manteuffel also opened the attack on a wider front than that of his right-hand neighbor, Waffen-SS General Dietrich, with the Fifth Panzer Army advancing over a 45-kilometer front across difficult terrain, with few roads and fewer bridges over the Ourth River. This enabled Manteuffel to feel for soft spots in the enemy line and direct his reserves to such points from well in the rear. This way of doing things was crowned with success, while the Sixth SS Panzer Army was soon stuck fast and unable to bring its reserves into action because the roads were jammed with traffic.

With the object of infiltrating rapidly and possibly unobserved through the enemy defensive front, Manteuffel had formed specially selected and trained assault detachments, independent of supplies and therefore extremely mobile. They also proved successful.

While Hitler had intended that the Sixth SS Panzer Army should deliver the main thrust of the offensive, Dietrich's forces could make only slight progress, while Manteuffel's army was not only successful from the start but also able to push elements of its 2d Panzer Division almost to the Maas River.

When an attack is making good progress and therefore appears to the men in the ranks to promise success, it is not surprising that their confidence in the commander grows and they give of their utmost to maintain the momentum of the assault and exploit their gains. But when an attack gets bogged down and the troops are forced to withdraw owing to the numerical superiority of the enemy, then signs appear that morale and discipline are being put to a severe test.

On 24 December 1944 the German offensive was finally brought to a standstill. The Americans had brought up considerable reinforcements, including the 82d and 101st Airborne divisions. In addition, the weather cleared, and the Allies could employ powerful air formations to which the Germans had no counter. On 3 January

1945 the Allies went over to the counterattack and major offensive action that prefaced a German retreat.

On 8 January 1945, Hitler eventually agreed to the army group's proposal to pull the German front back behind the West Wall—or Siegfried Line, as the British called it—since it was very obvious that large portions of the German force were in grave danger of encirclement. During this withdrawal by Manteuffel's army, which was undertaken under the most difficult of conditions of weather and terrain, bedeviled by lack of fuel and ammunition, there was never any feeling among middle or lower headquarters that the army commander had lost his grip on the situation.

Everything depended on the conduct, the discipline, and the staying powers of the frontline soldiers. They held out so magnificently that in spite of frequent confusion one could honestly describe it as an orderly withdrawal. The levelheaded and determined leadership of General von Manteuffel, the confidence his men placed in him, and the bravery of the German soldiers so shortly before the end of the war combined to accomplish a notable military achievement.

What made service under General von Manteuffel particularly pleasant for everyone concerned was his invariably friendly manner. He frequently suffered from severe attacks of migraine, but his leadership and behavior were never affected. What other commanders would often convey in the form of abrupt and not always friendly orders, took the form of a polite request from Manteuffel. I do not think that anyone could have disregarded any of his instructions, which were given in a calm and friendly voice but nevertheless clearly and decisively. For example, during the stress of the Ardennes offensive he turned calmly to one of his staff officers with the words "Would you be so kind as to drive back quickly to the general to deliver fresh orders to him?"

One day Manteuffel was standing in the doorway of a farmhouse, discussing the situation with one of his corps commanders and the latter's chief of staff. A sudden air raid on the village forced them to seek cover hurriedly in the cellar of the house. With a polite wave of the hand and a courteous, "After you, gentlemen," Manteuffel entered the shelter only after the others had preceded him.

Frederick the Great, who always wished for better understanding between his officers and the men, once said: "The soldier's contentment in the service rests primarily on his regard for his

245

superiors. A commander will never be disliked if his zeal is tempered with kindheartedness." It would seem to all who knew General von Manteuffel that this observation was meant to apply to him.

In the middle of February 1945, I was posted as chief of staff of the Fifth Panzer Army. I had known General von Manteuffel on the Eastern Front as a superb, versatile tank commander—the Zieten of modern times. Now I was to serve directly under him as my commander in chief during the retreat across the Rhine. I can only confirm that in his generous style of command his chief of staff was given a completely free hand in his sphere of operations.

Unfortunately, this period of harmonious cooperation was all too short lived, for on 2 March 1945—less than a month after I had joined his staff—Manteuffel was entrusted by Hitler with command of the Third Panzer Army, which was fighting against the Russians east of the Oder near Stettin. This army was supposed to thrust from Stettin toward the southeast to establish contact with the army group commanded by General Schörner, who was attacking from the area east of Goerlitz.

Manteuffel found his new army locked in heavy defensive fighting along the banks of the Oder River. The troops were so battleweary that there could be no thought of mounting a counterattack. In the midst of this unhappy situation, on 25 April, Field Marshal Keitel appeared at the front to get firsthand information about the situation from the commander in chief, Army Group Weichsel, General Heinrici and from Manteuffel. Without so much as a greeting to them, Keitel pounced on Heinrici, berated him for the withdrawal of his army group, and reproached him for the disorganization he had witnessed on his way there. He ordered Heinrici to intervene personally to rectify conditions on the roads, or, if necessary, a few people should be shot.

Heinrici vehemently rejected these demands, whereupon Keitel immediately relieved him of his command and offered it to General von Manteuffel, who rejected the offer out of hand "because of the shameless treatment meted out to the highly respected Colonel General Heinrici." Furthermore, he emphatically confirmed Heinrici's evaluation of the situation. Keitel's reply was to the effect that Manteuffel would be answerable to posterity for his attitude. Manteuffel's exact words in retort were: "Until this day all members of my family employed in the service of the state, either as officials or as army officers, have accepted their delegated responsibilities. I have no intention of trying to escape full responsibility myself."

Keitel left without another word, and in a dispatch to the Combined Staff of the Armed Forces, Manteuffel repeated his refusal of the proferred command.

At the end of April or beginning of May 1945 the 3d Panzer Army found itself deployed along the demarcation line between the Allies and the Red Army. Manteuffel sent his chief of staff to Montgomery's headquarters with an offer to surrender with his army. Field Marshal Montgomery at first refused the offer but the next day sent a staff officer to Manteuffel with the message that surrender would be accepted only if the troops came over unarmed and with discipline fully maintained. The surrender took place a few hours lated under full military discipline.

When I visited Manteuffel in Germany in August 1973, he passed on to me his personal impressions of Hitler's entourage, gained during his various visits to the Führer.

About Field Marshal Keitel he said:

Like so many of Hitler's entourage, Keitel was completely out of touch with conditions at the front and became more so the longer the war continued. He no longer understood the needs or the attitude of frontline troops. On several occasions when I tried to tell him something I had just told Hitler, I was put off with the words, "Manteuffel, you are young and so full of energy and drive. You are most certainly also well informed about the state of your troops, but in spite of your privileged position you should not approach the Führer with this sort of representation, objection, demands, and so forth. The man has enough to worry about already. You are just making his task more difficult."

On 2 March I had to report to Hitler when I passed through from the Western to the Eastern Front to take over command of the Third Panzer Army. As I entered the large audience room, Hitler yelled at me from afar, "All generals are liars!" I met this offensive accusation with a request, "I beg you to tell me when General von Manteuffel or any of his subordinate generals has ever lied to you." Hitler, visibly taken aback, became more reasonable, with the remark that he did not include me personally. After a lengthy and businesslike conference with Hitler, I reported this incredible incident to Keitel and added that I thought he should—in the interest of all general officers—protest against such unbelievable accusations. Keitel simply put me off with some meaningless remark.

Concerning General Jodl, Manteuffel had the following remarks to make:

Jodl had also lost contact with the front. He never took the opportunity of talking to me when I came directly from the front line to report to Hitler. On the few occasions when I saw him in Hitler's presence I could not help noticing his subservience toward Hitler and his arrogance toward his juniors, including myself, even though I was the commander in chief of an army.

Regarding Himmler:

We met one another during my visits to the Führer's headquarters. In the spring of 1945, when he became commander in chief of the Army Group Weichsel, I went to see him about taking over command of the Third Panzer Army in hopes of learning something about the situation and the intentions of his army group. Himmler overwhelmed me with a long-winded exposition of his political views. But about the military situation I learned nothing. In fact, he and his staff had no idea about the condition of their troops or their requirements, the supply situation, or other matters that I regarded as urgent. I was glad when he was relieved shortly afterward and had to hand over the Army Group to General Heinrici.

After his release from captivity in September 1947, Manteuffel was active in industry and also served as a municipal councilor in Neuse, on the Rhine. From 1953 to 1957 he was a member of the West German Parliament. When I spoke to him during my visit in 1973, I was specially struck by his modesty in attributing the successes achieved by units under his command to the fact that his men did their best to act in accordance with directives he gave them:

Our honor lies in doing our duty toward our people and our fatherland, as well as in the consciousness of our mutual obligation to keep faith with one another, so we can depend on each other. We must remember that, even in our technological age, it is man's fighting spirit that ultimately decides between victory and defeat.

When von Manteuffel paid a visit to the Pentagon in Washington, D.C., he was given photostatic copies of confidential reports by his superiors from his own personal file. They are well worth quoting:

When he was a battalion commander, on 1 April 1942: "Indefatiguable and a daredevil, a bold and dashing leader." And again on 27 July 1942:

Manteuffel has proved himself outstandingly during the Russian Campaign. Quick thinking, tactically able to take in the whole situation at a glance, always ready for action, brave and untiring, he carries through every assignment to complete success. A commander on whom one can rely in any situation.

From a report by Field Marshal Kesselring on 6 April 1943: "An outstanding Commanding Officer." And from General Balck on 25 January 1944: "Distinguishes himself time and again by surpassing bravery. He is always where the fighting is fiercest." On 1 February 1944: "Outstandingly brave and an excellent leader. There is no assignment which he cannot carry out splendidly." In a report dated 22 March 1944, Field Marshal von Manstein had this to say about Manteuffel:

A quite outstanding Panzer Divisional Commander. A conspicuous and enthusiastic leader, who excels in every respect. Always ready for action to the highest degree. Head and shoulders above the average.

On 13 March 1945:

Distinctly a natural leader with a strong personality. He possesses military ability of a high order and a keen eye for essentials. He knows how to impart his own natural enthusiasm to the men under him with assurance and success. Often tested as a commander of Panzer formations and as Army Commander, both in defence and attack. An exceptional Panzer commander.

In "recognition of his consistently heroic efforts," in February 1945, Manteuffel was awarded the Diamonds in addition to the Oak Leaves with Crossed Swords he had already earned to his Knight's Cross. He was the twenty-fourth member of the German armed forces to be thus honored.

The recognition accorded Manteuffel after the war by leading persons among Germany's former enemies strikes me as an indication that chivalry is not yet dead. He was invited to lecture at several universities and at military establishments, among them the Nato War College at Norfolk, Virginia; at Gettysburg; and at West Point. On several visits to the United States he was received as guest by Generals Eisenhower, Westmoreland, and Wedemeyer. In Britain, Field Marshal Montgomery met with him and his own former chief of staff, Sir Francis de Guingand, in a long discussion.

In his book *The Other Side of the Hill* the late Sir Basil Liddell Hart, the famous British military expert, gave his impressions of

General von Manteuffel, whom he often saw during the German's captivity and after his release. Sir Basil presented one of his own books to von Manteuffel with the inscription; "To a master in the art of mobility and surprise, with all good wishes." In another he wrote: "To a great commander of armored forces, in friendship and admiration."

Chapter 14

GENERAL
WALTHER WENCK

A Man Who Inspired Confidence

General Walther Wenck is of medium height and smart, soldierly appearance—a most likable person, and invariably charming not only to his superiors but also to his colleagues and those under him. Thanks to his self-confidence and the impression he gives of innate superiority, he exercises a measure of influence on his seniors, and at times of the most serious crisis he radiates an aura of imperturbability that affects everyone around him. Even in an apparently hopeless situation Wenck is never at a loss for some improvization, when his cheerful disposition and never-failing sense of humor stand him in good stead.

Born in Wittenberg on the Elbe River on 18 September 1900, Wenck belongs to the fourth successive generation of soldiers in his family. Too young to serve in World War I, he spent the years 1911 to 1918 in the Cadet Corps at Naumburg and at the Senior Cadet School at Lichterfelde. He then joined the Reinhard Volunteer Crops on 12 February 1919. He was promoted to noncommissioned rank on 27 August 1919, and at the end of April 1920 he transferred to the Von Oven Volunteers. On 1 May he was accepted into the Reichswehr.

Wenck began his regular service in the 5th Infantry Regiment but stayed with it only eight months before being transferred to the 9th Infantry Regiment, stationed at Potsdam and Spandau. He served with the 9th for twelve years, and on 1 February 1923 was promoted to second lieutenant. Later, as adjutant of the 3d Battalion, 9th Infantry Regiment—the infantry-training battalion of the army—he first came into contact with mobile formations during joint exercises with the training squadron of the Inspectorate of Motorized Forces. Such units were then in the initial stages of development. He caught the eye of the commander in chief of the army, General von Seeckt, the founder of the 100,000-man army.

After the general's dismissal from the High Command, Wenck was occasionally assigned to him as his aide-de-camp and escort, at Seeckt's request. At Christmas 1929, Seeckt presented Lieutenant Wenck with a personally autographed photograph.

On 1 May 1933, Lieutenant Wenck was transferred to the 3d Motorized Reconnaissance Unit. Promoted to captain on 1 May 1934, he was posted to the Kriegsakademie, or Staff College, in Berlin from 1 October 1934 until 5 October 1936. He was then transferred to the staff of the commander of the Armored Corps in Berlin, whose first commander was General Lutz. Colonel Heinz Guderian was Lutz's chief of staff. There Wenck saw the development of the German armored corps at first hand, his own task being to devise the best possible basic organization for such newfangled formations of armored troops. On 10 November 1938 he was appointed company commander in the 2d Panzer Regiment at Eisenach. Promoted to major on 1 March 1939, he became staff officer (operations) at 1st Panzer Division Headquarters on 1 April 1939.

On 1 September 1939, Wenck went into Poland with that division, under the command of Lieutenant General Rudolf Schmidt. At 1655 hours on 31 August 1939, there had arrived at the battle headquarters of the division the coded signal: "Case White, 1.9.1939; 0445 hours." The staff officer (operations) concluded his final briefing with an expression that was to become a byword in the division: "Come on, this is it. GO!" Wenck was awarded the Iron Cross, Second Class, on 18 September 1939, and First Class on 4 October 1939.

Early in the Polish Campaign it became customary with the 1st Panzer Division staff to send messages in rhyme. When an uncertainty reigned about the situation near Petrikau, Wenck revealed his poetic talent by signaling over the air to the adjutant of the 1st Lorried Infantry Brigade:

> My dear Gernsdorff, tell me now,
> Aren't you yet in Petrikau?

From then on messages were very often transmitted in this way, and the wireless operators found it amusing to think up rhymes, which also, incidentally, added considerably to the enemy's difficulties in decoding.

The campaign in the West, which began on 10 May 1940, found Wenck still staff officer (operations) of 1st Panzer Division, now under Major General Kirchner and part of General Guderian's 19th Motorized Corps, which was already generally referred to as a Panzer corps. Within the framework of the 19th Motorized Corps, the division was given the task of breaking through the Belgians' first line of defense in a thrust across Luxembourg, and the staff had prepared for this breakthrough in minutest detail long before orders for the attack were issued. The preparations had taken the form of a tactical exercise without troops, held in Koblenz and directed by General Guderian himself. The intention was to carry out Operation Sichelschnitt from a jumping-off point in the Moselle Valley, to breach the Maginot Line extension near Sedan and follow up with a turning movement north of the Aisne toward the Atlantic Coast.

On Guderian's instructions the staff officer (operations) of every division under his command had to draft and submit written operation orders covering the approach march to the assembly areas, the assault across the Maas River, air support for bridging the river, and so on. Guderian considered Wenck's orders—which were of necessity very comprehensive—to be sound after some minor details were altered. On the journey back from the "TEWT," Wenck suggested to General Kirchner, his divisional commander, that they run off twenty-five copies of his draft orders for their units, so that they would be readily available for the crossing of the Maas and the breaching of the Maginot Line at the appropriate time. Kirchner demurred. "Don't bother to do that," he told Wenck. "The real thing will turn out quite differently anyway."

But events proved the divisional commander wrong. Once the offensive had got under way, Wenck could quickly establish that all formation headquarters were acting in compliance with the TEWT decisions and that the enemy was reacting accordingly. All he had to do was issue his carefully worked out and already duplicated operation orders with a brief appendix. Assembly, attack, river crossing, and breakthrough went like clockwork. Fine staff work, first-class training, and the bravery of the men in the ranks achieved the outstanding success at Sedan.

255

In spite of a growing threat to the flank, on 14 May the commander of 1st Panzer Division decided to turn west and continue the thrust across the Ardennes Canal, since the division had to swing westward to fit the over-all situation and initiate the major drive toward the coast. General Guderian, who was invariably on the spot at decisive moments, arrived at the division's battle headquarters at this juncture, somewhat uneasy about the feasibility of the wheeling maneuver in face of French counterattacks.

Wenck's answer was typical. "Sir," he said, "you've taught us, 'Not a drizzle but a downpour.'" That clinched the argument in favor of swinging toward the coast.

On 17 May, while the supply columns of the 19th Corps were at Montcornet, Wenck happened to be there also, on his way back from Corps battle headquarters in Soize. French tanks attacked, and he was slightly wounded. He had been to corps headquarters for clarification of orders for a pause. "For the time being, no further movement westward across the Oise." Wenck vehemently expressed the opinion that the division could not consider any holdup of its forward drive while it was so favorably situated. Luckily, General List, commander in chief of the Twelfth Army, happened to arrive at corps battle headquarters shortly afterward. In Wenck's presence he approved Guderian's proposal to push forward a "reconnaissance in force." That was enough for Guderian—the advance by his Corps was to go on.

As became known only later, on account of the unprotected flank of the Panzer division pushing on toward the coast, Hitler had got cold feet and given the Army High Command orders for a pause.

When he arrived at the divisional battle headquarters at La Neuville-Bosmont, Wenck was jubilantly welcomed, walking with the help of a stick and hobbling along with his wounded foot in a thick camel-hair slipper. His penchant for making bold decisions on his own initiative as staff officer (operations) of the 1st Panzer Division was well illustrated by his orders for a surprise assault on Belfort on 17 June 1940, when he acted contrary to both corps and Panzer group orders, which had laid down the 1st Panzer Division objective for the day as the line Montbéliard-Héricourt. On the strength of his personal impression that the enemy facing his own battle groups was near collapse and that some hard knocks would quickly overwhelm all local resistance, Wenck decided to push on beyond the day's objective, toward Belfort. At 1850 hours he gave the order over the air to take Belfort by storm. He knew perfectly well that the order entailed a risk and might possibly even form a subject for consideration by a German court-martial, but he was prepared to take the chance. To prevent any last-minute orders for a withdrawal or a pause from reaching the troops, he never told the divisional commander what was going on, and by the time he eventually had to inform General Kirchner, who had been repeatedly asking whether the division had attained its objective for the day, Wenck revealed the truth.

"Sir, I have a confession to make," he admitted. "I ordered an assault on Belfort, and the division is already far beyond Mont-béliard, advancing on Belfort."

Kirchner got an almighty shock and was about to give his staff officer (operations) a real choking off. But then he put out his hand impulsively. "Wenck," he said, "we've always seen things through together. We'll do the same with this decision of yours, too. I think it was right."

Belfort was taken after some stiff fighting, and shortly afterward a dispatch-rider arrived from Corps Headquarters with the order, "Push on forthwith from Montbéliard to Belfort." Wenck told the dispatch-rider, "Report back to Corps that we are already in Belfort and having breakfast."

For this independent executive decision Wenck was promoted to lieutenant colonel on 1 December 1940.

General Guderian naturally arrived in Belfort soon after its occupation, and there he met the divisional staff, who had quickly established themselves in a hotel on the main street. General Kirchner was using the brief respite to take a bath, and Guderian, who could well appreciate the idea, gave instructions that Kirchner was not to be called from the bathroom. But the irrepressible Wenck had his own ideas about getting his general out of such comfortable luxury. Going out into the street, which led to a fort still in French hands, he stopped a passing 8-mm antiaircraft gun and ordered the gunner to drop it into action in front of the hotel and open fire on the fort.

An 88 makes a tremendous crack, and Kirchner understandably thought the hotel was under fire when he heard the first rounds go off. Leaping out of the bath, he appeared half-naked in front of General Guderian, who had himself been startled away from breakfast by the noise. There was loud laughter from all sides, as Wenck notched up another victory for his sense of humor.

Wenck went to the Russian Front on 22 June 1941 as a lieutenant colonel and staff officer (operations) of the 1st Panzer Division. The division's task, as part of the 41st Panzer Corps under General Reinhardt was to break through the frontier defenses at Tauroggen and then push on as rapidly as possible to the southern Dwina River and establish bridgeheads as a necessary preliminary to an advance on Leningrad. The division was now commanded by General Krüger, and Wenck's very daring handling of its operations in the Polish and French campaigns had become well known. What the other ranks especially appreciated was that he did everything possible to avoid any senseless sacrifice of blood.

On 17 July 1941 the enemy stepped up his air attacks on the Luga bridgehead held by the 1st Panzer Division, and continuous enemy air superiority began to wear out the troops. The commander of Armored Reconnaissance Unit 4 sent the following signal to 1st Panzer Division at 1125 hours:

> All those Russian pilots in the sky
> Are diving at us as they fly;
> Where is Professor Messerschmitt?
> He'd better hurry ere we're hit.

After calling up fighter cover for the unit, Wenck radiod back shortly afterward:

> Are our fighters there as yet,
> Or is it rat-tat-tat you get?
> Has our flak sent any crashing,
> Or are their bombs on you still bashing?

Still the victim of overwhelming enemy air superiority, the long-suffering reconnaissance unit advised:

> One of theirs has had its fill,
> Ten or more are bombing still.
> We report with much concern
> Two of ours will not return.

Wenck's repeated requests to Corps Headquarters for air cover were supported by the signal:

> At last, at last we cheer.
> There are aircraft in the air,
> But, alas, no Nazi bird . . .
> Only Bolshie planes are heard.

Inevitably the staff officer (operations) was repeatedly reprimanded by higher authority for such frivolity in his rhymed messages, but in spite of that his signals were sometimes imitated.

On 8 August 1941 the 1st Panzer Division was to push out from its bridgehead over the Luga at Sabsk in a northeasterly direction. Wenck and Lieutenant Colonel Went von Wietersheim were optimistic, and the latter's battle group broke through successfully. The division made a deep penetration into the Russian defensive system, but both flanking divisions had been held up, and on the night of 8/9 August corps ordered the 1st Panzer Division to pull back to its start line until further reinforcements, especially artillery, could come up. Von Wietersheim refused to give ground won with such heavy losses, and Wenck fully supported him. He managed to convince the corps chief of staff of the correctness of this decision, in the light of the over-all situation also, and the divisional commander—and later even the corps commander—supported Wenck's contention.

The 1st Panzer Division's forward thrust on 9 August now also helped the heavily engaged neighboring formations to fight their way forward, thus fully justifying the decision taken by von Wietersheim and forced through higher authority by Wenck.

On 9 September 1941 the 41st Panzer Corps attack on Leningrad began, and on 11 September elements of the division, with a Luftwaffe signals officer riding on a tank and directing Stuka attacks ahead of them, captured the village of Duderhof, southwest of Leningrad. Then Major Eckinger's battalion of the 113th Lorried Infantry Regiment stormed the vital Hill 167. From Lieutenant Darius, commanding the 6th Squadron of the 1st Panzer Regiment, Wenck received the radio signal in clear: "I can see Leningrad and the sea!"

But during the days that followed the division made little headway against ever-increasing enemy resistance.

On 17 September 1941, the division was pulled out of the Leningrad sector for a new assignment and transferred to Army Group Center while on the march. They moved south to the area of Ostrov to take part in the drive on Moscow, which Hitler had authorized far too late. The 1st Panzer Division fought its way through Cholm and Belyi to Sychevka, and on 11 October reached Subzov, across the Wasusa. They were near Rzhev, not far from the motorway to Moscow, which lay to the southeast. On 12

October they took part in the assault on Kalinin, the railway junction on the Volga, where the great river runs almost west to east north of Moscow. Irresistibly, the tanks quickly overtook Soviet motorized units and horse-drawn transport.

Where necessary, enemy vehicles were simply shoved out of the way and into ditches right and left of the road. Wenck reported to 41st Panzer Corps Headquarters: "Division advancing steadily on Kalinin. The Russians are persistently infiltrating our columns and are claiming right-of-way on the main road. Please give a ruling."

For once the Army High Command, which had intercepted the divisional wireless traffic, took up Wenck's joke and quipped, "As always, 1st Panzer Division has right-of-way."

On the evening of 15 October 1941 the staff officer (operations) of the 1st Panzer Division could report, "After heavy fighting, the road bridges over the Volga at Kalinin are in our hands, undamaged." But both motorized and Panzer units forming the spearhead of the drive on Moscow were by now almost bogged down on Russian roads that had become a morass of mud.

The well-known British military historian and authority General J. F. C. Fuller, summed up the situation, when he stated that "in all probability it was not so much the resistance of the Russians—strong though it was—or the effect of the weather on the Luftwaffe that saved Moscow, as the fact that the vehicles of the German front were bogged down in the mud." As the bitterness of the Russian winter increased, so did the bloodiness of the battles for Moscow. A greater asset even than the toughness of Russia's people and her soldiers, as Sir Basil Liddell-Hart has stated in his *History of the Second World War* was the primitiveness of her roads, most of which dissolved into bottomless mud.

At midday on 13 December 1941 the Russians broke through in a southerly direction, northwest of the 1st Panzer Division. Strong enemy forces threatened the division's line of withdrawal, which meant that Kalinin might soon have to be evacuated. The GOC of the Panzer Group, General Reinhardt, appeared at the 1st Panzer Division's battle headquarters and ordered, "Wenck, at least bring the men out for me—even at the cost of the equipment."

In this almost hopeless situation Wenck once again displayed his surprising imperturbability. His unshakable confidence that everything would turn out all right spread both to the men in the ranks and to their commanding officers. Calmly and deliberately preparations were made for a breakout by the division.

Wenck was now able to draw on his earlier experiences at Kalinin, where it had been possible to mislead the enemy by feint attacks and then to break through to the Volga because of the greater maneuverability of our tanks and artillery. On 14 December a typical, crystal-clear "Wenck order" was issued, covering the breakout by the 1st Panzer Division in every detail. Most of the vehicles set off toward the rear that same day. Short counterthrusts were planned to cope with enemy threats, but they were localized and limited in time. If possible, the whole division was to occupy defensive positions prepared by the 41st Panzer Corps in a single bound.

The breakout went exactly as Wenck had planned. On 15 December he signaled Corps: "0700 hours. All elements 1st Panzer Division safely behind the lines. Thank goodness!" For his achievement Wenck was awarded the German Cross in Gold.

On 5 February 1942, Wenck was posted to the Kriegsakademie in Berlin as an instructor, to pass on to the staff officers being trained there the lessons of his extensive experience. Like the men in the field, so the students at the Staff College were inspired by Wenck's infectious personality, and he became a shining example to them. He could tell them from bitter experience what attributes count for most in young staff officers in wartime—strength of character, readiness to accept responsibility, loyalty to one's commander, attention to the bigger picture so as not to get lost among details, and care never to make senseless demands on the troops.

Wenck was promoted to colonel on 1 June 1942, and three months later he was appointed chief of staff to the 57th Panzer Corps under General Kirchner, with whom he had served during the French Campaign. On 19 July this Panzer corps—now under the Seventeenth Army—began a daring thrust to Rostov-on-Don after breaking through the enemy line. As before, General Kirchner, with Colonel Wenck as his chief of staff, distinguished himself. They took the city by surprise and captured intact the big bridge over the Don. The drive by the Seventeenth Army toward the Caucasus began, and the 57th Panzer Corps pushed forward to Tuapse.

When the situation between the Don and the Chir became critical in the weeks before the great drama of Stalingrad, once again it was Wenck who contributed to the stabilizing of the front. On 21 November 1942 he received orders from the Army High Command to fly immediately to Morosovskaya in a special aircraft of the Luftwaffe, to take over the post of German chief of the general staff with the 3d Rumanian Army. Knowing how things stood with the Rumanians, he never hesitated a single second, and that very evening he reported to General Dumitrescu.

The next morning Wenck flew to the front in a Fieseler Storch. The line, as far as it still existed, ran along the bend of the Chir River, and we have his own description of it as it was formed that morning:

There was not much left of the Rumanian units. Remnants of the brave Battle Group Lascar were still fighting somewhere west of Kletskaya on the Don. All our other allies were in full flight, and with the inadequate means at our disposal there was no way of stopping the headlong retreat. This meant that I had to reply solely on the greatly reduced German 48th Panzer Corps, some emergency Luftwaffe field formations, and the available rear units of General Paulus' encircled Sixth Army, who were being formed into battle groups by energetic officers, and on Sixth Army and Fourth Panzer Army men who were returning from leave in dribs and drabs.

The only troops available to defend several hundred kilometers of the front line along the arc formed by the Don and Chir rivers were the battle groups under Lieutenant Colonel Spang, Colonels Stahel and Adam, and Staff Captain Sauerbruch, as well as some standby detachments from the services in the rear and from the Sixth Army. There were some tank crews and armored fighting vehicle squadrons without tanks and several Engineer and anti-aircraft units. Somewhat later, the main body of 48th Panzer Corps joined us, having somehow fought its way towards the south-west since 26 November.

So much for Wenck's report. After returning from the El Alamein Front in North Africa, I had just spent four weeks in the hospital. On 21 November 1942 I was in East Prussia with the chief of staff of the army, General Zeitzler, who informed me that I had been appointed chief of staff of the 48th Panzer Corps. At the same time he briefed me on the extremely critical situation at Stalingrad.

After reporting to the commander in chief of Army Group Don,

Field Marshal von Manstein, and being put in the picture still more precisely, at dawn on 29 November I left by air in a Fieseler Storch to join the advanced headquarters of the 48th Panzer Corps. Flying low, the pilot and I had to watch like lynxes to avoid landing among the enemy. There was no sign of any front line, and on my arrival at the corps battle headquarters I found that neither the corps commander, Lieutenant General Heim, nor his chief of staff was there any longer, so that in this really critical situation I could not even take over my job properly. It was real Hitler style! From the staff officer (operations) I learned, that, thanks to Colonel Wenck's energetic action, they had managed to bring the flight of the Rumanians to a halt. He had established some sort of front along the Don and Chir, using existing battle groups and rapidly organized blocking units. The 48th Panzer Corps—of which General von Knobelsdorff was to take command on 1 December—would have to act as a sort of "fire brigade" along the Chir.

It was my first meeting with this outstanding staff officer, Wenck. "Mellenthin," was all he said, "we're not always in such a mess. And we're going to straighten things out here, too. I need the 48th Panzer Corps especially for the job."

From the General von Manstein, Wenck received verbal orders: "You'll answer with your head if you allow the Russians to break through toward Rostov in your sector. The Don–Chir line must hold. If it does not, then not only the Sixth Army in Stalingrad but also Army Group A in the Caucasus will be lost."

Thanks to his tireless energy and inexhaustible resourcefulness, Wenck succeeded in sealing off every Soviet penetration. We also halted the Russians who had already broken into our positions and denied them the road to Rostov. After the war von Manstein presented Wenck with his photograph, inscribed: "To Panzer General Walther Wenck, in grateful recognition of his incomparable achievements as army chief of staff during the heavy fighting by Army Group Don/South in 1942/43 and in appreciation of his unfailing friendship—Erich von Manstein, Field Marshal."

On 28 December 1942, Wenck was decorated with the Knight's Cross of the Iron Cross. He had mastered a most difficult situation, and his success had proved decisive for the outcome of a major battle. One day before the announcement of the award, Wenck became chief of staff to the army detachment under Infantry General Hollidt, which also had under its command the 48th Panzer

Corps, of which I was now chief of staff. In the days that followed, with all our unfortunately unsuccessful efforts to relieve the Sixth Army in Stalingrad, I again had the opportunity of getting to know this chief of staff, who remained optimistic in the face of the greatest conceivable difficulties and was never without some solution to every problem that arose.

On 1 February 1943, Wenck was promoted to major general and on 11 March was appointed chief of staff of the First Panzer Army under General von Mackensen, who months later was to give the British and Americans some severe headaches at Anzio and elsewhere in Italy.

Shortly before Christmas 1942 a new major Soviet offensive broke through the Eighth Italian Army on the Don in the depths of a bitter winter, with snow deep on the ground and men sometimes freezing to death. The thrust by the Fourth Panzer Army to relieve Stalingrad had to be called off. Then, at the beginning of January 1943 the enemy also penetrated the Second Hungarian Army lines, and a whole Hungarian corps of 45,000 men capitulated. In the face of such disaster the Don Front simply dissolved—a sequence of events I have described in detail in the chapter on Field Marshal von Manstein.

After a difficult disengagement at the end of February the field marshal launched the First (von Mackensen) and 4th (Hoth) Panzer Army—with Wenck as chief of staff from the beginning of March, 1943—the enemy was repulsed and thrown back across the Donetz. This daring advance by German Panzer formations after a withdrawal of hundreds of kilometers, stabilized the southern front again in the area of Kharkov.

After the failure of the last German offensive in the region of Kursk during the summer of 1943, we fought only defensive and positional battles, as dictated by the senseless requirements of Hitler's "corporal's war," as he remembered things from World War I. Every inch of ground had to be contested, instead of using the wide-open spaces always available to us for mobile warfare in Russia. So, at the close of 1943, the German forces were driven back over the Dnieper, which was crossed at many points by the Russians.

At the beginning of 1944 the Russians encircled two German infantry corps near Cherkassy—altogether about 50,000 men. It seemed that Stalingrad was about to be reenacted on a smaller scale. Once again orders came from Hitler: "Hold on. Supply by air. Relief on the way. No breaking out." Panzer units of the First Panzer Army were also thrown in to allow the encircled forces to get out.

The pocket was only about 60 kilometers in diameter, and speed was essential.

Wenck, as resourceful as ever, did everything in his power to avert disaster, but the thrust by insufficiently powerful forces soon became stuck in the morass of mud. Vehicles sank axledeep. Even Wenck, having driven up to the spearhead of the attack once again—this time in a tracked vehicle—realized that the 14th Panzer Corps was literally stuck. He also knew that in fact the army had nothing more to put in. Every step forward would needlessly cost men's lives. Any breakout from the encirclement had to be achieved from the inside, and at long last Hitler sanctioned the attempt, though again it had been left too late.

Thanks to outstanding leadership, the bulk of the force was rescued by breaking out at Cherkassy, but all heavy armament and other equipment was lost, so that both corps were ineffective for some time to come.

By contrast, the encirclement of the First Panzer Army in the Kamenets–Podolsky Pocket, when their lines of retreat were cut off by Vatutin's First Ukranian Front forces and Konev's drive by the Second Ukranian Front to meet them along the Dniester, showed that a breakout could be successful. Though cut off from 17 March to 6 April 1944, the First Panzer Army got out and was ready to fight on immediately. The men of the First Panzer Army knew that they could count on it when they were told by the chief of staff, "Pappi" Wenck, and later also by Colonel Wagner of the staff, "Not to worry—we'll fix it!"

The army dubbed itself "the wandering pocket," and, by launching large-scale feint attacks in another direction, they succeeded in breaking out into the Buchach area, thus preserving for the army group a battleworthy force for further action.

On 24 March 1944 Wenck vacated the post of chief of staff to Army Group South; quite apart from what he had done for the First Panzer Army in the pocket, he had achieved a great deal toward its breakout, especially in the matter of supplies and encouragement to individual divisions.

On 22 July 1944 he left the Eastern Front to go to East Prussia as director of operations and deputy chief of staff at Army High Command headquarters. When he went to present his first report to Hitler and his close associates, Wenck described the situation at the front without embellishment and in typical frontline jargon. He ended with the words, "As you see, my Führer, the whole of the Eastern Front is like Swiss cheese—full of holes."

Field Marshal Keitel, the armed forces chief of staff, later warned him not to use such language in front of Hitler, and when Wenck the next day delivered a more moderate report, Hitler observed, "Wenck, I miss the liveliness of yesterday's report, which I liked."

Wenck's ingenuousness was well illustrated after the attempt on Hitler's life on 20 July 1944. He generally rode a motorcycle through the tight security around Hitler's bunker, though everyone else, including Göring, had to go on foot. Hitler's women secretaries often had cherry cakes with their tea, and Wenck, waiting in the anteroom for an interview with the Führer, let it be known that cherry cakes were his particular weakness. From then on there was always a piece for him, until one day all such treats were abruptly stopped. Hitler had decided to revoke all special privileges among his staff in view of the seriousness of the situation—and that included eating cake. Wenck never agreed with such a step, for he really did like cherry cake, and one of the women reported the fact to Hitler. To Wenck's great joy the next day there was cherry cake on the table for him again.

Thanks to his self-assurance, his intelligence, and his direct, frontline way of talking, which Hitler seemed particularly to appreciate, Wenck could occasionally bring some influence to bear on this obstinate egotist when it was needed to avoid direct calamity, but he could certainly not be numbered among the eternal yes men—Keitel in particular—with whom Hitler had surrounded himself.

In mid-February 1945 the Russians had already reached the Oder between Schwedt and Grünberg, but their flanks were vulnerable. An assault group under the command of Army Group Weichsel—now headed by Himmler, the Reichsführer SS—was supposed to drive into the flank and rear of these enemy forces from the area southeast of Stettin, but since Himmler was not competent to command such an operation, General Guderian, as chief of the general staff, wanted to second Wenck temporarily to Himmler as chief of staff for the important attack.

Hitler, though at first most indignant that "his Himmler" should be considered unfit for the task, after lengthy argument agreed to Guderian's request, and under Wenck's personal supervision the attack made good progress for a while, until he was unfortunately involved in a motor-car accident. He had taken over the vehicle from his exhausted driver, but was so worn-out himself that he fell asleep at the wheel and landed, badly injured, in the hospital. With Wenck, the driving force and outstanding chief of staff, lost to the counterthrust south of Stettin, the whole attack crumbled and came to a standstill. The episode provided a signal example of how decisively a man of real ability can influence the outcome of a battle.

Wenck again attracted general attention when, on 10 April 1945, he took over command of the Twelfth Army. Nine days previously he had been promoted to general of the Panzer troops retroactive to 1 November 1944, and now he was to head an army of Hitler's final enrollment of manpower, made up at the beginning of April 1945 from the last human and material resources available in central Germany. After assembling in the Harz, the army was to move west with the aim of liberating the Ruhr and eventually reestablishing an unbroken Western Front. It was just another of Hitler's incredibly utopian dreams, and things very rapidly turned out quite differently.

Colonel Reichhelm, the new chief of staff of the Twelfth Army and formerly staff officer (operations) with Field Marshal Model in the Ruhr Pocket, was summoned to report to Hitler at the beginning of April. In describing the situation, he made it clear that they must reckon on Model's forces in the Ruhr Pocket being wiped out very soon. Hitler retorted, "Army Group B may not surrender" and gave Reichhelm orders for the Twelfth Army's task, adding that it was also to regain the Rhine between Düsseldorf and Cologne as rapidly as possible. Model's group was expressly forbidden to surrender.

In the meantime, by 11 April the American Ninth Army under General Simpson had already reached the Elbe River south of Magdeburg—which is barely 130 kilometers west southwest of Berlin—and had established a small bridgehead on its eastern bank. That day Wenck and Reichhelm arrived at Twelfth Army battle headquarters, which was being set up in the Sapper School at Dessau-Rosslau, east of the Elbe and near the Harz. From the very first days they worked together a genuine feeling of mutual trust existed between Wenck and his staff, and this formed the foundation for the extremely grave decisions they were called upon to make. Wenck and his chief of staff shared the view that they should not attempt to carry out Hitler's unrealistic orders for a counterattack but should rather prepare for the inevitable end between the Oder and the Elbe and influence events as best they could by evacuating as many of their men and refugees as possible and by preventing any further destruction of villages and towns.

Wenck's Army had no Panzer units and only an antitank battalion as a substitute, with insufficient assault guns among the divisions. Army troops and antiaircraft units were almost totally lacking, and there was not the vestige of a German airforce in the area. He assumed that both the Americans and the Russians would now launch a final assault on Berlin, for the Twelfth Army had as yet no way of knowing that the Allies had agreed among themselves to a demarcation line along the Elbe and Mulde rivers.

The army battle headquarters, forced by circumstances, had to try to establish a stable defense farther west by employing the newly formed units in a mobile role, but Wenck expressly instructed that the destruction of all industrial plant and economically valuable installations, as ordered by Hitler, was to be prevented. Instead, the garrison commanders in the larger towns within his army's jurisdiction were to continue defending them only while they retained importance in relation to the planned movements of Wenck's army. Thus Wittenberg-on-the-Elbe, Brandenburg, and Rathenow were surrendered without any compelling reason and before it got to the point of desperate fighting within the towns.

By the middle of April the Americans had established a number of bridgeheads over the Elbe River, and Eisenhower gave orders to set up a consolidated front along the river and stop there before smashing a way into the nonexistent "Alpine Redoubt," a figment of the Allies' imagination.

The major Russian offensive directed on Berlin began on the day Eisenhower stopped on the banks of the Elbe, and it created a completely new situation for the Twelfth Army, upsetting all its dispositions, which, up to then, had mainly faced west. Now Wenck had to reckon on a possible Russian breakthrough toward Berlin, which would threaten his army in the rear. In view of the totally altered situation, he quickly decided to leave merely token defensive forces along the Elbe and to assemble east northeast of Magdeburg not only all available forces from Leipzig and Halle but also any remnants still west of the Elbe. They were to form a line of defense against the Russians. The moves were already under way by 17 April.

Wenck had received no instructions from the Combined Staff of the Armed Forces, and his decision again demonstrated his characteristic tendency to do what common sense dictated instead of attempting anything foolhardy. In face of the Russian onslaught it was now a matter of saving from ruin and annihilation as many German soldiers and refugees as possible by directing them toward the West.

On 21 April the first Russian tanks, followed by infantry rumbled toward the Twelfth Army defensive positions east of Belzig and were thrown back. Meanwhile, the Russians had already thrust beyond Berlin, north and south of the city, and were approaching its eastern suburbs. Hitler ordered the Ninth Army to turn about and link up with Wenck's army south of the city.

Field Marshal Keitel went in person to Wenck's battle headquarters. He greeted Wenck with the words, "We must rescue the Führer!"

Wenck, who knew how to handle Keitel, merely said calmly, "The army will attack."

What Keitel wanted was for the Twelfth Army to attack toward Jüterbog, make contact with the Ninth Army and then combine in a northward assault to relieve Berlin. After Keitel left, Wenck and his chief of staff held a council of war, and, even in so unpromising a military situation, they decided that the most important thing was to push eastward to force open an escape route for the Ninth Army, who were almost surrounded and in desperate straits. This would also save as many refugees as possible.

Wenck knew perfectly well that with his newly formed, weak divisions, lacking tanks and with little artillery, there was no hope whatever of relieving Berlin. Even the attempt would cost the lives of countless young men under his command, who were his personal responsibility. The last desperate radio-telephone call from Hitler to General Jodl on 29 April ran: "Where is Wenck? When is he starting?" In the Führer's bunker they seemed to be still hoping for the relief of the capital. Eighteen hours later Hitler was dead.

By 28 April, Wenck had secured his flanks as far as Wittenberg in the south and to a point southeast of Brandenburg in the north, to such a degree as to risk attacking with three divisions toward the northeast from the area of Belzig, midway between the two. It says a great deal for the confidence he had been able to infuse in his young soldiers—the last remaining recruits after nearly six years of war—that this attack was carried through with exemplary verve and dash and smashed obstinate Russian resistance.

They were able to free three thousand German wounded in Beelitz and to organize their immediate removal to the west. The left wing of the attacking troops reached Ferh and enabled the beleagured Potsdam garrison to reach safety behind the German lines. Though it could not relieve the Ninth Army, in this successful attack the Twelfth Army expended its last remaining offensive strength, and it had now to defend its own flanks to avoid being cut off from the Elbe by Russian formations. Yet there could be no thought of withdrawal until the rest of the Ninth Army had been rescued. Wenck had instructed them by wireless to break out toward Beelitz, and his front line there held until 1 May, when after ten days of heavy fighting the utterly exhausted remnants of the Ninth Army broke through the enemy lines. Thanks to the endurance of Wenck's young soldiers in this critical situation, when they themselves could at any moment have been encircled, some thirty thousand men streamed through the breach they had made and were saved.

The utmost speed was now imperative, and Wenck decided that, covered by defenses along the Havel River running through Rathenow, he would withdraw toward the Elbe north of Magdeburg. He hoped to obtain the Americans' consent to cross the Elbe on either side of Tangermünde so as to put his army out of reach of the Russians.

He sent General von Edelsheim, commander of the 48th Panzer Corps, to negotiate surrender terms. The chief of staff of the Ninth US Army conducted the negotiations on the Allied side, and the

Americans agreed to let the soldiers and wounded cross over to the American lines as prisoners of war, but they refused to accept any civilians whatsoever. The German deputation accepted these conditions only under protest, pointing out that thousands of civilians who had fled to the Elbe only wished to save themselves from the Russians. On receiving this news, Wenck said bitterly, "There is no help for it. We must try it. We can't just leave them here to be steam-rollered by the Russians."

During the night of 5 May they began ferrying the wounded, the unarmed men, and the noncombatant services across the river. Wenck himself went down to the crossing point and personally issued orders to use every conceivable means to move as many refugees across as possible, and the crossing proceeded smoothly while fighting units, still holding off the advancing Russians, slowly disengaged. The noise of battle came closer every minute.

The bridgehead on the eastern bank managed to hold out until the evening of 6 May. Then ammunition gave out. Wenck issued orders for the crossing of noncombatants to be completed by the morning of 7 May, and on that day, near the village of Ferchland, General Wenck, his chief of staff, Colonel Reichhelm, and some headquarters personnel crossed with the remaining soldiers in the last boat. Thus ended the Twelfth Army's final battle.

Thanks to his usual thoughtful, capable, and sympathetic leadership, Wenck had led some 100,000 soldiers within reach of his army across the Elbe and into American captivity. Civilians smuggled across the river numbered in the tens of thousands. This final battle had only been possible because young recruits, with a bare four weeks' experience in battle, had stood their ground with outstanding courage and discipline.

When Walther Wenck was released from American captivity, like all other career officers, he had to undertake a new profession. He accepted a subordinate post in a commercial firm in Dalhausen, and quickly made a success of his new career. He had a meteoric rise in industry. As has been true with others, so with Wenck. Apparently army training and, more particularly service on the German General Staff eased the way up in another profession.

A capacity for logical thought, correct evaluation of a situation followed by a clear decision, the art of treating people decently and influencing them positively, the ability to take a broad view, and, above all, loyalty towards one's colleagues—these are the per-

271

sonal qualities that Wenck brought to his business life. They assured his success. In 1950 he became a member of a management team of a large industrial undertaking specializing in the manufacture of coking ovens, and he was soon entrusted with the procurement of capital needed for the firm's reconstruction projects and with special assignments in foreign trade. On his first overseas trip in 1951 to Buenos Aires he procured for his firm a large order from the Argentine government and was received by President Juan Perón, with whom he had a two-hour discussion.

In spite of his lack of experience in commerce, Wenck's diplomatic ability and business acumen, his energy and brisk way of getting on with the job eventually earned the full recognition and appreciation of his firm, and he was appointed a director in 1953. In 1955 he became chairman of the board of directors.

As a former serviceman, Wenck faced something of a crisis of conscience when Franz Joseph Strauss, newly appointed minister of defense in West Germany, approached him with the offer of a post in the Ministry of Defense. It was not an easy decision for Wenck to make, but when the shop committee and the board of directors of his firm pleaded with him to remain with them, he decided to stay where he was. Through his travels to other countries, including the Orient he gained a worldwide perspective.

With his firm's consent, in November 1960, Wenck went to southern Germany to serve as general manager of a large firm of precision-instrument makers. When he retired some years later, a spokesman for the firm said at his farewell:

There are few men who are able to serve in the best sense of that word, or who are prepared to meet even the greatest challenges by putting their all into their tasks. But among them are those capable of leadership and of enthusiasm and unselfish loyalty. Walther Wenck can be counted among men of such exceptional character.

Manstein's criteria, set out in the Introduction to this book, apply to Walther Wenck, both as a military leader and as a captain of industry: "Intelligence, knowledge, and experience are telling prerequisites. . . . Strength of character and inner fortitude are . . . decisive factors. The confidence of men in the ranks rests upon a man's strength of character."

APPENDIX 1

THOUGHTS ON PRESENT-DAY TRAINING OF STAFF OFFICERS

Theory and Practice

In what General J. F. C. Fuller has justifiably called his "apocalyptic book *On War,* Carl von Clausewitz stated that "theory should never prescribe a rigid line of action." Such a danger exists when the new generation of military leaders is given a predominantly academic training, which leaves practice in the background. To quote Liddell-Hart, one is then training "philosophers, but not soldiers." It is certainly useful to teach certain subjects not directly related to military matters, the theory of education, sociology, psychology, political science, and the like, but one should not allow them to make inroads on the limited time available for subjects crucial to military training as such.

In many respects the present generation of embryonic military leaders faces a more difficult time than the years following World War I. Technology was not then highly developed, and, in addition, upon the outbreak of World War II there were many officers available who had had battle experience. There were staff officers who had undergone excellent training and had put their theoretical knowledge to the test on the battlefield before passing on their knowledge to another generation.

Today officers on the staffs of formation commanders must rely on pamphlets and books for guidance, for men with practical experience in the last war are becoming rare. Lack of practical experience can be partly compensated for by intensive study of military historical precedents, always provided that sufficient time is spent on such study and that military history is correctly taught.

Military history forms the basis of all military theory, and from that source springs a soldier's conduct in practice, as Clausewitz has explained. According to him, there are various ways in which to learn military history. The best method appears to be for the student to undertake a proper investigation of methods adopted in past wars. By this Clausewitz means that one should form carefully considered opinions on methods of command.

What actually happens during battle is not the main point of such study. The general staff officer should learn the practical side of warfare from studying the methods of command that have been adopted. However, theory without practice is only of limited value. Conversely, practice not backed by the theoretical mental effort, which makes the correct application of such practice possible, is insufficient for a military commander.

General Friedrich von Bernhardi, military author of the days before and after World War I, held the opinion that purely "routine" soldiers—that is to say, the strictly practical—will and must fail as soon as they are challenged by the great and difficult problems of modern warfare. They will always seek to solve such problems with the inadequate means with which they have become familiar in their own limited experience.

There was repeated evidence of the validity of this assertion during World War II, when generals who had achieved their rank on the grounds of outstanding bravery, failed to come up to expectations in the face of "great and difficult problems." It was especially so if they did not rely upon the advice of their staff officers.

Elsewhere Bernhardi stated that "those who have no time for serious military study, will never measure up to the demands of the future." Training of the rising generation of general staff officers must take this factor into account, and the most suitable time for "serious military study" is at the Kriegsakademie, or staff college. At this stage young officers are still particularly receptive and are not burdened with the cares that go with command of a formation of troops. Mistaken ideas and false lines of thought can still be rectified. Later, in the field lack of time renders this more difficult.

One may object that, in view of the abundance of material that has to be mastered at a leadership training school, there is not enough time available for military history. However, such time would be available, if:

1. Training at the college or academy lasted for three years, as it did for formation commanders' assistants in the Reichswehr until 1934, when it was shortened to two years.

2. Subjects such as sociology and political science were left out of the training program or made optional.

3. Intensive courses at universities or high schools were generally omitted, except in case of those few officers particularly gifted in the technological or other specialized fields.

4. So-called short courses interspersed during the time spent at the academy were abandoned so as to eliminate as far as possible any diversion from the main military branches of study, such as tactics, operational command, military history, logistics, and staff duties.

The General Staff Officer in Action

Field Marshal Alfred von Schlieffen originated the expression "Great achievements, small display; more reality than appearance." Because of his many-faceted training and education in clear, logical thought, the staff officer can unintentionally run into the danger of considering himself superior to the regimental officer and thus push himself into the limelight. A certain personal modesty is thus a special obligation laid on a general staff officer. He is and remains the assistant of his commanding officer, whom he helps by expressing his considered opinions and by relieving his GOC of all staff work.

It was General von Seekt who said, "General staff officers have no names," by which he meant the same thing as Field Marshal von Schlieffen, quoted above. Nevertheless, this self-effacement should be taken with certain reservations. Until 1938, in the old Imperial German Army as also in the Reichswehr, it was considered that an officer holding the appointment of a corps chief of staff or upward shared responsibility for steps taken by his GOC. If the chief of staff held an opinion fundamentally different from that of his superior officer, he had to submit his views in writing. However, if the GOC stood by his own decisions, then the chief of staff had to carry them out in complete loyalty.

Under Hitler this rule was abrogated. It was counter to his

"leadership principle," in accordance with which only one man could be responsible for measures of command. With the multiplicity of tasks with which a general will be faced in any future war, and with the abundance of subjects to be mastered, any single man will unquestionably be overloaded. An intelligent commander will therefore always pay attention to his senior staff officer and will gladly share responsibility with him, especially if the cooperation of the GOC with his chief of staff is harmonious, as it obviously should be (the reader has seen in the foregoing chapters instances where this was the case and where it was not).

Hitler's abolition of the Chief of Staff's coresponsibility also sprang from his intention to diminish the troops' high regard for the general staff, which to a great extent thwarted his plans.

In the difficult circumstances that are likely to exist in any future war, this regard will probably be increased. What should be avoided is any degradation of the military commander's assistant to the position of a mere receiver of orders, which may very easily lead to the creation of a lot of yes men. Anyone who has to bear responsibility will undoubtedly consciously strive to help not only his GOC but also the troops themselves. And where this sharing of responsibility exists between a senior staff officer and his GOC, the former is bound to become known. He will have a name in staff circles and among the troops.

In his day, Hitler also tried to abolish the "staff channels." Under this setup, general staff officers of the German Army could report direct to their immediate superior general staff officers on questions of command and personnel. They were thus in a position to pass on to their formation commanders information on those points as and when they deemed it necessary. It was evident that impartiality and tact had to be exercised and maintained. Tact is a matter of character, and in the selection of general staff officers today character still takes first place before all other considerations.

An understanding of history as well as breadth of intellect is required of a general staff officer. In a speech at the Führungsakademie Leadership School of the Bundeswehr in 1959 the late president of the Federal Republic of Germany, Theodor Heuss, said: "Improve yourselves and enrich your profession through an inner understanding of history and of the deep spiritual difficulties of our time so as to be worthy of the legacy of your profession."

And the former Defense Minister Schröder of the Federal Republic said of the leadership functions of general staff officers: "Only an officer of broad mental outlook with adequate knowledge of other walks of life and a high technical understanding can fulfill the requirements of military leadership on a higher level today and be the master and not the slave of technological potentialities."

In conclusion, I must stress that the present and future general staff officer, by comparison with the product of our former staff training, which purposely left political knowledge and interest in politics out of consideration, must be more familiar with political and social forces and tendencies. In addition, on account of the frantic development of weapons, he must also have much better scientific and technical knowledge.

We must acknowledge that the topmost military organization on the German side during World War II—deliberately developed by Hitler—exhibited serious shortcomings. No real command of the armed forces existed. The common interest and the whole picture were not considered, as each arm of the service sought to extract what benefits it could, with Göring and Himmler the most blatant examples.

From the book *Bekenntnisse zum Soldaten,* by Ulrich de Mazière, the last inspector general of the Bundeswehr, it is clear that the present-day general staff officers of all arms of the service are being trained particularly in the field of command as a whole. The essential basis of general staff training remains unaltered; it is merely considerably expanded, particularly through Germany's obligations to NATO.

On this point, in an address to the Leadership School of the Bundeswehr in Hamburg, Mazière wrote in the above-mentioned book: "The Bundeswehr is an Allied Army. It exercises its activities in military forces fulfilling their task within an Alliance. Many of you will be given assignments on integrated staffs. The declared policy of German defence policy is to strengthen and maintain the Atlantic Alliance."

APPENDIX 2

A FUTURE WAR AND ITS GENERALS

"History will condemn only those nations that make no attempt to defend themselves." It has always been the duty of generals and the general staff to consider in advance all possibilities of national defense. A prerequisite for this purpose is to achieve clarity about the intentions and potential strength of this or that prospective enemy, as well as about the nature and form that a future war may take.

Such considerations often fall within the field of the conjectural or the unknown, and one such unknown quantity rests on continuous changes in the world, on frequent changes in government, and particularly nowadays on technology.

In his book *Military Strategy,* Soviet Marshal V. D. Sokolovsky says with undoubted justification that formerly generals and general staffs often prepared themselves to fight the next war according to the methods of the last. Such an approach fails to take account of the unknown, and because of its paucity of ideas is sure to lead to bitter disillusionment and defeat. Sokolovsky reckons that under existing circumstances no kind of war is improbable; in a more limited sense it can only be said that there are "more probable" and "less probable" forms in which war may manifest itself.

A war may begin with conventional methods. Tactical nuclear weapons may then be brought into action and such a war, can then soon—or perhaps only later—escalate into unlimited nuclear warfare. It can be accepted as certain that the instability of present-day international political relations favors rather than hinders escalation in the form the conflict takes. The massively destructive weapons of our day therefore lend exceptional importance to the problem of escalation.

In all deliberations of this nature one will certainly do well to become intimately aware of the train of thought adopted by Soviet politicians and military strategists. In his book Marshal Sokolovsky enlarges upon the possibilities, methods, and kind of fighting in a future war as follows:

The employment of new-style weapons in a future war of intercontinental missiles and nuclear armament will substantially change the objectives of those responsible for the conduct of hostilities and will result in a revolutionary change in the methods of fighting and warfare in general.

. . . this raises the question what, under such circumstances, the main military strategical objective of a war can be—the wiping out of the enemy's main forces, as was the rule in the past, or the annihilation and destruction of targets in the enemy hinterland and its disorganization.

Sokolovsky provides the answer: "Both objectives must be attained simultaneously."

But such demands can be met only if the military strategy adopted is based on the offensive from the outset. Sokolovsky makes no bones about it when he states that Soviet strategy is to grasp the initiative from the beginning, which means that decisive importance must be attributed to the opening phase of any future war.

This line of thought should therefore form the basis for conducting any future war, and the foundation for appropriate deliberations and measures taken by generals and the general staff. As already mentioned, according to the Soviet view one must prepare oneself for all possible forms of warfare and methods of combat in any future conflict, and naturally prepare most of all for what appears to be the most probable in the existing situation.

Serious consideration of the subject begins with the defensive system of a state. A system of defense styled to meet a specifically expected threat, as, for example, a conventional or short-lived nuclear war, will most certainly be outstripped by events that are bound to follow. Every system of defense must leave room for all eventualities, so that political and military leaders under the pressure of actual circumstances do not fail to set their defensive sights sufficiently high to meet any situation without having to abandon their original ideas as ineffectual. For states the size of those in Europe such a requirement presents an enormous financial problem. From the point of view of cost they may not be in a position to solve the problem on their own, to say nothing of defending themselves.

The inescapable deduction from all this is a division of labor and costs within the framework of an alliance, a coalition such as NATO has been for the Western world since 1949, with European and American states linked in a unique form of military union. Peaceful protestations and corresponding "treaties," disarmament negotiations, and arms-limitation resolutions absolve neither politicians nor commanding generals from their duty to exercise every possible care for the security of their own states.

On Strategy

Much can be said about the definition of "strategy." Here we present only three possible meanings, to which particular attention should be paid in our present time and situation.

1. "Strategy is the science of anticipating events" (Vorausdenkens).

2. "The best strategy is always to be really powerful" (Clausewitz).

3. "One's own strategic ideas should always emanate from the strategy of the enemy, which means that all dogmatic ideas on the subject are false" (Sokolovsky).

On Politics

The military strategist should not be in any doubt that political strategy takes precedence over the military. In support of this thesis are a number of statements by prominent men, both political and military. Lenin, in his commentary on General von Clausewitz' *On War,* remarks that politics should be the reason, war merely the instrument, and not vice versa. Consequently, the military standpoint must be subordinated to the political.

Churchill stated that the military strategist is the politician's adviser. How he acknowledged military opinion as advisory to politics is shown by his conversation with Lord Dowding, commander in chief of the Metropolitan Fighter Command, in May 1940. Churchill asked him whether Britain was in a position to offer France additional and adequate air support in her dire distress. The French reckoned that without massive air assistance from Britain they would be unable to hold the German attack. Lord Dowding declared that twenty-five squadrons had to be held intact for the defense of Britain. Since there were no more available, there could be no question of sending air formations to France. This military standpoint clinched the decision of the politician. The French had to look after themselves and were thus left to their political and military fate.

Regardless of the priority of political over military strategy, in any future war the closest dovetailing of political and military leadership must be regarded as vital. An acknowledged expert of Soviet politics, the Austrian Lewtzkyz, expresses himself on this point as follows:

> The more political success becomes dependent upon military action, so much the closer will be the interdependence of political and military leadership. This presupposes that the military must become involved in purely political strategy to a degree previously unknown, and can play a decisive role even in purely political decisions. The success of political actions and the reduction of the risks attaching to them depends upon how closely cooperation between the political and the military leadership has been knit.

From what one can gather from reports from the Soviet Union, in that country there exists the closest collaboration between political and military leadership, born from experience during World War II. Such collaboration will be necessary for all parties taking part in any future war if a great common objective is to be attained. The supreme military commander must in future be drawn into all political decision making, and a right of participation is his due. A prerequisite, naturally, is that he has learned to apply his mind to political matters.

The commander in chief of the German Reichswehr in the 1920's, General von Seeckt, was often invited to attend important sittings of the German cabinet. To the government's advantage, his opinions on both the internal and the foreign political situation were listened to. In a future conflict, such politico-military cooperation cannot be too close.

From the foregoing it follows, as was the case on the German side in the war of 1914–18, that there can be no pure, absolute military strategy. Quite apart from the precedence of the political side, present-day military strategy is composed of other factors, which senior military commanders and the staff have to take into serious consideration. They include industry, morale, and technology.

The French general and military authority General André Beaufre, speaks very pointedly on this method of deliberation when he states that the idea of strategy is today far removed from the purely military way of thinking. In addition to the political, it also includes the psychological, economic and technological viewpoints.

On Industry

Marshal Sokolovsky is speaking in the same sense as General Beaufre when he says:

Military strategy is to a large extent dependent upon the economy. In the execution of his strategic plans the supreme commander is more than ever dependent upon the material potentialities provided by his country's economy.

Further on he states:

Not only is war itself dependent upon economic conditions, but they also influence the army's style of fighting, that is to say, the methods by which the war is waged or, in other words, strategy. Every repudiation of the principle that strategic objectives must match the war resources at the disposal of the state leads to risk in warfare and thus to defeat.

As an example of the validity of this observation the command of the German Army under Ludendorff in World War I can be cited. Because of indecisive and weak German political leadership, Ludendorff felt obliged to interfere in the political and economic, as well as the military, direction of Germany. He was thus no longer merely "the adviser of politics" but its dictator. He interfered in the economy through coercive measures, because the political leadership had, among other things, neglected to make the appropriate economic preparations for war at the proper time. Ludendorff was thus to some extent forced to take into his own hands all the reins required for the direction of the war. In accordance with his character, he often did this in a way that was thoroughly reckless, without the necessary understanding of politics or the economy.

Colonel Bauer, who was one of his closest collaborators, later said of his chief, Ludendorff: "In economic affairs he had no grounding whatsoever. As far as he was concerned, all political problems were purely military problems."

In spite of his undisputed talents and knowledge in the military sphere, Ludendorff thus lacked that degree of special understanding which is required by a top-ranking military commander, or, to use the words of Chief of the General Staff Beck, "that harmony of personality demanded by Clausewutz." In terms of both human nature and technical knowledge, Ludendorff was overtaxed.

During World War II, Hitler maintained that he fully grasped the significance of economics for waging war. In fact, his knowledge of economic matters often astounded the experts. Nevertheless, he failed to bring this knowledge and understanding into a satisfactory combination with his military strategic objectives. In the course of the Russian Campaign, he neglected the main strategic objective, which was the final annihilation of enemy forces, in favor of capturing areas important from the point of view of food supplies or of taking the doubtless important oil fields of the Caucasus.

On Morale

Among the basic elements of morale are honor, loyalty, trustworthiness, a sense of duty, diligence, a love one's country, and a forward-looking mind. Nowadays it is difficult to escape the impression that these moral fundamentals are lacking to a considerable extent in the Western world. A nation's will to defend itself and also the steadfastness of its army largely depend upon whether its citizens are consciously aware of these moral values. One of the principal tasks of any nation's political and military leadership is therefore persistently to raise the people's morale and to make it the obvious basis of all action.

Morale does not develop suddenly or of its own accord. It is the result of example, of the actions and superior spirit of individuals among an elite coterie of people. Moral virtues are numbered among idealistic concepts. A man without ideals has no incentive. But those ideals can be developed only in association with known reality, with which the political and military leadership has to reckon.

The morale of a nation and its fighting forces are a single, indivisible whole. An army founded on conscription will fight with conviction only if it knows itself to be identified with its homeland. Failure to pay attention to morale, or the neglect of it by government or military leadership, implicitly carries within itself the seeds of defeat. All authorities in a position of leadership must therefore strive to present their objectives and methods convincingly to the people. Otherwise they cannot develop or maintain morals.

How highly Napoleon, among others, valued morals may be gathered from his saying: "Moral factors are far more decisive to victory than a ratio between numbers."

On Technology

"Military strategy in the future is no longer a purely military domain, for the scientist and the technician must be drawn into it to a large extent. They belong together." This opinion of General Count von Kielmannsegg agrees with that of Marshal Sokolovsky, who is convinced that the complicated techniques of modern warfare require a great number of service personnel, especially engineers and technicians, whose viewpoints and judgment must be given due regard. It would thus be ill-advised to devote exclusive or even particular emphasis to one of these sectional fields or, in other words, to foster specialization. Pure specialization always tends to have a splintering effect on the whole. The military leader of the future must not allow himself to be led into a position where he cannot see the wood for the trees. Bias and prejudice, in no matter what direction, are serious disadvantages for a military leader.

On Generals

Sir Basil Liddell-Hart, in his book on the German generals of World War II, says that they "were the best finished products of their profession anywhere. They could have been better if their outlook had been wider and their understanding deeper. But if they had become philosophers they would have ceased to be soldiers."

It is left to the reader to judge to what extent the German generals delineated in these pages justified Liddell-Hart's opinion of them as "excellent products of their profession" from the human and moral and also from the professional points of view. In many cases a lack of a "wider horizon" may be discernible. It does not stem from any absence of mental ability or inadequate education, but far more from their training in accordance with certain traditions. In former times the main stress of general staff training lay clearly on the best possible execution of more or less purely military tasks. In the future this simply can no longer hold good. Future warfare imperiously demands a supreme command that possesses not only a "wider horizon" but also a "deeper understanding" of everything included in the concept of military strategy. In this respect, what assistance can future generals be offered from the experience of World War II?

From descriptions of possible developments in a future war, as envisaged by Soviet military strategists, it becomes obvious that any such war will confront war leaders and commanding generals with considerably greater demands than those confronting leaders in the past. Quite apart from a broadly based education and a comprehensive training covering many fields, it will be important for generals to have extraordinary strength of character and, as Field Marshal von Manstein put it, "to possess and give evidence of great fortitude." The Greek philosopher Heraclitus taught that "a man's character is his destiny." Only strong and well-founded characters will measure up to the demands of a future war, and their destiny may then well be that of their nation and their people.

Besides knowledge and ability, besides willpower, initiative, and elasticity in the use of available means, a military commander should never lose his sense of what is attainable. Hitler, who regarded himself as a military leader, certainly had great willpower. But he had no eye for the necessary relationship between the setting of operational objectives and available forces; his demands did not match the capabilities of men and material.

Strong characters must always possess moral as well as physical courage. They must be prepared to swim against the stream. In other words, they must be prepared to show the courage of their convictions, which may sometimes be uncomfortable for others. To give evidence of the courage of one's convictions under a dictator, as history has shown, can be extremely perilous. As can be seen from the memoirs of Soviet generals, such courage was completely lacking among virtually all of them—with the possible exception of Marshal Zhukov. As has been reported, they "feared Stalin more than they did the Germans." The courage of one's convictions has nothing to do with lack of obedience or refusal of duty, even when one disagrees with the supreme political or military commander on fundamental principles.

Every leading politician and every general must be able to exercise sufficient authority, for a state and its highest courts can influence the course of events to only a limited extent and then only indirectly. The military commander or general must know how to delegate such authority as he himself possesses to his subordinate commanders. It is only thus that he can expect them to exercise initiative, which should never be repressed.

In his memoirs, Marshal Zhukov states: "Strict centralization of the Supreme Headquarters is a pressing necessity for the successful conduct of war. But this does not exclude independent initiative by commanders at the front; rather, it actually requires it." Hitler rejected this obvious requirement. He seldom tolerated personal initiative. Although all the reins for the conduct of the war were in his hands, there was no question of a strictly centralized Supreme Headquarters. From about 1942 the Russian front was controlled by the Army General Staff (OKH) while the other theaters of operations were the domain of the Combined Staff of the Armed Forces (OKW).

A possible nuclear war will require strict centralization. That will also be the case in a war waged by a coalition, where the employment of nuclear weapons and also the allocation of tasks to the various allies can be controlled only by the very topmost authority if proper coordination is to be attained and the major strategic goals successfully reached.

As already stated, none of this excludes personal initiative, provided commanders have been trained to think in terms of the overall picture. The supreme command must refrain from interfering in individual or minor operations. During World War I, General Luddendorff interfered with the direction of individual operations and even in the command of smaller formations. Hitler did the same thing during World War II. Both—as Field Marshal von Rundstedt once put it—conducted "corporals' wars." They thus lost a view of the entire field of operations and eventually of their own war aims. In addition, they impeded individual initiative by their commanding generals, which is so necessary for the immediate conduct of battle.

Military leaders who have never actually held frontline commands easily lose a feeling for the spirit of the fighting troops and an understanding of their capabilities. As Marshal Sokolovsky says, "The importance of a commanding officer rests on inseparable unity between himself and his troops." Such "inseparable unity" can exist only when the commander knows the needs, the spirit, and the capabilities of his troops through personal experience. In theory this is seldom possible.

During World War I the first German chief of the General Staff, General von Moltke, had not commanded any troops for many years. Even during the war itself he was never in contact with the front. Consequently, he could have no notion of what actually happened in battle, or of the troops' capabilities and the difficulties they might suddenly be called upon to face. Accordingly, he did not truly command but groped about in circumstances that were unintelligible to him.

During World War II the leading generals of the Wehrmacht, Field Marshal Keitel and General Jodl, had not served as formation commanders. They had no understanding of what the troops wanted.

Ultimately, modern military strategy requires that its leading brains should prevent war, and should do so by being constantly prepared for it. The task of future generals must therefore be to attend to this preparedness for war, so as to assist in surmounting crises that could lead to war. Preparedness for war depends upon long-term planning. That is only consistently practicable if generals are left undisturbed in their appointments for long periods. They must be in a position to put their plans into effect.

In a future war the challenges that military commanders and generals will have to face will be extraordinarily difficult ones. It will be possible to meet such challenges only if a strong character is available as a foundation on which to base all deliberations, conduct, and deeds. Anyone destined to be a military leader should bear in mind the words of General von Seekt: "The basis of human greatness is neither intellect nor knowledge, but character." Everything—ability, achievement—springs from that. Character is the decisive factor among soldiers, among military commanders.

Conclusion

The foregoing chapters on the personalities and character of German generals of World War II, as well as what has been said about future generals, lead to certain conclusions. Even in this age of atomic weapons the needs for mobility are not eliminated. On the contrary, the modern general must also take the necessary steps against the increased effect of firepower by employing increased mobility and superior speed. A prerequisite for this is mobility of thought and action.

The present-day general must guard against specialization in face of the ever-increasing variety of technical fields open to us. His task as a general, and not as a specialist, is primarily to coordinate the various fields through his own persuasive powers and not to allow himself to be diverted from taking an over-all view.

Especially at the Stalingrad catastrophe, which was caused by the failure of Germany's allies, our military leaders endured bitter experiences. Hitler would not listen to the warnings of experts, who proposed to put in German units as "Corset busks" among allied troops—as was done in the Alamein Line. We had too little contact with our allies and did not understand their mentality, fighting morale, or military equipment. The general of today has the advantage of being able to move about within the framework of allied forces in peacetime, of learning that the fighting forces of various nations also have diverse mentalities. Their organization and equipment differ from one another, as do their training and fighting doctrines.

Finally like the generals of yesterday, so should today's generals live according to the precept of the old Tübingen evangelist Friedrich Oetinger:

God give me the patience to suffer those things which I cannot change, the courage to change those things I can, and the wisdom to distinguish the one from the other.

SOURCES

Alman, K. *Panzer Vor.* Rastatt, Erich Pabel Verlag, 1966.

Auchinleck, Field Marshal Sir C. Auchinleck Papers. Manchester, England, Manchester University Library.

Balck, General Hermann. Unpublished Diaries.

Bandulet, Bruno. *Adenauer zwischen West und Ost.* Munich, Weltforum Verlag, 1970.

Barnett, Corelli. *The Swordbearers.* London, Eyre & Spottiswoode, 1963.

Beaufre, General André. *Abschreckung und Strategie.* Berlin, Propylaen Verlag.

Bialer, Seweryn. *Stalin and His Generals.* London, Souvenir Press.

Carell, Paul. *Unternehmen Barbarossa.* Berlin, Deutsche Buchgemeinschaft.

Carsten, F. L. *The Reichswehr and Politics.* London, Oxford University Press, 1966.

Churchill, Sir Winston. *The Second World War.* London, Cassell & Co., 1948.

Clausewitz, General Carl von. *Vom Kriege.* Berlin, Vier Falken Verlag.

Dingler, Colonel H. J. Personal notes and reminiscences.

Erfurt, General. *Die Geschichte des Deutschen Generalstabes, 1918–1945.* Göttingen, Musterschmidt, 1957.

Fraschka, G. *Mit Schwertern und Brillanten.* Rastatt, Erich Pabel Verlag, 1970.

Fuller, General J. F. C. *Die Entartete Kunst: Krieg zu Fuhren, 1789–1961.* Berlin, Verlag Wissenschaft und Politik, 1964.

Gallo, M. *The Night of the Long Knives.* Godalming, Fontana Books, 1972.

Goerlitz, Walter. *Paulus and Stalingrad.* London, Methuen & Co., 1963.

Grabert, H. *Sieger und Besiegte.* Tübingen, Verlag der Hochschullehrer Zeitung, 1966.

Guderian, General Heinz. *Errinerungen eines Soldaten.* Heidelberg, Kurt Vowinkel Verlag, 1960.

Hilbrunn, Otto. *Konventionelle Kriegführung im Nuklearer Zeitalter.* Frankfurt am Main, Verlag E. S. Mittler & Sohn, 1965.

Hoffmann, A. *Widerstand—Staatsstreich—Attentat.* Munich, Verlag Piper & Co., 1969.

Horne, Alistair. *To Lose a Battle.* London, Macmillan, 1969.

Jung, H. *Die Ardennenoffensive, 1944–1945.* Göttingen, Musterschmidt Verlag, 1971.

Karst, General H. Miscellaneous published papers.

Kern, Erich. *General von Pannwitz und Seine Kosaken.* Oldendorf, Verlag K. W. Schütz, Jr., 1971.

Kleist, Peter. *Die Europäische Tragödie.*

Kurowski, A. *Deutsche Offiziere in Staat: Wirtschaft und Wissenschaft.* Herford and Bonn, Maximilian Verlag, 1967.

———. *Armee Wenck.* Heidelberg, Kurt Vowinkel Verlag.

Lewitzkyj, Boris. *Die Marschälle und die Politik.* Cologne, Markus Verlag, 1971.

Liddell-Hart, Sir Basil. *Deutsche Generale des Zweiten Weltkrieges.* Econ Verlag, 1969.

———. *Grosse Herrführer.* Econ Verlag, 1968.

———. *History of the Second World War.* London, Cassell & Co., 1970.

———. *Lebenserinnerungen.* Econ Verlag, 1960.

———, ed. *The Rommel Papers.* London, Collins, 1953.

———, ed. in Chief. *History of the Second World War.* London, Purnell.

Maizière, Ulrich, Inspector General of the Bundeswehr. *Bekenntnis zum Soldaten.* Hamburg, R. v. Deckers Verlag, G. Schenk, 1971.

Manstein, Field Marshal Erich von. *Verlorene Siege.* Bonn, Athenaeum Verlag, 1958.

Mellenthin, Major General F. W. von. *Panzer Battles.* London, Cassell & Co., 1955; Norman, University of Oklahoma Press, 1956.

Meyer-Welcker, Colonel *Seeckt.*

Model, Colonel H. *Der Deutsche Generalstabsoffizier.* Bernard & Gräfe, 1968.

Moll, Otto E. *Die deutschen Generalfeldmaschälle.* Rastatt, Erich Pabel Verlag, 1961.

Mueller, K. *Das Heer und Hitler.* Deutsche Verlaganstalt, 1969.

Nehring, General Walther K. *Die Geschichte der Deutschen Panzerwaffe.* Frankfurt am Main, Verlag Ullstein, 1969.

Orpen, Colonal Neil. *War in the Desert.* London and Capetown, Purnell, 1971.

Playfair, Major General I. S. O. *History of the Second World War: The Mediterranean and Middle East.* Vols. II and III. London, H. M. Stationery Office, 1956, 1960.

Ruge, Admiral Friedrich. *Rommel und die Invasion.* Stuttgart, K. F. Koehler Verlag, 1959.

Schukow, Marshal. *Erinnerungen und Gedanken.* Deutsche Verlaganstalt, 1969.

Shirer, William L. *The Collapse of the Third Republic.* London, Heinemann, 1970.

———. *The Rise and Fall of the Third Reich.* London, Secker and Warburg, 1960.

Siewert, General G. *Schuldig: Die Generäle unter Hitler.* Bad Nauheim, Podzun Verlag, 1972.

Sokolovsky, Marshal. *Militärstrategie.* Switzerland, Hober & Co. Verlag, 1965.

Speer, Albert. *Erinnerungen.* Berlin, Propylaen Verlag, 1969.

Speidel, General H. *Zeitbetrachtungen.* Haase und Kohler Verlag, 1969.

Stoves, Major Rolf. *I Panzer Division.* Podzun Verlag, 1961.

Thorwald, J. *Das Ende an der Elbe.* Stuttgart, Steingrüben Verlag, 1950.

Uhle-Wettler, F. *Leichte Infanterie im Atomzeitalter.* Wehr und Wissen, 1966.

Wagener, L. *Heeresgruppe Sud.* Bad Nauheim, Podzun Verlag.

Wallach, Colonel J. L. *Das Dogma der Vernichtungschlacht.* Bernard & Grafe, 1967.

Westphal, General Siegfried. *Heer in Fesseln.* Bonn, Athenaüm Verlag, 1950.

Young, Brigadier Desmond. *Rommel.* London, Collins, 1950.

Zeitzler, General Kurt. *Deutsche Soldaten Kalender* and *Deutsches Soldatenjahrbuch.* Munich, Schild Verlag, 1962–74.

———. *The Fatal Decisions: Stalingrad.* London, Michael Joseph, 1956.

———. *Wehrkunde.* (Various volumes.)

———. *Wehrwissenschaftliche Rundschau.* Frankfurt am Main, Verlag Mittler & Sohn, 1970.

INDEX

Aachen (Aix-la-Chapelle), Germany: 12, 152, 217

Aerial warfare: 34, 78, 169, 218–19, 233, 262

African Campaign: 59–82, 97

Afrika Korps: 60, 63–64, 67, 70, 72, 74–76, 82; defeated, 113

Alexander, Gen. Harold: 48, 50

Algiers: 134

Allies: 25, 26, 47, 52, 156, 164–66, 183, 217, 232, 247, 268

American forces: 113, 144, 156, 163, 215, 218–22, 237, 244, 264

Amiens, France: 59, 167, 198

Anschluss: 42

Antonescu, Marshal Ion: 46, 135

Antwerp, Belgium: 152, 217

Anzio, Italy: 264

Ardennes: 25–26, 98; offensive, 1944–45, 152–57, 172, 182, 217, 225, 235–36, 243–46, 256

Armored Corps Training School, Wünsdorf, Germany: 240

Armored warfare: 26, 63–65, 85, 229–36, 242–48; and General Guderian, 86–89; on Eastern Front, 106–23, 195–218; on Western Front, 255–57, 261, 267; on Russian Front, 257–63

Army Group A: 25, 26, 36, 46; *see also* Army Group South

Army Group B: 25–26, 81, 111, 113–14, 152, 156, 164, 232, 267

Army Group Center: 182–83, 259–61

Army Group Don: 34–36, 114, 119, 263

Army Group G: 170, 189

Army Group North: 28, 181; in Courland, 182; in Ukraine, 213

Army Group South: 25, 32, 106, 206, 235; *see also* Army Group A

Army Group Weichsel: 246, 266

Army High Command: 9–10, 26, 256, 260, 262

Auchinleck, Gen. Sir Claude: 65, 76, 80, 83

Austria: 12, 14, 23, 48, 50

Balck, Gen. Hermann: 86, 96–97, 113, 162, 172, 189–223

Battle of the Bulge: 154–55

Belgium: 25–26, 58, 162

Bengasi: 60, 62, 69, 72–73

Berlin, Germany: 9, 14, 19, 24, 57, 152, 155–56, 183, 229, 267–70

Bessarabia: 48, 181

Bizerte: 241

Blomberg, Werner von: 6, 8, 10–12, 15, 23, 104; as war minister, 5, 13, 23, 89, 129

Bock, Col. Gen. Fedor von: as commander of Army Group B, 25, 93, 107–108; replaced by Hitler as army commander in chief, 149

Bordeaux, France: 163

Bormann, Martin: 180

Bradley, Gen. Omar N.: 164, 218

Brauchitch, Field Marshal Walter von: 12, 14; as army commander in chief, 15, 59, 95; replaced by Hitler, 149

British: 25, 59, 152, 264

British Intelligence: 62, 74

British 12th Corps: 163

Brussels, Belgium: 152, 167–68

Bug River: 43, 181

Carpathians: 180–81, 214

Caspian Sea: 44

Caucasus: 45–46, 107–108, 111, 135, 178, 261, 263; oil fields in, 30, 94, 106, 108; and German assault, 31–44; withdrawal from, 34, 36